Labor against the Regime

Modern Intellectual and Political History of the Middle East
Fred H. Lawson, *Series Editor*

Select Titles in Modern Intellectual and Political History of the Middle East

The Autocratic Parliament: Power and Legitimacy in Egypt, 1866–2011
Irene Weipert-Fenner

Everyday Politics in the Libyan Arab Jamahiriya
Matteo Capasso

Killing Contention: Demobilization in Morocco during the Arab Spring
Sammy Zeyad Badran

The Logic of Cooperation in Autocracies: Political Opposition in the Third Yemeni Republic
Jens Heibach

Ottoman Passports: Security and Geographic Mobility, 1876–1908
İlkay Yılmaz

Outcasting Armenians: Tanzimat of the Provinces
Talin Suciyan

Politics as Worship: Righteous Activism and the Egyptian Muslim Brothers
Sumita Pahwa

Why Alliances Fail: Islamist and Leftist Coalitions in North Africa
Matt Buehler

For a full list of titles in this series,
visit https://press.syr.edu/supressbook-series
/modern-intellectual-and-political-history-of-the-middle-east/.

LABOR AGAINST THE REGIME

WORKERS' MOBILIZATION IN EGYPT, 2004–2011

NADINE ABDALLA

Syracuse University Press

First Edition 2025

25 26 27 28 29 30 6 5 4 3 2 1

For a listing of books published and distributed by Syracuse University Press, visit https://press.syr.edu.

ISBN: 9780815638520 (hardcover)
9780815657316 (e-book)

Library of Congress Cataloging in Publication Control Number: 2024027849

This book is dedicated to my mother, Mona Baramki,
and my husband, Hany Fawzy.
Moreover, I extend this dedication to the relentless fight
for social justice within Egypt's labor movement,
and to all the movements across the globe that are striving
for their inherent right to live with dignity and freedom.

Contents

Acknowledgments

The creation of this book stands as a refined iteration of my PhD thesis. Its realization has been made possible through the invaluable support of numerous institutions and individuals, for whom I am profoundly grateful. Their guidance, advice, revisions, and unwavering encouragement have been instrumental in this endeavor.

I extend my heartfelt gratitude to my mentors, whose unwavering support has been pivotal throughout my PhD journey. At the forefront is Jean Noël Ferrié, my supervisor, to whom I owe immeasurable thanks for his sage advice and the substantial time he dedicated to enhancing the quality of my research. His unwavering backing has not only contributed to the fruition of this work but has also been instrumental in my academic growth.

I would like to sincerely express my appreciation to Amr El-Shobaki for his unwavering guidance during my time as a research assistant at the Al-Ahram Center for Political and Strategic Studies (ACPSS) in Cairo as well as our collaboration in various academic and professional endeavors. His support and encouragement have been a guiding light in my professional journey, and his mentorship has profoundly contributed to my learning and development, both personally and academically. Without his enduring support, the accomplishments I celebrate today would not have been attainable.

I am deeply thankful to Jean Marcou for his crucial role as the former director of the French section at the Faculty of Economic and Political Sciences (FEPS) at Cairo University that played a key part in initiating my academic journey. His influence during my student years at FEPS in Cairo continues to resonate, as does the support he offered for me to pursue my master's degree in Paris.

My sincere gratitude extends to Dina El-Khawaga for her consistent interest in my work. Her dedicated feedback, insightful comments, and encouragement have been invaluable sources of motivation.

I fondly recall my time at the Arab Forum for Alternative Studies (AFA), where I shared both triumphs and challenges with the team. Special recognition goes to Mohamed Al-Agati and Habiba Mohsen, my long-standing friend, for their unwavering companionship and support.

I express my thanks to the Swiss Confederation Scholarship of University Studies (Bourse d'Etude Universitaire de la Confédération Suisse) for the doctoral fellowship that enabled me to develop the theoretical framework of my thesis. The fellowship, hosted at the Lausanne Institute of Political and International Studies (IEPI), University of Lausanne (Unil), Switzerland, allowed me to benefit from Mounia Bennani-Chraïbi's invaluable feedback on earlier versions of this research.

I am equally grateful to the German Institute for International and Security Affairs (Stiftung Wissenschaft und Politik) (SWP) in Berlin for providing a doctoral fellowship. Their logistical and intellectual support greatly facilitated the finalization of my thesis with the highest possible quality. I extend my thanks to the SWP team for their exceptional support, leading to enriching academic exchanges that sharpened my arguments and elevated my academic profile. I wish to give special recognition to Muriel Asseburg, whose incredible support played a crucial role in the successful completion of my thesis and, consequently, this book. Her generosity, insightful intellectual exchanges, and exceptional management skills are elements I will forever cherish, as they significantly eased my journey.

I would also like to extend my gratitude to the Volkswagen Foundation for providing me with a grant to translate my thesis into English. This opportunity arose within the scope of the research project, "Socioeconomic Protests and Political Transformation: Dynamics of Contentious Politics in Egypt and Tunisia against the Background of South American Experiences," a collaborative effort in which I participated. The project was administered by The Peace Research Institute Frankfurt (PRIF) in Germany, in partnership with the Arab Forum for Alternative Social Studies (AFA) in Beirut and the Faculty of Law at Sfax University in Tunisia. Within this context, I wish to offer special thanks to Irene Weipert-Fenner and Jonas

Wolff for their invaluable support, scholarly exchanges, guidance, and the cherished moments we shared. Their contributions will always hold a special place in my memories.

Appreciation is extended to the Center for Economics, Juridical and Social Studies (Centre d'Etudes et de Documentation Economiques, Juridiques et Sociales-Cedej) for the fellowship that supported the transformation of my thesis into a book. I especially thank Karine Bennafla, Marine Poirier, and Marie Vannetzel for their support during my time there and the enriching academic exchanges we shared.

I am profoundly thankful for the Arab German Young Academy for Sciences and Humanities (AGYA) for the two fellowships that facilitated the transition from thesis to book form, as well as for addressing reviewer suggestions. These fellowships were hosted at the Center of Middle Eastern and North African Politics at Freie Universität, Berlin, led by Cilja Harders. I am profoundly grateful to her for providing exceptional intellectual and moral support that significantly influenced my experience at the center, making it a second home for me in Berlin. The academic guidance she offered and her deep engagement with my research are aspects that I will always hold dear and never forget. Special appreciation is also reserved for the Europe in Middle East and Middle East in Europe (EUME) fellowship program in Berlin, particularly Georges Khalil for his invaluable intellectual, moral, and logistical support.

I express my gratitude to the American University in Cairo for providing me with grants that facilitated the proofreading and indexing of my manuscript. In this regard, I wish to extend special thanks to my mentors at the Department of Sociology, Egyptology, and Anthropology (SEA) at AUC, Hanan Sabea, Helen Rizzo, and Ian Morrison for their unwavering support, invaluable guidance, and the time they dedicated to mentoring me in both academic pursuits and career advancement. Your ongoing support, assistance, and mentorship are deeply appreciated. Your encouragement during the toughest times is something I will always remember. I would also like to convey my thanks to my colleagues at SEA, Dina Makram Ebeid and Yasmine Ahmed, for the wonderful times we shared, their supportive presence, and the warmth they brought into our day-to-day interactions.

I am deeply grateful to Georges Fahmi, Tewfik Aclimandos, Virginie Collombier, and Youssef El-Chazli for their priceless contributions to the process of reviewing earlier version of this work. Their dedicated time and effort in offering insightful comments and corrections are greatly acknowledged. I extend my gratitude to Mostafa Bassiouni and Dina Bishara for our consistently engaging discussions, and I appreciate Nourane Helmy for her readiness to assist whenever required.

I would also like to express my thanks to Laura Gribbon for her meticulous proofreading of this manuscript, especially given the time constraints. Your dedication is truly appreciated. I also wish to express my gratitude to Salma Mostafa and Stephanie Amin for their support and assistance in carrying out the essential transliteration for this book, as well as the requisite reference styling and formatting. Their contributions were of paramount importance in bringing this work to fruition.

A heartfelt appreciation is extended to Ahmed Badawi, Amal Dib, Amgad Mohamed, Dina Al-Sharnoby, Doreen Khoury, Hassan Saber, Hoda Salah, Ragui Samy, and Sherry Basta, whose steadfast support sustained me throughout the writing journey. Special recognition goes to Amr Salah, Dina Wahba, Hanan Badr, Hania Sobhy, Marwa Taher, Rabha Allam, and Salma Al-Nakash for their unwavering encouragement and morale boosts that accompanied me during the writing process. Our shared moments hold a special place in my heart.

The creation of this book would have been insurmountable without the invaluable contributions of Abdel Moneim Emam, Nasser Abdel Hamid, and Mohamed Abul Dahab. Their generosity in providing access to information and facilitating communication with interviewees from Mahalla Al-Kobra city is beyond measure. My deepest gratitude goes to them for making this book a reality. Their assistance, support, and profound intellectual exchanges are something I will always remember. I take this opportunity to express my deep gratitude to Ahmed Eid, who facilitated my connection with Emam and Abdel Hamid. Without his help, this work would not have come to fruition.

I extend my thanks to the leaders of the labor movement in the Mahalla company, as well as the leaders of the state—employees of the Real Estate Tax Collectors' Movement, for their precious collaboration, enthusiasm, and patience throughout our numerous interactions. This book is dedicated to them and their compelling struggle for their rights.

This acknowledgment would be incomplete without expressing gratitude to my father, Hani Abdalla, whose strong support transcends geographical boundaries, and to my sister, Marianne, for her love, care, and logistical assistance, which eased many tasks.

I want to extend a special thank-you to my mother, Mona Baramki, the person who believed in me the most, consistently stood by my side, provided encouragement, and enveloped me in love. Words fall short in describing the depth of my gratitude toward her. Her influence and affection will forever be interwoven with my essence, and I hold her sacrifices during my travels in high regard. My achievements will always serve as a testament to her steadfast support and extraordinary love. This book is dedicated to her, the person I hold dearest, who has always viewed my successes and accomplishments as her own.

Last but not least, I extend my heartfelt thanks to my husband, Hany Fawzy, whose priceless moral support has been a constant during this arduous writing journey. His genuine concern for the successful completion of this book holds immense value for me. His positivity and care have fortified my perseverance and resilience in the face of challenges. His sacrifices during my writing retreats will forever be remembered. This book is dedicated to the person I cherish the most, the one who believed in my success and made it his own.

Abbreviations

CTUWS	Center of Trade Union and Workers' Services
ETUF	Egyptian Trade Union Federation
FDI	Foreign Direct Investment
IMF	International Monetary Fund
ITUF	International Trade Union Federation
NDP	National Democratic Party
PSI	Public Service International
RETA	Real Estate Tax Authority
SCC	Strike Coordinating Committee
WTO	World Trade Organization

Labor against the Regime

Introduction

Egyptian workers played a significant role in the 2011 uprising that led to the downfall of the Mubarak regime. Their participation in the protests began as individual citizens rather than members of specific organizations (Abdalla 2012a; Alexander and Bassiouny 2014; Duboc 2015). After the initial wave of protests subsided, workers started striking and demanding their rights. These labor strikes quickly spread across the country, causing disruptions to the economy and government operations (Abdalla 2012b; Alexander and Bassiouny 2014). While the exact impact of these protests on the decision to remove Mubarak cannot be fully measured, they certainly increased pressure on the Supreme Council of the Armed Forces (SCAF) and contributed to the regime's dismissal of Mubarak (Duboc 2015).

However, the labor activism in Egypt did not start in 2011. Prior to the regime's breakdown, the country experienced a significant wave of social and labor protests, which began in 2004 in response to the government's acceleration of neoliberal policies. These policies led to immediate hardships and exacerbated socioeconomic inequality. The number of labor protests increased dramatically, with millions of Egyptians participating in strikes, sit-ins, and other forms of protest between 2004 and 2008 (Beinin 2009; 2011).

These demonstrations were not limited to specific sectors but encompassed various industries, both in the public and private sectors. The demands of these protests focused on improving living conditions and increasing wages and bonuses. Many of them were short lived due to administrative and security constraints imposed by the Mubarak regime. However, they marked a significant shift in the participation of different sectors of society, especially with the participation of workers in certain sectors of the economy—which, until then, had been spared from protests—such as civil servants, who previously had been reluctant to protest against the state (Bishara 2018).

These labor mobilizations had several distinct characteristics. First, they focused strictly on socioeconomic demands and did not challenge the Mubarak regime's policies or its patron-client relationship with workers. In addition, the workers rejected any politicization of their demands and alliances with political organizations, emphasizing their protests as solely economic in nature (Abdalla 2015). Also, they refused to challenge the regime's institutions, including the state-controlled Egyptian Trade Union Federation (ETUF), and the establishment of independent unions was not considered. In return, the Mubarak regime almost rarely resorted to violence against labor protests. The security forces didn't tend to use force against protesting workers, unlike in the 1980s and 1990s (Alexander 2010, 248). With a few exceptions, the regime reacted with varying degrees of containment, indifference, and concessions (Bishara 2018, 43).

Case Studies, Research Questions, and Main Argument

During the five years leading up to the 2011 uprising, most labor protests were either short lived, like the partial strike by postal employees in May 2009 against administrative restrictions on promotions,[1] or failed to compel the government to address their demands, such as the Ministry of Education administrative staff's protests for increased bonuses in March and April 2009.[2] Alternatively, some protests demobilized after achieving their objectives, as seen in the case of locomotive engineers who disbanded after securing owed bonuses in January 2009.[3]

In contrast, the Mahalla workers' movement (2006–8) and the RETA state employees' movement (2007–9), which are the primary case studies

1. "Al-tashdidat al-amniyya tuhbiṭ idrab muwazafi al-barid" [Security Threats Abort Postal Workers' Strike], 2009, *Al-Youm Al-Sabi'*, May 7, 2009.

2. Hatem Salem, 2009, "Idariyu al-ta'lim: i'tisamat wa ihtijajat" [Education Employees: Sit-Ins and Protests], *Al-Youm Al-Sabi'*, August 30, 2009.

3. "Million junayh khasa'ir alsika al-hadid bisabab idrab al-thalath sa'at" [A Million in Losses Due to the Railway Strike], 2009, *Al-Masry Al-Youm*, January 24, 2009.

of this research, stand out as the only two movements that actively contested and challenged the rule of the Mubarak regime. They not only succeeded in satisfying their financial demands, inspiring and triggering other protests, but they also stepped outside of the strictly socioeconomic framework of workers' demands (in the case of the Mahalla workers) and successfully challenged the state corporatist system (in the case of the RETA movement). This means that the Mahalla labor and RETA employees' movements were perceived as being overtly oppositional to the Mubarak regime. This fact reinforces their significance, and the importance of understanding the dynamics of their contentious interaction with the different players of the Mubarak regime, as well as the different outcomes this contention generated.

The Mahalla Company—a public-sector firm with about twenty-four thousand workers, representing one-quarter of the textile workers in the public sector in Egypt—had a long history of activism and building strong organizational structures. The workers of the company organized a strike on December 7, 2006, claiming their right to the two-month bonuses that the company management had refused to give them. This strike was a crucial event in the upsurge of labor militancy, which began toward the end of 2004. The movement not only succeeded in 2006, despite the constraints imposed by the regime, but it also triggered another strike just one year later, on September 23, 2007, demanding the satisfaction of other financial demands specific to their movement. Emboldened by its success in 2007, the movement made a decision that partially challenged the state corporatist system: it demanded the dissolution of the textile trade union committee (affiliated with the ETUF), located within the company. These committees were perceived as being representative of the state among the workers (rather than the other way around), particularly since the trade union elections on November 13, 2006, which were marked by fraud. This decision, which started to produce similar attitudes among workers in the textile sector, was considered by the Mubarak regime as being challenging to its power.

One year later, the Mahalla labor movement organized a strike on April 6, 2008, to claim a minimum wage for all Egyptian workers. This demand marked a transition from simple, narrow economic demands to national-scale demands. In other words, it marked a position that directly called into question the socioeconomic policies that framed the regime's relations with workers. The political opposition declared its solidarity with the labor movement, thereby leading to the gradual politicization of workers' claims. While, the Mubarak regime's security apparatus, in contrast to the 2006 and 2007 strikes, forced the labor leaders to demobilize the workers in 2008, the forcibly canceled strike was followed by the biggest uprising in Egypt since 1977, as people took to the streets in Al-Mahalla al-Kubra city to protest against the worsening economic situation. Although the labor movement of the Mahalla Company was weakened by the time of the 2011 uprising, in its aftermath the demand for a national minimum wage became the leitmotif of labor activism in Egypt.

The RETA employees' movement—which had neither a history of activism nor strong organizational structures for mobilization—succeeded in achieving its goal after several successive scattered mobilizations that were disconnected in space and time. It evolved into a social movement strong enough to oblige the government to meet its demands despite the restrictive measures imposed by the regime. In addition, its innovative repertoire of protest actions influenced the mobilizations that succeeded it. For the first time in the recent history of social movements in modern Egypt, this movement held a sit-in on December 3, 2007, directly in front of the Cabinet, asking for parity with their colleagues in Cairo. The location of the sit-in gave them unusual visibility and somewhat normalized the turn to "street politics" a few years before the regime's breakdown.

Following this successful sit-in, on December 20, 2008, Kamal Abu Eita, the movement's leader, made the historical decision to build the first independent trade union in Egypt since 1957, the role of which was to represent the employees of the RETA independently of the framework of the ETUF. Unsurprisingly, this decision directly challenged the state corporatist system and thus questioned the pattern of state-labor patron-clientelist relations. The RETA movement's achievement was to open the door to revising state-labor relations—namely, the rules of workers' representation before the 2011 uprising. Other groups followed this example and likewise founded new trade unions, even before the ouster of Mubarak in 2011: the teachers, retirees, and health technicians, on July 14, April 26, and December 31, 2010, respectively. After 2011, hundreds of "independent" trade unions emerged and joined forces in several federations. Today, while the demands of organized labor for a new social pact, and its call for politico-institutional revisions—such as freedom of association and wage redistribution—continues, though its capacity to achieve its goals remains limited.

Against this background, in this book, I address the following research questions:

1. How did the Mahalla labor movement (2006–7) and the RETA (2007) emerge and succeed in the context of the authoritarian regime of Mubarak?[4]
2. How and why did these two movements choose to oppose the Mubarak regime and challenge the patron-client relation it had maintained with the workers?[5]
3. How and why did the RETA movement succeed in its endeavor of forming an independent union on December 20, 2008, while the Mahalla labor movement was repressed and demobilized after its call for a minimum wage in the April 6, 2008, strike?

To answer these questions, I argue that the leaders' strategies, tactics, and actions—influenced by their different biographies, relation to politics, and the social base they enjoyed (or not) within the movement—had a significant influence on both movements' internal and external dynamics in the context of the authoritarian regime of Mubarak (2006–10), and on the eve of its breakdown in 2011.

4. The term "movement success" refers primarily to its ability to exert the necessary pressure to compel the regime to respond positively to its demands, despite the constraints imposed by the latter.

5. "Opposition to the regime" suggests the transition from strictly economic claims, which were accepted by the Mubarak regime, to other claims, which were prohibited within the prevailing framework. In fact, they were considered to be in direct opposition. The specific issues of contention were twofold: the demand on a national scale for a minimum wage for all workers in Egypt, calling into question the socioeconomic policies of the government, thus opening the door for political organization to ally with the workers; and the establishment of a new trade union by the Real Estate Tax Collectors, a move that challenged the state corporatist system in Egyptian institutions.

In the case of both movements, their leaders worked intensively on mobilizing their colleagues to demand their economic rights by exploiting their support networks—those they had largely constructed through the fraudulent trade unions elections of 2006. As mentioned, and as will be discussed more in detail in the first chapter, the changing strategy of the regime, which stopped resorting to the repression of labor protests, especially with the mid-2000s, presented a political opportunity that encouraged labor activism to thrive. In the case of the Mahalla movement, which enjoyed a long history of activism and strong mobilizing structures, the perception of political opportunities by the movement's leaders was not necessary for them to decide to mobilize their colleagues. In fact, they weren't able to detect such political opportunities before the movement's mobilization. On the contrary, the leaders mobilized the movement members to ask for the two months' worth of bonuses based on their belief that success would not be hard to achieve, given the movement's long history of successful activism. In the case of the RETA movement, which didn't enjoy such a history of activism or such strong organizational structures as the Mahalla movement, the leaders' realization of the changing strategy of regime players was essential in motivating them to mobilize their colleagues to take advantage of political opportunities and, thus, to request equal salaries to their colleagues in Cairo. In both cases, the activism of these leaders and the success of their tactics led to the circumvention of security pressures and, consequently, the success of their early mobilizations. This encouraged them to go even further in their activism.

In both movements, the leaders had a great impact on the movement's capacity to push the government to achieve its socioeconomic demands. In the case of the Mahalla labor movement, strong mobilizing structures were an important but insufficient condition for guaranteeing the movement's capacity to survive and to succeed in challenging the players of the authoritarian regime of Mubarak. In contrast, the choices, strategies, and tactics deployed by the movement's leaders were a necessary prerequisite for success. In the case of the RETA movement, the leader's choices and decisions were not only crucial for its success in confronting the regime's players, but also, and importantly, in building the movement's weak or even nonexistent mobilizing structures in a restrictive political context.

Leaders' agency in both movements included: exploiting arising political opportunities, putting forward effective strategies and resonant framings, allowing the persistence of the movement (in the case of the Mahalla labor movement), and achieving success in protests until the formation of a social movement on a national scale (in the case of the RETA movement). In this regard, leaders' agency can only be understood through a dynamic and interactional perspective. Leaders' actions and strategies do not just enable them to exploit opportunities and respond to the constraints imposed by the players of authoritarian regimes, but also allow them to generate new opportunities for the movement to expand and to consolidate its structures (as in the case of the RETA movement), or to persist and sustain itself for several days despite security pressures (as in the case of the Mahalla movement).

The decision of the Mahalla movement leaders to challenge the Mubarak regime, and to ask for a minimum wage for all workers, can be explained by the presence of a group of politicized leaders within the movement who were opposed to the regime. They considered the regime's changing strategy and the movement's previous successes as opportunities for increasing their activism and opposition to regime policies. In the same vein, the politicization of some of the RETA movement's leaders, and their cognitive vision of sociopolitical change, encouraged these leaders to exploit the victory they had obtained, by forcing the government to meet their economic demands after ten days in front of the Cabinet. In this sense, the presence of politicized leaders at the top of a social movement, and their ability to achieve previous successes, are necessary conditions in opposing the players of an authoritarian regime.

The Mahalla labor movement's unsuccessful attempt to oppose/challenge the regime players can be explained by two factors: first, the presence of a group of leaders within the movement (similar to other labor movements that emerged in the Egyptian context since 2004), who advocated for a consensual position with the regime, and considered demands that were strictly financial to be their priority. Second, their possession of a social base within the movement that was broad enough to prevent its mobilization in a threatening manner to the regime. To avoid repression, the strategy of this nonpoliticized group of leaders, who also possessed a large social base within the movement, pushed it to cancel the call for the April 6, 2008, strike, thereby demobilizing the movement. The other group of more politicized leaders—whose social base was much weaker within the movement—failed to mobilize the movement to strike. However, their persistence in calling for the strike, a persistence that was amplified by the privately owned press, put the regime's security apparatus on a state of alert. The latter resorted to a level of repression that the movement wasn't equipped to deal with.

In contrast, the RETA employee's movement was able to challenge regime players and to successfully contest the regime's corporatist system, as it was led by a group of politicized leaders who had a strong social base within the movement. They were able to exploit this to convince the movement's members of the necessity of building a new trade union independent of the state corporatist structure, for the first time in Egypt's history since 1957. To achieve their vision, the leaders capitalized on the construction of a strong collective identity for the movement over the ten days of the sit-in. They produced narratives and framings that enabled them to persuade the movement's constituencies to embrace their choice, despite the risks. Through the narrative they formulated, the movement leaders managed to turn the threats or risks that the movement feared (e.g., risk of repression) into opportunities to be seized (e.g., remaining united to preserve their power). In the same vein, through the strategies they implemented, they succeeded in obliging the government to recognize their union and stopped any attempts by the regime players to block their oppositional initiative. In this sense, the presence of politicized leaders, who enjoyed a strong social base within the movement and were able to formulate effective strategies and resonant framings, was a necessary condition for it to succeed in its oppositional endeavor to the players of the authoritarian regime.

Theoretical Framework and Contribution

This research falls within the framework of social movement theory and contentious politics. It adopts the "strategic interaction paradigm" (SIP) as a framework of analysis for this book's two main case studies. The SIP approach provides a relational perspective, focusing on the strategic interactions among different players in various arenas. While the SIP approach has mainly been used to analyze social movements in democratic contexts—with a few exceptions, such as Volpi and Jasper (2018)—the relational approach taken in this book is particularly valuable, as it examines strategic interactions in authoritarian settings within the Middle Eastern context. In that respect, this research takes into account the critics addressed to the political process model (PPM) and the political opportunity structure (POS) for being structural, nondynamic, and nonrelational.[6]

The Strategic Interaction Paradigm (SIP) was introduced by Jasper and Duyvendak (2015) in their coedited volume. It focused on studying players and arenas in social movements. Players are seen as engaging in strategic action with specific goals, while arenas are defined as spaces where interactions take place with something at stake (Jasper, 2015a). This paradigm breaks down constructs like "the state" and "movements" into different players and arenas, emphasizing strategic interactions between the players (Duyvendak and Fillieule 2015; Jasper and Volpi 2018). In that sense, the SIP highlights their actions and strategies, including their attempts to block opponents and achieve their goals. By focusing on the interactions between players and analyzing their choices and decisions, the SIP offers a more nuanced understanding of social movements. Additionally, the language of players and arenas helps in highlighting the importance of time, interaction, and processes. Both sides are always moving and interacting during this contentious process (Jasper 2015a, 22–23). All actions are reactions, and because of this, interaction necessarily unfolds over time (Jabola-Carolus et al. 2020, 640). To analyze the interaction and

6. The PPM (political process model) developed by Doug McAdam (1982) consists of three analytical tools: political opportunity structure (POS), mobilizing structures, and frame analysis. The model suggests that mobilization and social movements occur when there are political opportunities, which refers to the existence of favorable political conditions and the absence of constraints that limit a movement's capacity for action (Tarrow 1998); mobilizing structures, which are formal and informal entities through which people engage in collective action (McAdam, Mayer, and Zald 1996); and the framing of collective action, which focuses on the use of cultural symbols and ideas by social movements to shape the meaning and interpretation of their actions (Benford and Snow 1986, 2000).

trace its evolution over time, the weight of past decisions, accumulations, understandings, and expectations is taken into consideration (Jasper 2021, 245). The identities, biographies, careers, and cultural backgrounds of the various players are also taken into account, as they influence how players attribute meaning to the world around them, and, thus, their decisions and choices. In fact, the emphasis on actions and choices in the SIP approach enables a deeper understanding of political action as an engagement between players over shared interests; it recognizes the trade-offs, dilemmas, and compromises they face as they navigate different arenas. By expanding their possibilities and limiting options for opponents, players strategically position themselves and seek to generate social change (Jasper 2014).

In this research, I adopt Samer Soliman's (2011) definition of "state" and "regime." Soliman sees the state as "the sum total of public institutions that rule over a specific territory, with their organizational structures, laws and regulations, and formal and informal rules" (24). A regime, according to Soliman, is "the organization of individuals who lead the state" (25). It is the management and leadership of an organized ruling coalition that transforms the state, which is a structure, into an agent (7). Therefore, the regime incorporates "the president of the republic, top security officials, the council of ministers (government), and the high public officials who lead and direct diverse state institutions and organs—individuals, human beings with flesh and blood" (25).[7] Accordingly, in this study, I investigate the "game" of moves and countermoves between the various subplayers of the Mubarak regime (government, Mahalla Company management, the representatives of the state corporatist structure [the ETUF], and the security apparatus) and the key players of the two labor movements studied in this book in the different arenas (of labor-related rights, trade unions affairs, and street politics). I confer greater importance to the dynamics of the strategic interactions between the actors/ players in the different arenas, as well as their goals and capabilities. I argue that this interactive

7. Soliman (2011) notes that despite the difference in the regime's policies from Nasser to Sadat to Mubarak, certain characteristics remained unchanged—namely, the authoritarian nature and clientelist relations.

approach is even more significant in authoritarian settings, where protesters face the risks of repression and, thus, have to negotiate, innovate, and implement strategies to challenge other players who seek to restrict their actions.

Along these lines, this research pays particular attention to the actions of movement leaders. It recognizes them as key players in social movements who make strategic decisions, inspire others, and influence collective action (Morris and Staggenborg 2004). They play a very important role in the development of collective action (Jasper 2014). Leaders must select the most influential frame among a large array of resonant beliefs, amplifying some and amending others, which is important in achieving the movement's goals (Robnett 2013). However, the role of leadership in social movements has been underresearched, and existing studies often take a structuralist approach (Erikson and Bob 2006; Morris and Staggenborg 2004; Ganz and McKenna 2019). Leaders' agency as players in comparison to the constraining conditions imposed on them has been downplayed in social movement studies. The literature on contentious politics has neglected the importance of leaders' practices and actions as well as the fact that the leaders of movements make choices among several options, and that these choices affect the mobilization capacity of the movement, as well as its outcome (Morris 1999). Leadership is frequently treated as a dependent variable rather than an independent variable with a significant impact on movement dynamics (Robnett 2013).

This research aims to address this gap by examining leaders' actions, strategies, and framings and highlighting their impact on movement mobilization and outcomes. Given the authoritarian regime's capacity to repress opponents, the strategies and choices of movement leaders gain heightened significance. In authoritarian contexts where mobilizing structures are often lacking at the movement's inception, leaders' agency and strategies become crucial in capitalizing on opportunities to build and mobilize their movements. Leaders' framing strategies play a vital role in recruitment, sustainability, and, notably, the movement's resilience in the face of repression, particularly within authoritarian settings.

In sum, this research focuses on the strategies, tactics, and framing choices of movement leaders, considering them crucial for understanding the dynamics of the movement as well as its outcomes. The analysis of these strategies and framings is presented in a relational and interactional perspective, taking into account the temporal evolution of the movement. Importantly, it also takes into consideration the influence of leaders' political careers, experiences, relationship with politics, and their social base within the movement when examining their choices and strategies. This recognizes the impact of these factors on their decision-making processes. Therefore, I argue that leaders with different political conceptions and positions within their movements make different strategic choices, which influence the internal and external dynamics of their respective movements.

Relevant Literature and Contribution

The literature on the labor movement in Egypt encompasses various perspectives and themes. One aspect of the research focuses on the history of state-labor relations and labor activism in Egypt, examining different approaches and frameworks. Beinin and Lockman (1988) employed a historico-Marxist approach to examine the development of the Egyptian labor movement and its connection to politics from the late nineteenth century until the rise of the Nasserist regime. They argue that the working class emerged as a result of Egyptian capitalism and British colonialism, with workers advocating for economic demands alongside nationalist aspirations for independence. Goldberg (2019) critiques the Marxist analysis and calls for a deeper examination of workers' social interactions and their place within broader society. Goldberg's critique highlighted the importance of the fascinating ethnographic research of Shehata (2009) in two public textile factories in Alexandria in which he personally worked. He highlighted the role of the shop floor and workers' everyday experiences in shaping their collective identity. Distinctive practices and rituals within the factory contribute to workers' sense of belonging and differentiation. Contrary to the Marxist approach taken by Beinin and Lockman (1988), Posusney (1993, 1997) adopted a different approach in her analysis of state-labor relations and workers' collective action from 1952 to 1980: the moral economy. She argues that workers perceive their wages and benefits as entitlements in exchange for their contribution to national economic development. The relationship between the state and workers is characterized by a patron-client relationship, where workers support the state in return for economic privileges and job security. In contrast to Posusney, who argues for workers' acceptance of controlled unions based on the moral economy, and differing from Beinin and Lockman (1988), who view state corporatism as imposed by the postcolonial regime, Goldberg (1992, 2019) supports the rational choice paradigm as an explanatory model for workers' decisions in the postcolonial era, particularly in their relationship with the state.[8] According to Goldberg, state corporatism was a rational choice for both union leaders and workers due to the limited opportunities in open labor markets, as workers preferred administered markets with state-regulated wages. This perspective acknowledges workers' agency and the potential for their choices to evolve based on circumstances and opportunities.

Another aspect of the literature focuses on state corporatism and its deficiency—for example, Paczynska (2006, 2009) explores organized labor's response to privatization processes in Egypt and other countries. She finds that organized labor in Egypt and Poland had a significant influence on the reform program, while labor in Mexico and the Czech Republic struggled to shape restructuring plans. The availability of resources ensuring that the voices of organized labor, such as the Egyptian Trade Union Federation (ETUF), are heard during privatization debates, and the cohesiveness of the ruling party and relationships with labor prior to reforms, are identified as key variables influencing workers' responses. Aidi (2009) disagrees with the notion that ETUF's leadership was able to block privatization due to its influence and financial independence. Instead, he attributes the slowdown of privatization to the regime's inability to control rank-and-file workers and incorporate them into the new economic system. Aidi compares Mexico and Egypt, highlighting the more

8. According to the rational choice approach, collective action is the result of aggregated individual preferences, formed by a desire to maximize their impact. In the workers' case, this means that engaging in collective action is the result of a calculation of costs versus benefits. When the expected benefits (remunerations, jobs, privileges) exceed the expected costs (salaries not received, loss of work or repression), the workers organize collective action.

exclusive ruling party and corporatist structure in Egypt, which hindered the regime's control over workers. Hartshorn (2018, 2019) extends Aidi's analysis by explaining the collapse of state corporatism in Egypt and Tunisia prior to the 2011 uprisings. He blames the collapse on a combination of structural adjustment, flexibilization, and loss of political power. The contraction of the public sector through privatization and flexibilization undermined workers' employment and wages, leading to protests. The Mubarak regime's increasing control over the state corporatist structure and the rise of neoliberal policies disconnected the organization from rank-and-file workers. This led to the organization of collective action and alternative structures outside the auspices of the ETUF. Bishara (2018) addresses the variation in labor groups' responses to authoritarian institutions by creating independent organizations, with a specific focus on the Mahalla labor movement and the RETA employees' movement. She builds on Aidi's analysis and presents a sequential model that explains the timing and variation of labor group exits from the corporatist structure. She emphasizes macrostructural factors such as the erosion of corporatist gains and the regime's control over the structure while noting that, additionally, group-level factors, including the history of activism and financial benefits, play a role. In this respect, Bishara also highlights the importance of leadership in advancing oppositional goals and shaping strategies.

Shifting the focus on the discussions addressing the features and characteristics of the cycle of labor protests (2004–11), El-Mahdi (2011) argues that the wave of labor protests in Egypt starting from 2006 cannot be explained solely by rational choice or the restoration of gains, as suggested by the moral economy theory. Instead, she asserts that these protests reflect the neoliberal rupture of the labor-state pact that existed since 1952. This rupture is manifested in the state's withdrawal from the economy and the reduction of repression against workers to attract capital. While economic and wage demands still dominate the labor movement, El-Mahdi argues that the recent protests differ in tactics, with longer strikes and the inclusion of political demands such as management dismissal, minimum wage, and independent unions. This challenges the moral economy perspective and signifies a break from the old authoritarian state-labor relations, opening the possibility for a new democratic reality. Duboc (2015), on the other hand, contends that labor protests in Egypt before 2011 displayed a form of "non-contentious politics." Workers rejected the politicization of their demands, which was a pragmatic response to the restrictive political context and a tool to avoid repression while achieving economic demands. She emphasizes the performativity of workers' acceptance of the regime's rules in order to win concessions. Alexander (2010, 2013) and Alexander and Bassiouny (2014) focus on the democratic character of the labor protests and their role in shaping the pre-2011 revolutionary dynamics. Alexander (2010) argues that a shift occurred from a bureaucratic model of leadership dominated by the state-controlled ETUF to a more democratic model. Structural adjustment policies increased state control over the ETUF, leading to decreased legitimacy among workers and challenging the ETUF's authority. This created opportunities for alternative structures, such as independent unions, and the emergence of democratic practices within the labor movement. These practices allowed for debates, dialogue, and workers' participation in decision-making, leading to the creation of "spheres of dissidence" where alternative visions of society could be articulated (Alexander 2013).

Finally, with regard to the social movement analysis of the wave of labor protests post-2004, to their credit Beinin and Duboc (2013) authored one of the first scholarly works to adopt a critical perspective of social movement theory in the analysis of workers' movements in Egypt (during the period of 2004–12), taking into account the challenges imposed by the authoritarian context. This article featured in Beinin and Vairel's (2013) collective volume, which offers a critical analysis of social movements in the Middle East and North Africa (MENA) region, including labor protests in Egypt. Beinin and Vairel (2013) argue that social movement theory, often based on cases in the democratic north, can be still relevant in studying mobilizations in authoritarian contexts. They criticize the political process model (PPM) for its structuralist bias and adopt a more dynamic framework: McAdam, Tarrow, and Tilly's "dynamic of contention" (2001), which they consider better suited for studying movements in the MENA region. Contrary to the PPM, Beinin and Duboc (2013) show that the labor movement in Egypt operated with limited resources and weak organizational structures and often relied on informal networks

in-depth analysis of the dialectics between the leaders and their followers, showing how these interactions reinforced the persistence of workers protests over time. I demonstrate that the agency of leaders plays a pivotal role in formulating and communicating alternative visions for society, as exemplified by the RETA movement. Moreover, I emphasize the varying effects of leaders' connections to their followers on their ability to convey progressive visions, thereby influencing the movement's dynamics and outcomes, as observed in the case of the Mahalla labor movement.

Third, my analysis of the Mahalla labor and RETA employees' movements, based on the SIP, offers a comprehensive, interactive, and relational framework for analyzing the dynamics of labor protests. This framework goes beyond the dynamic of contention framework adopted by Beinin and Vairel (2013) in their collective volume. The SIP focuses on the interactions between different players, rather than solely focusing on contextual factors or structures. It provides a better understanding of the actions, strategies, and tactics employed by various players in contentious arenas. In my research, I delve deeper into the strategies and tactics employed by movement leaders, demonstrating how their actions and choices facilitated the transformation of scattered protests with weak organizational structures and limited resources into a nationwide movement with strong mobilizing structures, as seen in the case of the RETA employees. Basing my analysis on the SIP, I explain how the movement's interactional dynamics, including the dynamics of the leaders' strategic interaction with regime players, promoted the gradual formation of the movement's mobilizing structures. This is a point that Beinin and Duboc (2013) fail to thoroughly explain. While the authors acknowledge the eruption of labor protests in Egypt pre-2011 despite limited resources and weak organizational structures, they neither provide a comprehensive explanation of the process through which these movements may built and transformed into stronger entities nor delve into the role of leaders in facilitating this transformation.

In sum, I believe that prior studies on the labor movement in Egypt have lacked a systematic focus on the interactive and contentious dynamics between regime players and key players within these movements. In sharp contrast, this research enhances the existing body of scholarship on Egyptian labor activism and social movements within the context of authoritarian regimes. It explores the influence exerted by leaders, analyzing their choices through an interactive and dynamic perspective, thus highlighting their significance in understanding the outcomes of the movement, whether classified as "success" or "failure."

Structure of the Book

The first chapter discusses the sociopolitical context of labor protests during the late Mubarak era (2004–11). In this chapter, I present three characteristics that distinguished this period of time and influenced the movement leaders' choices. To begin, I discuss the pact that governed state-labor relations in the postcolonial era, the changes or the rupture that neoliberal policies introduced to that pact, and the workers' responses. Next, I take an in-depth look at the state corporatist structure and the deficiency of its cooptation mechanisms pre-2011. Special attention is given to the high interference of the security forces in the 2006 trade union elections, a fact that rendered the organization completely ineffective. Finally, I analyze the political opportunities available since 2004, due to a change in the regime's strategy, embodied by the relative liberalization of the mass media and the declining repression of workers' protests, elements that led to a significant increase in the frequency of labor protests. In the chapters that follow, I discuss how the movement leaders exploited these opportunities and the outcomes this generated.

In the second chapter, I emphasize the mechanisms of emergence and success of the Mahalla movement in 2006, and the role of the movement leaders in achieving such an outcome. I present a sociological and historical analysis of the Misr Company for Spinning and Weaving in Al-Mahalla al-Kubra City and explore the multitude of informal networks maintained by the workers within the company. Then, I shed light on the sociological and activist backgrounds of the movement's leaders, and their consequently divergent positions, which later influenced their choices during the strategic interaction with the regime players in the arena of work-related rights. This analysis of the movement's internal dynamics—with regard to the demands proclaimed and the strategies pursued—is necessary for analysis of the movement's outcomes. I emphasize the tactics and framings that were employed by the leaders in response to the regime players' moves to end the 2006 strike, and their impact on the success of the 2006 strike in achieving the movement's economical demands.

In the third chapter, I look at the way the movement leaders interacted with the openings in the regime players' strategy in the arena of labor-related rights, and the dynamic of the strategic and contentious interaction between the movement players and the regime players. I investigate the movement players' failed attempt to challenge the ETUF (one of the regime's subplayers) by asking for the dissolution of the trade union committee inside the company (which is affiliated to the ETUF). This contentious episode is crucial for understanding the entire dynamic of the movement through the lens of the divergent strategies of its players vis-à-vis the regime players. I go on to analyze the mechanisms through which the leaders exploited the media (especially the privately-owned press), as well as the dynamics of the strategic alliance between the media and the movement. Finally, I explore the dynamics of the 2007 strike and the strategic interaction between the government and the movement leaders and examine the tactics that were pursued by the latter to ensure the survival of the movement during the six-day strike.

In the fourth chapter, I first examine the movement's internal dynamics, which led to the decision to make the minimum wage for all workers in Egypt the driving demand of the 2008 strike. Next, I investigate the process through which political organizations arrived on the scene after the movement chose to present a demand that was national in scope. I emphasize the media's role in transferring workers' demands from the local to the national level and on transforming the economic framing of these demands into a political one in a context of the politicization of labor. From there, I analyze the dynamics of this contentious and strategic interaction between the regime players and the movement players. I shed light on the strategic trade-offs and dilemmas that faced the movement's players, and the different choices made by the movement's leaders based on their different cognitive visions. Then I discuss the repertoire of repression deployed by the security apparatus in response to both the confrontational strategy chosen by the group of politicized leaders, and the outcomes that these contentious interactions generated either at the level of the company and the city of Mahalla.

In the fifth chapter, I describe the process and the dynamics of the emergence (and development) of the RETA movement as a "player." I thus explain how the limited mobilization of the RETA movement in the Giza governorate produced an *upward scale shift*, leading progressively to the formation of a social movement of national scope, despite the movement's geographical dispersion and weak organizational structures.[10] I start by presenting an analysis of the sociological profiles and activist careers of the movement's leaders. Next, I analyze the process of the spread of the movement's protest from Giza to the other governorates, and the process through which the movement's mobilizing structures were gradually formed during this contentious and strategic interaction with the regime players in the arena of labor-related rights and in the arena of street politics. In this regard, I emphasize the movement leaders' tactics and decisive influence on the success of the process.

In the sixth chapter, I emphasize the dynamics of the RETA employees' sit-in on December 3, 2007, which was established in front of the headquarters of the Cabinet for ten consecutive days. I explore how the RETA movement leaders successfully carried out this mobilization, thus obliging the regime players to meet their demand for parity with the RETA employees based in Cairo. In this sense, I investigate the strategic choices made by the movement's leaders to avoid repression, and the tactics they used to neutralize the security apparatus during the ten days of the sit-in. I examine how the movement players decided to create, and succeeded in founding, an independent union, an action characterized—by the regime players—as oppositional or challenging to their power. I explain how, through the interactional and contentious dynamic of the sit-in, a collective identity was formed, and how this permitted the construction of a strong social movement that was able to challenge the state corporatist structure of the ETUF (one of the regime's subplayers). Finally, I discuss the decisive role of the leaders in this endeavor, with a focus on the narrative and the framings they formulated to persuade the movement's

10. Upward scale shift involves coordination of collective action at a higher level (whether regional, national, or even international) than its initiation (Tilly and Tarrow 2015, 125).

security apparatus, coupled with media coverage, enhanced the visibility, sustainability, and frequency of these protests in the years preceding the uprising.

Accentuation of Policies of Economic Liberalization and Its Impact

During the 1930s and 1940s, Egypt underwent substantial industrialization, leading to the emergence of a significant working class. This working class, despite not constituting a majority, played a pivotal role in labor activism, tightly connected with the nationalist struggle against British colonialism. The workers perceived economic and political demands as inseparable (Beinin and Lockman 1988).

With Nasser assuming power in 1952, a state-labor patron-client relationship characterized state-labor relation. Government and worker behavior and choices were governed by the moral economy approach (Posusney 1997), emphasizing a reciprocal implicit agreement. The state guaranteed workers a decent standard of living, and, in return, workers provided political support and contributed to the national development project, particularly in the public sector (Posusney 1997; Pratt 2001; Waterbury 1983).

Contrary to this, Goldberg proposed a rational choice approach post–World War II, highlighting the demand for secure jobs as the key concern for the working class. While some skilled workers benefited from open labor markets, most preferred state-regulated wages in exchange for job security and political loyalty. The exchange of job security and state-regulated benefits for political obedience can thus be considered a preferential claim of the organized sector of the workforce in the public sector, that which the regime had incorporated into the corporatist structure it founded in 1957 (Goldberg 1992, 2019). The rational choice approach emphasizes workers' agency and the temporality of their decisions, aligned with the regime's choices. While suitable for understanding labor movements challenging regime policies, it falls short in analyzing specific policies prompting worker protests and the diverse repertoire of actions expressing discontent.

According to the moral economy approach, the breach of the implicit pact between labor and the state—characterized by declining wages, subsidy removal, and privatization—elicits worker discontent, driven by heightened job insecurity and loss of profits previously ensured by the public sector. Policy alterations unrelated to these concerns generate less anger. This means that the erosion of workers' earnings through a direct reduction of salary would generate more resistance than that caused by inflation, the impact of which would be less direct for workers (Posusney 1997, 17–21). This highlights a shift observed in 2008, when Mahalla workers demanded a minimum wage for all Egyptian workers, due to rising inflation, deviating from the established pattern.

To express their anger, labor refrains from striking except as a last resort, emphasizing their commitment to not hinder production despite grievances. Instead, workers employ symbolic protests like refusing to collect wages, affecting government finances, and resorting to facility occupations and sit-ins (Posusney 1997, 156). This strategic approach underscores their dedication to their pact with the state, even as the state falls short.

Following the collapse of the Nasserist project, Sadat and Mubarak leaned toward economic liberalization. Structural issues, overstaffing, reduced output per employee, and escalating subsidies posed challenges to the Nasserist model (Goldberg 1992, 157). Foreign exchange shortages and inadequate domestic resources hindered policy goals, exacerbating the budget deficit. The regime faced a dilemma as its pursuit of rapid economic growth, which required a high level of investment, and therefore of savings, clashed with the drive to increase citizens' consumption, exacerbated by dwindling foreign reserves (Ikram 2006, 12; Farah 2009, 36).

The government's response to the deficit exacerbated economic conditions, opting for import restrictions instead of devising strategies to boost them. By 1974, the balance of payments deficit reached \$326 million, with a projected current account deficit of about \$1.4 billion in 1975. Industrial production suffered from underutilization, plummeting to 32 percent in 1974, reflecting the challenges in sustaining the Egyptian economy during this period (Ikram 2006, 16–17).

Sadat's post-populist transformation marked a significant shift in Egyptian economic policies following the 1973 October War, leveraging the war's legitimacy and changing international dynamics (El Shafei 1995, 18; Ikram 2006, 18; Farah 2009, 78). His *infitah* or "open door policy" aimed at global market integration and foreign investment, leading to a reconfiguration of the social contract established by Nasser (Pratt 1998, 17). However, these economic reforms, emphasizing public-sector efficiency and promoting the private sector, came at the expense of pro-labor measures introduced by Nasser, altering the relations and dynamics between the state and the working class (Pratt 1998, 16).

The regime's new direction triggered labor protests from 1974 to 1977. Mahalla workers, in March 1975, and public transportation workers in September 1975, engaged in strikes demanding improved conditions (Farah 2009, 79). The popular slogans chanted during this period were rooted in the moral economy. They reflected workers' attempts to return to a period when their wages and social status were higher than they had become under Sadat. For example, in 1975, the strikers came up with the catchphrase "During the defeat, people could still eat" (Beinin 2009, 71).

The IMF-sponsored austerity program in 1976 further intensified public discontent, resulting in large food riots on January 18–19, 1977 and subsequent repression of the political left (Adly 2021, 168; Beinin 2009, 71). Although GDP grew substantially during Sadat's infitah era (1974–82), averaging 9.1 percent annually, this growth was propelled by factors like petroleum exports, Suez Canal revenues, remittances, and tourism, rather than increased productivity in sectors vital for the Egyptian labor force (Ikram 2006, 24–26; Waterbury 1985, 73). Infitah's anticipated foreign investment failed to materialize as expected, with gains concentrated in financial services (Waterbury 1985, 76). Structural issues, such as the lack of competitiveness-increasing policies, remained unaddressed under Sadat, leaving the public sector dominant and financial commitments to welfare programs unchanged (Ikram 2006, 24; Waterbury 1985, 80–81). The economic reforms led to the disorganization and marginalization of the working class and repression of the Left by the end of the 1970s (Beinin 2009, 71).

Following a decade of infitah, Egypt faced, under Mubarak, severe economic challenges, with external debt soaring from $3 billion in 1974

hesitancy in implementing privatization measures swiftly was also influenced by concerns about social and political instability, as highlighted by Soliman (2011), Kienle (2004), and Ferrié (2006). Aidi (2009) suggests that the regime's inability, rather than unwillingness, to expedite privatization is rooted in its lack of control over the workers. The Egyptian Trade Union Federation's (ETUF) structural incapacity to represent workers complicated the regime's plans for labor (further discussed in subsequent sections).

Workers, grappling with deteriorating social and financial conditions, protested against the adverse effects of privatization, which, in turn, discouraged private investment (Pratt 2001, 116–17). The government responded with partial social compensation for affected workers, including early retirement policies and the formation of shareholder collectives among public sector workers (Farah 2009, 82). Simultaneously, the regime resorted to repression to quell protests. Given that privatization was put forward gradually, repression was easy to carry out, because the security apparatus only had to deal with localized protests (Pratt 2001, 118).

As liberalization and privatization increased, labor protests surged. Between 1998 and 1999, there were 287 of them, including 90 strikes, marking the most significant labor agitation since 1952 (Aidi 2009, 143), compared to only 37 in 1988/89—that is to say, before the start of privatization (Pratt 2001, 120; Aidi 2009, 142; Paczynska 2009, 188). Worth noting is that, by the end of the 1990s, real wages declined in almost all sectors of the economy, and, by 2000, half the population was living below the poverty line (Paczynska 2009, 187). This does not make it surprising that the period from 1998 to 2003 saw an average of 118 labor protests per year (Beinin and Duboc 2013, 212).

In addition, the repertoire of protest actions changed during this period in comparison with the second half of the 1980s. Recourse to strike as a mode of protest was more frequent, with eight strikes occurring in 1990, twenty-six in 1991, twenty-eight in 1992, sixty-three in 1993, and then the bloody strike of 1994 in the Kafr al-Dawar plant (Aidi 2009, 142). However, these labor protests did not indicate a willingness to abandon the moral economy contract. Instead, they underscored workers' commitment to the postcolonial pact, even as the government deviated from it.

The nature of labor claims did not pose a real threat to the state; rather, they strengthened the regime's position by reaffirming the moral economy and limiting workers' negotiating leverage (Pratt 2001, 120–22).

In the 1990s, weak connections with political parties limited the labor movement ability to frame their claims as part of a broader struggle (Albrecht 2013, 54). The influence of political parties in this era experienced a general decline, largely attributed to state restrictions on party politics, resulting in a political arena marked by stagnation during the Mubarak era (El-Shobaki 2010, 2011). Partisan structures were depleted of their capacity for action, and leftist parties, traditionally allies of the labor movement, saw a decline (Beinin 2009, 72). Beinin (2009, 72) notes that the Tajammuʻ Party, representing the traditional Left, strategically supported the Mubarak regime against the Muslim Brotherhood and Islamist insurgency, anticipating state repression or Brotherhood control over potential labor protests. This strategic choice aimed to provide the party with more flexibility under authoritarian rule, leading to informal negotiations on labor issues with the government (Clement 2007, 106).

Additionally, the fall of communism globally in the late 1980s had repercussions for Egyptian politics, causing former communist parties, including the Egyptian Communist Party, to virtually disappear from the political scene (El-Mahdi 2010). By the end of the 1990s, these once-strong parties were reduced to a mere dozen activist leaders, as many had already left a decade earlier. The traditional Left witnessed a gradual decline, ceasing to be a reliable or effective ally of the labor movement, thereby contributing to labor's permanent "disconnection" from political parties and a process of gradual depoliticization. The only exception was that a few members of various movements belonged to the rather politicized generation of the 1970s and 1980s. These two factors will be key to understanding the behavior and choices of the leaders of the various social movements discussed in chapters to follow.

During the third period from 2003/4 to 2011, Egypt experienced a notable acceleration in economic liberalization, particularly in privatization under prime minister Ahmed Nazif's Cabinet. The government passed the unified labor code in 2003, legalizing short-term contracts and layoffs, eroding the job security that was a significant labor benefit during the

Nasser era (Aidi 2009; Paczynska 2009). Economic reform became a top priority for the Mubarak regime in 2002, prompting the appointment of Gamal Mubarak, wealthy businessmen, and international finance experts to key positions within the NDP (Collombier 2012, 4). This marked a shift from state bureaucrats and academics to openly neoliberal technocrats and businessmen (El-Mahdi 2012, 139). The Nazif government announced ambitious plans to privatize the majority of public enterprises, resulting in the privatization of seventeen enterprises in its first year and fifty-nine for $2.6 billion in 2005–2006 (Beinin 2011, 186). Privatization revenues reached 2.5 percent and 1.9 percent of GDP in 2005–6 and 2006–7, driven by major privatizations like the sale of the Bank of Alexandria and the partial privatization of Telecom Egypt (Rutherford 2008, 223). Between 2004 and 2008, Egypt more than doubled its privatization revenues compared to the previous decade (Roll 2013, 7).

Furthermore, measures were implemented to open up Egypt's economy to trade and foreign investment, including a reduction in tariff and nontariff barriers and tax reforms. Tax on imports decreased by an average of 9 percent in 2004, and a law introduced in 2006 standardized the tax on companies at a rate of 20 percent (El-Naggar 2009). Trade as a percentage of GDP increased from 46.1 to 65.1 percent between 2002/3 and 2006/7, and foreign direct investment (FDI) rose from 2.2 percent to 5.3 percent of GDP from 2004 to 2007, although it remained concentrated in the oil, energy, and construction sectors, rather than being diverted to export-oriented sectors (Diab 2017).

The IMF praised these economic reforms, highlighting a growth rate that more than doubled from 3.2 percent to 7.1 percent between 2002/3 and 2006/7 (Bush 2012, 59). However, this growth was accompanied by the rise of monopolies, increased inequalities, poverty, and the deterioration of social conditions, leading to the 2011 uprising. The inefficiency and lack of transparency in governance structures resulted in crony capitalism, corruption, and a failure to redistribute growth equally among the population (El-Mahdi 2012; Bush 2012). The period between 2004 and 2011 also marked the intertwining of private wealth and political power as businessmen joined the NDP and entered parliament post the 2000, 2005, and 2010 elections (Soliman 2011; Adly 2012, 2020). Politically connected

figures benefited from privatization and deregulation, while workers faced wage stagnation and rising unemployment, contributing to economic inequality (Joya 2017, 343).

Contrary to the neoliberal expectation of a "trickle-down effect," social measures accompanying liberal reforms and the redistribution of economic growth were lacking (Collombier 2012, 4). The state's retreat from social services and welfare intensified with the implementation of the neoliberal agenda, resulting in the reproduction of poverty and downward mobility (El-Mahdi 2012). The percentage of Egyptians living on less than two dollars per day grew from 19.6 percent in 2004 to 25.2 percent in 2010. Simultaneously, inflation rose significantly, and real wages declined after the devaluation of the Egyptian pound in 2003 (Aidi 2009, 173). Inflation rates increased from 4.7 percent in 2004–2005 to 10.9 percent in 2007 (El-Naggar 2007, 171). The ratio of wages and salaries to GDP declined sharply, falling from 48.5 percent in the late 1980s to less than 20 percent in 2007 (El-Naggar 2009, 49). The global food crisis exacerbated the situation, with prices of essential commodities rising sharply from 2005 to 2008 (Beinin and Duboc 2013, 211). In December 2007, a 40 percent increase in the price of 144 food items led to a major social crisis, aggravated by shortages of subsidized bread in the spring of 2008 (Beinin and Duboc 2013, 211).

High inflation rates particularly impacted the small real wages of civil servants and public sector workers, leading to a significant reduction in their purchasing power. Government reports indicated that 6.8 million government and public sector employees lost half their salaries in 2007 (Aidi 2009, 173). Consequently, most public-sector workers and their families were considered "poor," living on less than two dollars per day per person, reflecting the dire economic conditions faced by a substantial portion of the population (Beinin 2011, 187). In 2007, the basic monthly salary of industry workers was approximately 105 EGP per month ($19; Beinin 2011, 187), keeping in mind that the average base salary of textile workers in the first half of the 2000s was 250 EGP ($36). It should be noted that in the public sector, allowances and bonuses increased the monthly salary by approximately 400–450 EGP ($57.60–$64.80; Beinin 2009, 75). As for civil servants who worked thirty years, they received a salary of approximately 730 EGP ($105.20; El-Naggar 2007, 179). This is important because

it explains the reason why state employees, like the real estate tax collectors, considered themselves part of the labor movement during this period of the second half of the 2000s. As Rabab El-Mahdi (2011, 398) stated, the recent developments in capitalism made the distinction between the two categories more difficult, since some "blue-collar" workers in the industrial sector were better paid than the state's "white-collar" employees. That is why, in this book, I will refer to both categories as being part of the labor movement. Worth noting is that both categories were also affiliated with the ETUF.

Between 2004 and the eve of the Mubarak regime's breakdown in 2011, Egypt experienced an unprecedented wave of labor protests, with public-sector workers and civil servants leading the charge as early as 2004 (Adly 2012, 211). This period marked the longest and most substantial wave of labor protests since the end of World War II (Beinin and El-Hamalawy, 2007b). The 2004 annual report of the Land Center for Human Rights reported that, from 1998 to 2004, there were approximately 1,000 collective actions. One-quarter of them were held in the year 2004 alone (approximately 266), an increase of 200 percent compared to 2003, which had approximately 86 (Beinin 2009, 77). In fact, 70 percent of the labor protests that took place in 2004 were organized after the Nazif government assumed office in July 2004 (Beinin 2009, 187).

By the end of 2006, the success of the labor movement strike in the Misr Spinning and Weaving Company at Al-Mahalla al-Kubra, north of Cairo, had a trigger effect on other protest movements. During the time frame of the first Mahalla strike on December 7, 2006, and the second Mahalla strike on September 23, 2007, the number of workers participating in strikes nationwide increased from 198, 414 workers to 2 million in May 2007 (El-Mahdi 2010, 147). With this stimulus, the number of social mobilizations increased significantly in 2007, virtually tripling, compared to 2006. These mobilizations in fact multiplied from 266 in 2006 (including 80 in the governmental sector and 79 in the public sector) to 614 in 2007 (including 255 in the governmental sector and 145 in the public sector), and then to 609 in 2008 (including 267 in the governmental sector and 107 in the public sector), 432 in 2009 (including 189 in the governmental sector and 67 in the public sector) and 371 in 2010 (including 165 in the governmental sector and 34 in the public sector; Beinin and Duboc 2013, 214–15).

Two key factors contributed to the rise of worker protests: the enactment of Act 12 of 2003, which removed workers' job security, and the acceleration of the privatization process. These factors exacerbated the long-term deterioration of workers' conditions, eroding their economic gains from the Nasser era and signaling a significant departure from the moral economy contract with the government (Beinin and Duboc, 2013). The wave of protests reflected a neoliberal rupture with the post-1952 labor-state pact, both ideationally and materially, as the state retreated from the economy in discourse and action, accompanied by a decrease in repression of workers and the emergence of new media and increasing possibilities for circulation of information (El-Mahdi 2011).

In that respect, I argue that this wave of labor protests, which emerged on the eve of the breakdown of the Mubarak regime in 2011, was characterized by both discontinuity and continuity with the moral economy: while the workers' repertoire of actions aligned less with the moral economy framework, the nature of their claims remained generally aligned with it. However, I contend that the reluctance of workers to confront the regime in their protests was not solely rooted in their purported belief in a partnership with the state, as posited by the moral economy. Rather, it can be attributed to pragmatic considerations within a constrained political context. As asserted by Duboc (2015, 34), labor does not explicitly recognize the regime's power. Instead, it expresses a form of acceptance of the authority, leveraging it to secure economic gains while steering clear of coercion. An important characteristic of this kind of noncontentious politics is, thus, its performativity. Contrary to El-Mahdi (2011), who affirmed that this wave of protests experienced the rise of new demands with a political aspect—such as those asking for company management dismissal, a minimum wage, the replacement of union committees, and the establishment of independent unions—that challenge the moral economy pact, I argue that these demands were the exception rather than the rule. With the exception of the Mahalla labor movement, which raised the challenging demands of the minimum wage in 2008 and withdrew confidence from the trade union committee of the textile union within the company in 2007, and the RETA state-employees, who built an independent union in 2008, the claims that arose during workers' protests remained limited to those of a strictly economic and sector-based nature.

This situation underscores the need to understand and assess the oppositional choices made by the leaders of the two movements at stake in this book and to analyze the effect of the tactical innovation in the Real Estate Tax Collector Movement's repertoire of actions that led to its success in achieving its demands and challenging the Mubarak regime.

State Corporatism or Inefficient Co-optation?

At the end of the struggle for independence, Nasser constructed an authoritarian political formula drawing on what Schmitter (1974, 86) called "state corporatism," a form of representation designed to link the associative interests of civil society with the state's decision-making structure. This corporatism aimed to incorporate social groups into vertical mobilization structures for national development, presenting itself as a form of socialism. Organizing society into functional, vertical groups, it restricted pluralistic and competing interests, serving as a means of controlling and supervising various social groups and their access to material resources (Gobe 2006, 172).

During the Nasser era, state-worker relations were marked by an explicit agreement between trade union leaders and the regime, aligned with the moral economy. Union leaders supported the Nasser regime and refrained from striking in exchange for guarantees on workers' economic demands, particularly job security. As a result, in 1952, the regime enacted laws to contain labor activism in return for ensuring job security and the improvement of working conditions such as Act 317 of 1952, prohibiting strikes and limiting trade union pluralism, leading to the creation of a single union in each employment category (Pratt 1998, 9).

In 1957, Nasser established the Egyptian Federation of Trade Unions (ETUF), its executive council appointed by the government. This move illustrated the regime's tactic of co-opting labor movement leaders to exert control. The ETUF, created after purging opposition activists, particularly those with communist leanings, was linked to a parent ministry overseeing its finances and activities (El-Shafei 1995, 15). The ETUF had increased powers in collective negotiation, supported various services for its members, and enjoyed privileges like establishing savings funds and cooperatives and athletic and cultural clubs for its members. All of this was partially financed through compulsory membership (Bianchi 1986, 432).

In 1961, the ETUF was granted a formal monopoly of representation, becoming the single official union organization with a hierarchical structure representing workers in any given industry (Paczynska 2009, 87; Aidi 2009, 70). In 1964, the centralization of the corporatist system was reinforced through the reduction in the number of national trade unions from fifty-nine in 1959 to twenty-eight in 1964. This made the coordination of collective action more difficult, since unrelated industries and unions were placed together in the same structure (Pratt 1998, 12).

The ETUF comprised three levels of organization: the trade union committee at the base, consisting of organization-related committees (such as the case of the Mahalla Company workers) and professional committees (such as the case of the state employees of the Real Estate Tax Collectors) representing workers in specific factories or professions; general trade unions, numbering 23, representing various professions, each with multiple trade union committees at workplaces, totaling 1,809 committees; and the General Federation, with a board of directors composed of the 23 representatives of the general unions.[1]

However, Nasser's institutional structure lacked representative channels for mid-level and low-level leaders, limiting their ability to express the preferences of their constituencies or rise in the hierarchy (Aidi 2009, 72). This structural lack of integration and representation increased with the regimes of Sadat and Mubarak, who sought to increase the cooptation of the leadership at the upper echelons of the federation, thereby increasing their disconnection from the middle and lower ranks of the institution—a problem that (as will be explained) would be accentuated even more with the level and degree of fraud that the 2006 trade unions elections witnessed.

1. Mostafa Bassiouni, 2009, "Azmat al-tanzim al-niqabi fi Misr" [The Crisis of the Trade Union Organization in Egypt], Center for Socialist Studies, November 2009, http://www.e-socialists.net/node/5115 (accessed June 16, 2024).

Under Sadat's presidency (1970–81), despite the illusion of political liberalization with multiparty elections in 1977, workers faced dissatisfaction due to economic liberalization policies. In response to protests at the Mahalla Company in 1975 and the bread riots in 1977, Sadat introduced legal reforms increasing the centralizing and the state control over the corporatist structure; simultaneously intensifying the scrutiny of union leaders (Bianchi 1986, 432–38). Act 35 of 1976 in particular expanded the federation's powers as well as the authority of the minister of labor over its activities and funding. The act also incorporated the trade union leaders within the state bureaucracy, giving them the right to participate in discussions of the laws relating to social and economic development (Pratt 1998, 19). Act 1 of 1981 extended union leaders' terms, perpetuating their leadership at the top of the union hierarchy and granting them the right to issue executive decrees on union affairs. However, local committees were not allowed to sign collective agreements without the permission of the union in question (Pratt 1998, 20), limiting the capacity of lower-level unionists to resist economic liberalization reforms (Aidi 2009, 150). These structural constraints isolated top-level unionists from their bases, exacerbating disconnection (El-Shafei 1995; Aidi 2009).

As early as 1991, Mubarak initiated structural adjustment policies, promoting divestiture through Law 203 of 1991 (Hartshorn 2019). This legislation introduced bureaucratic and managerial changes essential for economic reforms, strategically keeping the federation away from economic policy negotiations and benefiting the businessmen who were participating in them (Hartshorn 2019; Pratt 2001). The implementation of economic liberalization, especially privatization, entailed even closer control of the trade union organization. This control would come about through a series of legal reforms aiming at co-opting upper union echelons and preventing vertical rotation within the organization, reminiscent of Sadat's regime (El-Shafei 1995; Pratt 1998; Alexander 2010).

During the 1990s, the government amended Act 35 of 1976 governing union affairs (Amendment 12, 1995), extending union leaders' terms from four to five years (Alexander 2010) and allowing them to remain in leadership positions at retirement age, provided they stayed in the same sector of the union they represented (Pratt 2001, 117–18). As a result, the rotation of federation executive committee leaders ceased after the 1996 elections, favoring the regime-friendly old guard (Pratt 1998, 34–35). These amendments aimed to consolidate the power of the loyalists at the expense of younger leaders potentially more radical in opposing privatization. Regime loyalty within the ETUF was further strengthened by reserving a cabinet position for the federation and promoting an executive member to the Ministry of Manpower. By the 2000s, the majority of ETUF's leadership were also members of Mubarak's party, as was the minister of manpower (Hartshorn 2019, 40).

In 2003, as economic liberalization intensified, a unified labor code, No. 12, was enacted, depriving public-sector workers of job security (by allowing contracts for temporary work in the public sector) but granting the right to strike, albeit only under ETUF auspices. In reality, however, the ETUF never authorized a strike or any sort of collective action. Contention over work-related issues was thus pushed out of the formal system, and wildcat strikes become the only possible way to express grievances (Hartshorn 2019, 35).

Postenactment, the regime ensured the permanence of loyalists in trade union leadership through oversight of election rules by the Ministry of Labor. As Clément (2007, 69) points out, several bureaucratic rules enabled the regime to eliminate oppositional candidates through, for example, the requirement that candidates obtain the signatures of the three cochairs and have their applications stamped by the union, as well as limiting its issuance to one or two days before it was due to be filed. Moreover, the applications had to be submitted to one of the twenty-two Department of Labor offices issuing the candidacy certificates. The candidates who managed to overcome these obstacles faced new difficulties at the time of submitting their applications, as state security agents checked each application and pointed to the candidates who should be denied certificates (73).

These bureaucratic hurdles are important in understanding the dynamic and results of the fraudulent trade union elections that were held on November 13, 2006, and that were followed by the largest wave of labor protests in Egypt since World War II. The executive committee seats of the federation and fourteen unions within the General Union were all won by acclamation, while, at the lower levels, 45 percent of trade union committee seats (805 out of 1,807) were determined in the same manner, with the remaining 1,002 seats subject to elections (Sharara 2009, 71). Government intervention, a recurring theme in Egyptian trade union history, reached unprecedented levels in 2006 compared to previous elections in 1980 and 1990, extending beyond the upper echelons of the union hierarchy to encompass fraud at all organizational levels of the federation (Bishara 2018).

In these trade union elections, government and security interference and, thus, electoral fraud occurred via two mechanisms: for one, a substantial number of candidates were prevented from participating, extending even to the local level. Clément (2006, 109) notes that out of thirty-five thousand registered candidates, ten thousand to thirty thousand were excluded, with most permitted candidates selected by the federation's president in collaboration with the Ministry of Labor and state security, and with the assistance of the companies' management. Direct security intervention on the election day—the second mechanism—aimed to thwart the success of certain candidates who might have otherwise escaped exclusion (Bishara 2018, 41–42). An example is Kamal Abu Eita, leader of the RETA movement, as will be discussed in chapter 5.

Hence, starting from the late 1980s and early 1990s and following the successive measures of governmental control over the ETUF, it is hard to believe that this institution was able to deliver in any capacity, either on behalf of the regime or the workers. However, Paczynska (2006, 2009) argues that the powers granted by Sadat to the ETUF, with the aim of decreasing workers' opposition to his rule, increased the federation's financial and political independence vis-à-vis the regime. This independence allowed ETUF to resist Mubarak's economic liberalization policies in the 1990s, especially regarding privatization. Sadat's grants included procedural prerogatives, such as participating in government discussions concerning any policy changes that would have an economic or social impact on workers, and economic privileges, such as using public funds and compulsory worker contributions to establish financial resources, making ETUF one of Egypt's wealthiest interest groups (Bianchi 1986; Paczynska 2006, 2009).

Contrary to Paczynska (2006, 2009), Aidi (2009) assumes that ETUF faced a structural problem from its inception, as it lacked representative channels for mid- and low-level leaders to express constituents' grievances. This explains the slowdown of privatization in the 1980s and early 1990s, as the regime was unable to incorporate workers into the liberalized economic system without facing strong resistance. I agree with Aidi that this structural dysfunctionality of ETUF rendered the institution incapable of conveying meaningful support for the regime's plans. I also argue that the Mubarak regime exacerbated this problem by strengthening control over ETUF. As noted by Hartshorn (2018, 2019), structural adjustment policies (which led to, e.g., the contraction of the public sector, privatization, loss of job security, the laying off of workers, and stagnated wages), combined with increased control measures (through the combination of new laws and cooptation of leaders), rendered ETUF leaders isolated from their base and unable to connect with rank-and-file workers. The supposed close ties with the regime failed to halt neoliberal reforms that negatively impacted workers, highlighting the weakened influence of ETUF in safeguarding workers' interests (2019, 41). This situation pushed the workers to find other channels to express their dissatisfaction, either through legal measures and the courts, via the support of human rights and labor rights NGOs, or via the organization of collective action and alternative structures outside the auspices of the ETUF (2019). The largest wave of worker protests since World War II emerged in the mid-2000s, signifying the failure of the ETUF to represent and control workers effectively.

The extensive fraud that marked the 2006 trade union elections generated two important results of particular significance for the development of the two social movements at stake in this book. One result was its severance of the disconnection between the ETUF and rank-and-file workers, exacerbating the existing crisis of representation. Fraud infiltrating the lower echelons of the union, prompted workers to act and protest independently (Bishara 2018, 41). The acceleration of economic liberalization policies since the mid-2000s, coupled with fraud in the 2006 trade union elections, triggered the largest wave of labor protests in Egypt since World War II, setting the stage for the 2011 uprising. As pointed out by Hartshorn (2019), the collapse of corporatism in Egypt marked not only the erosion of an economic system but also key support structures for the regime.

The other result was that union leaders, denied positions within the ETUF due to activism, leveraged workplace networks and those built during their electoral campaigns for collective action against the regime and the ETUF (one of its subplayers), as the two movements under study in this book will show. As Hartshorn (2018, 343) has highlighted, the case of the Mahalla workers and the RETA state-employees marked the emergence of a "labor lacunae": spaces in the political and economic structures that witnessed increased authoritarian management and accelerated economic liberalization, thereby leading to substitute methods of corporatist bargaining and inclusion by coercion or neglect. This opened the door to increasing militancy.

Some activists, disillusioned by the fraudulent interventions, abandoned the idea of "reforming from within" through participation in the union's elections, opting to establish new, more representative trade union structures independent of the coopted ETUF (Bishara 2018, 42). The wave of workers' protests after 2006 opened the door, as Alexander (2010) points out, for the emergence of a more democratic model of leadership, challenging the bureaucratic top-down approach represented by the ETUF. The Real Estate Tax Collectors movement, for instance, founded the first "independent union" since 1957 in December 2008, reflecting a broader trend toward democratic organizational structures and questioning the traditional leadership model within the ETUF.

Change in the Mubarak Regime Strategy: More Sustainability for Labor Protests?

The postcolonial regimes in Egypt, marked by centralized executive power and party hegemony, underwent significant changes with Sadat's arrival. While retaining corporatist structures implemented by his predecessor, Sadat introduced a dualist strategy, allowing the emergence of pluralistic economic and political entities. This included a move towards a multiparty system, greater media freedom, and limited civil society organizations, albeit under strict control to maintain party hegemony (Shehata 2009, 21–25).

The Mubarak regime, characterized as a "liberalized autocracy," sustained political liberalization without transforming into a democratic regime (Brumberg 2002, 2003; Vairel 2013). This mixed strategy maintained corporatist control while allowing the growth of pluralistic structures. Political liberalization served as a survival strategy for the regime, balancing democratic elements with tight control over power levers (Shehata 2009, 33–34). During 2004–6, Mubarak permitted even greater political liberalization in response to growing US pressure for Middle East democratization following the events of September 11, 2001. In a 2003 speech to the National Endowment for Democracy, George W. Bush urged Egypt and other Middle Eastern countries to embrace political reforms.[2] On June 20, 2005, US secretary of state Condoleezza Rice delivered a speech at the American University in Cairo, emphasizing the inevitability of a fully free and democratic world. Rice specifically advocated for Egypt to establish free elections, stressing the need for these elections, including parliamentary ones, to adhere to objective standards defining every free election.[3] In this context, on February 26, 2005, Mubarak proposed the amendment of article 76 of the Egyptian Constitution, allowing for the first time the establishment of presidential elections in September 2005. This limited or relative opening introduced by the regime can be understood as part of its survival strategy, as it allowed it to face American attempts to export democracy, to increase its legitimacy externally, and to extend its social base internally (Abdalla 2006).

Two protest cycles emerged during this period. The first, from 2004 to 2006, saw the formation of the Egyptian Movement for Change, Kifaya (Enough), symbolizing political opposition to Mubarak's continued rule and his son's intended succession—hence the movement's name, "Enough." Its slogan was, "No to the continuation of this reign, no to succession" (*La lil tamdid wa la lil tawrith*). Kifaya, led by political elites and intellectuals, marked a departure from previous limits on speech and

2. "President Bush Discusses Freedom in Iraq and the Middle East," remarks by the president at the twentieth anniversary of the National Endowment for Democracy, White House, November 6, 2003, http://www.whitehouse.gov/news/releases/2003/11/20031106-2.html.

3. Condolezza Rice, 2005, "Remarks at the American University in Cairo," US Department of State, June 20, 2005, https://2001-2009.state.gov/secretary/rm/2005/48328.htm.

political action (Albrecht 2013, 73). The movement openly criticized the president, breaking a long-standing taboo, with private media amplifying its rhetoric and enlarging the circle of political discussions (Albrecht 2013, 73; Ben Nefissa 2008, 20–21). Kifaya introduced "street politics" (relatively speaking), organizing public gatherings and demonstrations in Cairo's city center and challenging the regime's red lines (Albrecht 2013, 72–73). Despite its innovation and impact, Kifaya remained largely elitist and limited in scope, failing to establish broad connections to more popular sectors (Vairel 2013, 44).

The Kifaya movement, symbolizing political opposition to Mubarak, significantly influenced Egypt's youth, providing an alternative political outlet (Allam 2012, 26–27; Mohsen 2012, 76; Abdalla 2012, 51). Some of the young people of Kifaya formed the movement Youth for Change, which participated in most of the events organized by Kifaya from 2005 on (Mohsen 2012, 76). Other young Kifaya members later played crucial roles in the formation of new political parties, such as Ayman Abdel Nour's Al-Ghad Party and Osama al-Ghazali Harb's Al-Jabha al-Dimuqratiya Party, emphasizing the desire for change through youthful and viable entities (Abdalla 2012, 51–55). The dedication of young activists to both the Kifaya movement and newly formed political parties, along with the rise of blogging from the mid-2000s, encouraged segments of politicized youth to envision the possibility of change (Allam 2012, 26–27; Mohsen 2012, 76; Abdalla 2012, 51). This sentiment played a pivotal role in the significant contentious episode of April 6, 2008. In the landscape of growing cyberactivism, two political activists affiliated with Al-Ghad and Al-Jabha al-Dimuqratiya utilized Facebook as a political mobilization tool for the first time (Shehata 2007, 5; Duboc 2009b). They employed the platform to advocate for a national strike on April 6, 2008, expressing solidarity with the Mahalla Company workers. The virtual call to action eventually led to the establishment of the 6th of April movement.

The second cycle of protests, spanning from 2004 to 2010, primarily focused on social issues, with the political openness of 2004–6 creating a conducive environment for protest actions. However, the increase in labor protests cannot be solely explained by political openness during this period. The rationale behind this is that labor protests had already experienced a surge in tandem with the liberalization of economic policies in the 1980s–1990s, within a more oppressive context compared to the conditions in the late 1990s and mid-2000s.

Instead, the sustainability of labor protests, especially during the mid-2000s wave, warrants closer scrutiny. I argue that it can be attributed to substantial changes in the regime's strategy. One shift was that the regime allowed the liberalization of the privately owned press and media, leading to the emergence of newspapers and satellite channels that became strategic allies of the labor movement. This departure from previous restrictive legislation, notably Act 148 of 1980, was marked by the enactment of Act 396 of 1996. This new legislation simplified the process for newspaper ownership, requiring approval only from the Cabinet, as opposed to the more stringent conditions of Act 148. This liberalization coincided with ongoing privatization in the 1990s, fostering an investment-friendly environment for privately owned media (Ezz El-Arab 2008). As a result, a new generation of Egyptian newspapers, including *Al-Usbu‘* (January 20, 1997), *Sawt Al-Ummah* (December 6, 2002), *Al-Masry Al-Youm* (January 19, 2004), *Al-Fajr* (June 3, 2005), *Al-Dustur* (March 23, 2005), and *Al-Badil* (August 18, 2007), emerged. Privately owned newspapers achieved a more credible outlook and garnered a broad readership; however, as highlighted by Ezz El-Arab (102–5), they faced challenges related to professionalism. Notably, *Al-Badil* and *Al-Dustur* newspapers, with their leftist inclinations, emerged as strategic allies of the labor movement. Additionally, private media, especially satellite television channels like Dream TV, El-Mehwar, and On TV, emerged during this period of increased privatization (Kheir 2012). By 2006, Nilesat 101 had over eighty TV channels and four hundred radio channels, facilitating political debates in the public sphere (Abdulla, 2006, 93). This newfound openness allowed discussions on once-taboo political topics, including criticism of state institutions or the president's family, fostering a new type of interaction between the state and society (Ben Nefissa and Moisseron 2007, 19–20). These media outlets served two interconnected functions crucial for sustaining labor protests: providing visibility for protest actions and raising the cost of repression. Media coverage of social and political protests influenced public opinion, thereby providing protesters with a degree of protection as well as encouragement.

It is not surprising that the next crucial change in the regime's strategy revolves around a decrease in regime repression. While the early 2000s saw a decline in violent security interventions in political protests, particularly evident with the Kifaya movement in 2005, a subsequent period of relative political deliberalization in 2007 brought about increased security crackdowns on political protests (Albrecht 2013, 16). Interestingly, security forces adopted consistently nonrepressive measures toward labor protests during the 2004–10 period, in stark contrast to the 1980s and 1990s (Alexander 2010, 248). In fact, during 1981–94, the Mubarak regime had always responded to labor protests with a mixture of concessions and repression (Posusney 1997, 163). In various instances spanning 1984, 1985, 1986, 1989, and 1994, security forces forcibly entered factories where workers had initiated sit-ins, resulting in the arrest of a substantial number of workers. Tragically, during these episodes, particularly in 1984, 1989, and 1994, confrontations between security forces and workers led to the loss of lives (Bishara 2018, 43). For example, organized strikes at the steel plant in Helwan (1989) and the textile factory in Kafr al-Dawar (1984–94) were suppressed with deadly violence (Beinin 2010, 35). However, by the late 1990s, there was a notable easing up on security crackdowns (Clément 2006, 107), with the regime opting for containment (e.g., cordoning off protest sites), indifference, and concessions rather than concessions and repression (Bishara 2018, 43). The transition to a more hands-off approach by security forces became a prevailing trend by 2006, notably after the Mahalla movement's labor strike at the end of the year. Security forces generally contained protests by surrounding premises or encouraging punitive measures by company management against organizers but without recourse to violence against them. The exception was the crackdown on the Mahalla Company labor protest in 2008.

While accurate information explaining the regime's shift in security strategy is challenging to obtain, a set of hypotheses shed light on potential reasons for this change—for example, the absence of a significant political threat to the regime since the late 1990s, particularly with the decline in influence of leftist political parties, as mentioned previously, coupled with the depoliticization of the labor movement which decreased worker mobilizations (Clément 2006, 107). Additionally, the liberalization of the media made it difficult for the regime to resort to repression without international consequences (El-Mahdi 2011, 396). Moreover, as highlighted by El-Mahdi (2011), a new political elite ascended to power, prominently comprised of businessmen and technocrats, notably affiliated with the NDP Policy Committee led by Gamal Mubarak, the president's son. This elite, distinct from the previous military-centric bureaucrats with a repressive stance, prioritized economic reform and relied heavily on foreign investors and private investment; consequently, they were averse to jeopardizing their reputation by resorting to forceful intervention in factories and companies (396).

Despite the uncertainty regarding the exact reasons, it is evident that the Mubarak regime's response to labor protests underwent a transformation since the late 1990s and especially with the mid-2000s. The decline in repression, while not a significant factor in the emergence of the Mahalla protests in 2006, played a role in reducing the cost of labor protests, facilitating their increased frequency. In a climate of media liberalization and easy dissemination of information, the decline in repression encouraged other labor movements to thrive.

Conclusion

In summary, the period from 2004 to 2011 was marked by three key characteristics that significantly influenced the choices and actions of leaders of the analyzed movements: first, a rapid implementation of economic liberalization policies alongside a decline in living standards since the mid-2000s. The implemented policies, signifying a departure from the postcolonial pact, were characterized by labor claims that were strictly economic in nature, avoiding direct challenges to regime players. This holds significance in analyzing the leaders' evolution within the two movements, shifting from purely financial demands in 2006 and 2007 to more confrontational demands against regime players in April and December 2008. Second, the significant extent of fraud in the 2006 union elections impacted leaders who were excluded from the process, motivating them to mobilize for future protests through the networks formed during those elections. Finally, changes in the regime's strategy, involving a decrease in repression and media liberalization. These factors prompted the leaders to shift from primarily financial demands in 2006/7 to more oppositional demands against the regime in 2008. The forthcoming chapters delve into how these leaders navigated these changes, interacted with regime players, and effectively orchestrated subsequent protests, ultimately compelling the government to address their grievances.

2

The Hero Reappears?

The Emergence of the Mahalla Labor Movement

Introduction

In this chapter, I begin with a sociological and historical examination of the Misr Company for Spinning and Weaving in Al-Mahalla al-Kubra, highlighting the distinctive company structure that facilitated strong social networks among workers. These networks forged solidarity bonds and a collective identity, ultimately culminating in the 2006 mobilization. In contrast to structural theories, in my analysis I delve into the complexities of the social players, scrutinizing their personal and collective histories. Drawing upon the strategic interaction paradigm, I explore the biographical and sociological characteristics of movement leaders as strategic players, explaining how these factors shape both the internal and external dynamics of the movement. Understanding the sociological and activist profiles of leaders proves crucial for deciphering their choices, strategies, and, consequently, the outcomes of the movement.

I also analyze the framing and tactics employed by movement leaders in response to regime attempts to end the 2006 strike. Through an analysis of the strategic interactions between key players from both the movement and the regime, I offer a dynamic perspective on how these contentious interactions unfolded and the resulting outcomes. The decisions and actions of movement leaders aimed to strengthen worker solidarity, enabling the mobilization to persist despite security threats and ultimately achieving success in securing financial demands from both the government and the company's management. I argue that the success of the 2006 mobilization created new opportunities for the sustained success of the Misr

Company's labor movement, underscoring the role of contentious interactions in guiding the movement's players to perceive and interpret existing political opportunities.

The Misr (Mahalla) Company: Governmental Control and Financial Problems

The Mahalla Company, located in the city of Al-Mahalla al-Kubra, includes a number of spinning and textile plants. It is also one of the largest cities in the governorate of Al-Gharbiyya, north of Cairo. The company, which owns the largest spinning and weaving factory in the Middle East, was founded on August 26, 1927, as the first Bank of Egypt project, led by Egyptian economist Talaat Harb, founder of the modern Egyptian economy. From the outset, the company hired two thousand workers. Currently, it has about twenty-four thousand workers, one-quarter of all textile workers in the public sector in Egypt.[1] The Mahalla Company is affiliated with the Spinning and Weaving Holding Company (Al-sharika al-qabida lil-ghazl wa al-nasij), run by the Ministry of Investment (previously the Ministry of Trade).[2] Under Act No. 203 of 1991 and its decrees, the holding company controls any public-sector companies relating to spinning and weaving, such as the Mahalla Company.[3] The holding company comprises thirty-two companies: twenty-three spinning and weaving companies, and nine cotton companies. This type of company is founded upon the recommendation of the minister of investment and approved by the prime minister.[4] Its director (or chairman of the board of directors) is also determined by the same Act No. 203, which stipulates that a holding company must include a board of directors and a general assembly, which is responsible for the formation of the board of

1. From an undated booklet on the internal structure of the Mahalla Company, published by the company itself.

2. Referred to in this book as the "holding company," for the sake of simplification.

3. See website of "Al-sharika al-qabida lil-ghazl wa al-nasij" [The Spinning and Weaving and Clothing Company], http://www.mpbs.gov.eg/Arabic/Affiliates/Holding Companies/Pages/HoldingCompaniesDetails.aspx?id=5.

4. See Article 1, Chapter 2 of Act No. 203 of 1991.

directors.[5] The general assembly also chooses its president for a three-year renewable term.[6] However, this structure is merely theoretical, because, on the practical level, it is the minister of investment who directly appoints the chairman of the board of directors, as clarified by the director of the Center of Trade Union and Workers Services (CTUWS) (Dar Al-Khadamat Al-Niqabiyya wal-'Umaliyya), an NGO for the defense of workers' rights, during the strikes of 2006–8 (Saher, interview with author, August 4, 2009). This was the case, for example, for holding company ex-director Mohsen al-Gilani, in position until May 28, 2012 (he was also ex-president of the global group Amonisto and Co. of the Delta Spinning and Weaving Co.).[7] At the end of his term, the new minister of investment appointed General Fouad Abdel Alim, former chairman of the board of directors of the Mahalla Company, to preside over the holding company and train a new board of directors.[8] This complex web of connections highlights government influence over these companies.

Act No. 202 of 1991 stipulates that companies affiliated with the holding company, like the Mahalla Company, be founded upon the suggestion of the holding company's board of directors, following the approval of the minister of investment. The board of directors of the companies affiliated with the holding company must include a minimum of five and a maximum of nine members.[9] The chairman of the board must also be designated by the General Assembly.[10] However, this designation process is also only theoretical, because, on a practical level, the chairman of the board of directors of these companies must be appointed by the holding

5. See Article 3, Chapter 2 of Act No. 203 of 1991.

6. See Act No. 203.

7. See the biography of Mohsen al-Gilani on the website of "Al-sharika al-qabida lil-ghazl wa al-nasij" [The Spinning and Weaving and Clothing Company], http://www.textileholding-gov-eg.com/a-mohsen.htm (accessed July 23, 2024).

8. "Abdel Alim ra'isan lil-qabida lil-ghazl khalif Al-Ghilani" [Abdel Alim Succeeds El-Ghilani in the Presidency of El-Sherka El-Kabeda], 2012, *Al-Youm Al-Sabi'*, May 28, 2012.

9. It should also include the president of the trade union committee of the company, but without counting his vote.

10. See Act No. 203 of 1991.

company's chairman of the board of directors (Saher 2009), which shows the vicious cycle of governmental control and lack of transparency. This is, in fact, what happened with the Mahalla Company's chairman of the board of directors from 2006 to 2007, Abdel Fattah al-Gebally, who was a former official in the company, and with his successor (at the end of 2007), General Fouad Abdel Alim, ex-director of the Arab Company and Bolvar Spinning and Weaving, also affiliated with the holding company (Saher 2009).

Since the late 1990s, the Mahalla Company's earnings—which previously exceeded 4 billion Egyptian pounds (EGP) per year—had been steadily decreasing, while its debts increased due to economic liberalization policies enacted by the government.[11] These policies led to the lifting of price controls on cotton, which is necessary for textile manufacturing. Indeed, a few weeks after the 2006 strike, minister of labor Aisha Abdel Hadi acknowledged that the crisis at the Mahalla Company was not a random occurrence. She affirmed that the textile sector's decline resulted from inadequate government policies, particularly the hasty removal of price controls on cotton. This, coupled with an accumulation of interest on company debt, exacerbated the crisis.[12] Ibrahim Abu Saa'da, a former company worker and ex-member of its Board of Directors, confirms this fact. However, he provides more details concerning the Mahalla Company. He explains that the increase in company debt and the considerable losses that it has accrued go back to the year 1996, when the government decided to lift price controls on cotton. The price of a ton of cotton reached 18,000 EGP. Cotton production in Egypt is only 4.5 million quintals (1 quintal = 100 kg.), 3 million of which are exported. The rest was left for internal consumption. The Mahalla Company uses 1 million, and the remainder

11. Al-Sayed El-Turki, 2006, "Bil-arqam wa al-watha'iq: khitat al-hukuma li-takhrib sharikat ghazl al-Mahalla li-salih rijal al-a'mal" [With Numbers and Documents: The Plan of the Government to Destroy the Mahalla Company for the Benefit of businessmen], *Al-Dustur*, December 20, 2006.

12. "Wazirat al-quwwa al-'amila ta'tarif: al-siyasat al-mutarakima al-khati'a sabab ahdath ghazl al-Mahalla" [The Minister of Labor Admits: Bad Policies Are behind the Events of the Company of Mahalla], 2006, *Al-Jumhuriyya*, December 26, 2006.

is distributed to other companies in the textile industry. He added that, to make up for the lack of domestically produced cotton, Egypt imports from Syria, Pakistan, and India, which is much less expensive (a ton costs only 13,000 EGP) than cotton produced by Egypt, but its shorter fiber means lower quality (El-Turki 2006, 2).

The imported cotton negatively influenced the company's profitability. The imported short-fiber cotton damaged the company's machines, which deteriorated. Consequently, the company's product quality steadily declined, and importers purchased less and less. The Egyptian privately owned newspaper daily *Al-Dustur* published several annulled contracts with foreign importers in Europe and the United States because of the company's declining product quality and defects in the exported products. It cited the example of a canceled contract (138/16/2005) between the Mahalla Company and the Italian Technocabrique Company. The contract stipulated the import of 750 tons of spun cotton at 1.7 million EGP. It was revoked because the fabric that was sent to Italy was defective (El-Turki 2006, 2). Most of the importers terminated their contracts with the Mahalla Company for the same reason and even demanded that it provide them with an explanation for the visible deterioration in product quality during the last few years.[13] It should be mentioned in this context that the company succeeded in turning a profit up until 2005: in 2004 and 2005, it saw financial gains of 140 million and 72 million EGP, respectively. With bank interest payments of 98.4 million EGP in 2004, and 106.2 million EGP in 2005, this resulted in a net profit of 19.2 million in 2004, and 5 million in 2005.[14]

In 2006, and with the advent of new chairman al-Gebally in the month of March, the company's financial situation became even more grave

13. They could not understand the reason behind this deterioration because the company has an international reputation.

14. Mohamed Abul Dahab, 2008, "Al-jam'iyya al-mumumiyya li-sharikat ghazl al-Mahalla 21 October al-qadim wa masadir: al-arqam al-awaliyya lil-mizaniyya tu'aqid wujud khusarat 144 million junayh" [The General Assembly of the Mahalla Company Convenes Next October 21 and Sources: Preliminary Figures Confirm Losses of 144 Million Egyptian Pounds], *Al-Dustur*, October 15, 2008, 2.

because the net profits began to transform into losses as a result of bank loans taken out by the company's management. Its debts increased considerably. The company had financial gains of 102 million, and bank interest payments of 115.1 million, so these gains were transformed into a net loss of 5 million. After the strike of 2006, the minister of the investment made the decision to cancel the company's debt to strengthen its financial position.[15] Nevertheless, in 2007, the situation worsened dramatically, when its profits were transformed into rather substantial losses. The company saw losses of 13.1 million, with bank interest payments of 33.1 million EGP, and net losses reached 43.7 million EGP (Abul Dahab 2008, 2).

It is worth noting that the company's General Assembly decided, on November 27, 2007, to dismiss the company's director, Abdel Fattah al-Gebally, after accusing him of corruption. This decision, however, was made as a result of the strike in September 2007. To placate the workers, the minister of investment accepted his resignation, which had been one of the demands of the 2007 protests. Moreover, an inquiry commission was formed by the General Assembly to detect corruption within the company.[16] The commission reported several forms of corruption in the administration or in financial resource management, such as the presence of a number of al-Gebally's relatives, who occupied key positions and enjoyed special privileges; al-Gebally's questionable financial expenditures, such as outlays for the development company's social club and cinema, as well as debts estimated at one million EGP under the names of unknown clients; and negligence in the maintenance of equipment damaged by the defective cotton (Bedir 2006, 2).

This corruption resulted in a company with inefficient machinery and defective fabric that was not being exported. This state of affairs led to increased losses and the refusal to provide the workers with their bonuses,

15. Nagwa Tantawy, 2006, "Ijma' min al-nuwab wa al-hukuma 'ala tahiyat al-'umal" [The Agreement of the Parliament and the Government Regarding the Congratulations of the Workers], *Al-Isbu'*, December 18, 2006.

16. Fathy Bedir, 2006, "'umal ghazl al-Mahalla yutalibun bi-muhakamat ra'is al-sharika" [Workers of the Mahalla Company Request the Judgment of the President of the Company], *Al-Wafd*, December 10, 2006.

since the company was no longer profitable (El-Turki 2006, 2). It also explains the movement leaders' insistence on receiving the bonuses the workers were due, despite the losses. As stated by one of the movement leaders, they fulfilled the tasks assigned to them, and the company's low productivity was primarily attributed to corruption and inadequate maintenance of the equipment they were obligated to work with (Soad, interview with author, February 7, 2010).

In 2008, with the arrival of new director Fouad Abdel Alim Hassan (by mandate), the losses tripled and reached approximately 145 million EGP. At the first Annual Meeting of the General Assembly under Hassan's mandate, on October 21, 2008, the losses were unveiled: 144, 750,000 EGP. The problems of corruption and mismanagement increased all the more under Hassan's mandate: the losses tripled. Domestic sales decreased by 455, 989 million EGP to 391, 105 million—an estimated 64, 884 million EGP less than the previous year. Exports decreased by 396, 570 pounds to 357, 373 million EGP—a difference of 39, 197 million EGP in comparison with the previous year. Total company sales thus declined by 852, 559 million EGP to 748, 478 million EGP.[17] This was a decrease of 104 million EGP from the previous year, a fact that bears out the company's poor resource management.

Finally, it is important to mention that these gradually increasing losses of the company led the leaders of the movement to wonder about the government's intentions to privatize it under the pretext of increasing profits. As stated by two leaders of the movement, there had always been concerns among the leadership that this scenario might unfold. They feared that, in the event of privatization, each factory associated with the company would be sold individually. Essentially, the largest assembly of workers in Egypt—a significant factor in its ability to apply pressure—would be systematically and irreversibly dismantled, which was their foremost concern (Reyad and Ashraf, interview with author, January 31, 2009).

17. This data was collected by the author from the *Al-Dustur* newspaper correspondent in the city of Al-Mahalla al-Kubra.

A Multitude of Social Networks and Bonds of Solidarity

In view of the substantial workforce, the Mahalla Company was divided into multiple divisions, as articulated by one of the leaders of the movement: the Spinning Division, which in 2010 had approximately five thousand workers, was historically one of the most demanding sections in terms of physical effort and the number of working hours and, as a result did not hire women; the Weaving Division, which encompassed approximately fifteen plants and two thousand workers; the Fabric Treatment Division; the Medical Cotton Division, which boasted the largest wadding factory in the Middle East; the Wool Division, which had approximately three plants and two thousand workers; the Clothing Division, which had approximately five thousand workers, including many women; and the Silk Division. Other divisions were related to engineering (the water factory, the central electrical system, garage equipment), and to administrative work. The Engineering Division had approximately three thousand engineers and workers, while the Administrative Division had approximately five thousand employees (Wahid, interview with author, April 11, 2010).

The company structure has historically been hierarchical in nature. At the summit of this hierarchy were the high-level employees in the administrative departments. They were mostly civil servants with university degrees. In the middle of the hierarchy were the technicians in the engineering departments. They had technical diplomas, which means they had completed middle school and then studied in technical institutes. At the base of the hierarchy were the workers in the spinning, weaving, cotton, and clothing departments. They had generally completed their primary education or middle school studies and sometimes had no schooling at all (Saher, interview with author, February 7, 2009). This was not just a matter of hierarchy, but also a class demarcation between high level employees and technicians on the one hand, and the workers on the other. A small example of this is that the middle- and high-level employees had their own door to enter the company that the workers did not have the right to use. The workers' quarters were much more modest than those of the employees, ensuring that they remained not only economically but also socially disadvantaged (2009). It is worth noting that almost all the leaders of the mobilization in 2006 were either from the middle or the base of this hierarchy. Furthermore, the leaders of the 2006 strike were spread throughout the departments, which facilitated the formation of social ties between workers through daily social interactions.

The company is located on an area of 600 acres, of which 340 were devoted to production, and 260 to social services and housing. Factory workers have always lived either in the villages and towns around Mahalla, or in factory housing, which included homes, pools, parks, social clubs, libraries, nurseries, poultry farms, a training center for the workers, a sanitary drainage station, a theater, a scout's organization for the center, a hospital, and 50 acres of agricultural land.[18] The company structure consisted of several factories on the one hand, and, on the other, everything needed to live there. Homes and places of entertainment were thus designed to create a multitude of informal networks among the workers. It was no longer a factory in the strict sense of the word, but, rather, a social structure, a way of life. It was a community of workers with social bonds. This situation makes it quite different from other Egyptian companies like those situated in the new private industrial complexes of 6th of October City (Sitta October), or 10th of Ramadan (Al-'Ashir min Ramadan). In these locations, the workers are quite scattered in factories that are at a distance from each other (El-Mahdi 2010, 157–58; Abdalla 2017; 2020).

In addition, matters between Mahalla Company workers were not confined to the workplace but took place in a context of day-to-day family relationships, including spouses, parents, and children. The public companies traditionally recruited the children of workers. This tradition was all the more marked in the Mahalla Company, which had a higher percentage of women in the workforce because of the production of knitted and crocheted goods (Duboc 2011, 11). Entire families worked at the company.

One of the workers explained it this way:

> I've been working in the business for ten years now. This is where my father also worked, and where my wife, my mother, and my sister still

18. From an undated booklet on the internal structure of the company of Mahalla, published by the company itself.

> work. This is the case for almost all the families working at the company. Here we represent generations from the same family. (Interview cited in El-Mahdi 2010, 158)

The factory played a central role in the makeup of employee social networks within the movement. These networks reinforced a sense of belonging to the factory as a social, rather than a strictly professional, unit. The factory was a source of ties outside of work, both through matrimonial bonds and social or economic relationships (Duboc 2011, 10–11).

Reyad (2009), a company labor leader, explained:

> One day, I lost my salary of 500 Egyptian pounds. I was sad, and I didn't know what to do, but when one of my friends found out, the news spread quickly in the company. Five hundred workers each paid one pound and they gave me my salary.

In this framework, informal credit groups (*gam'iyat*), prevalent among company workers, also give a good picture of how well they are integrated into solidarity networks. The "*gam'iya*" (credit group) is a lending system based on its members' monthly contributions. One person is designated the responsibility of collecting the money and must ensure that each member receives the amount borrowed, according to an agreed upon schedule. In Mahalla, workers often used this system to finance wedding arrangements, to cope with the costs of health care, or to buy home appliances. This system is based on a relationship of trust between the members of the *gam'iya*, and imposes moral obligations with regard to monthly payments (Duboc 2011, 12).

Hence, bonds of solidarity were visible through the daily relations of the workers, who were prepared to use their networks to help each other. These bonds were shaped by what Jasper (2014) calls "affective loyalties." Jasper (108) defines affective loyalties toward individuals, groups, places, and ideas as being "these basic orientations toward the world [that] include love, respect, and trust—as well as their negative counterparts like hate or mistrust" (108). In the case of the Mahalla workers, affective loyalties toward the factory and the community of workers did not only include love, respect, and trust toward their counterparts in the movement but also mistrust toward regime players. These bonds of solidarity and this shared network of friendship and militancy thus formed the basis of a strong collective identity, reinforcing the individual's identification with the community and developing a sense of belonging to it.

As highlighted by Duboc (2011, 13), social and family ties between workers emphasize the division between them and those who benefited from their work—namely, "management, the official trade union and the government representatives"; therefore, the term "worker" is used to designate any person hired to work in the factory who was prepared to question the legitimacy of these groups (Duboc 2011, 13). Hence a distinct *boundary* between the "we" and the "them" was established, mirroring the strong collective identity of the movement that was constructed and shaped in opposition to the regime players.[19] This explains why company engineers such as Yasser and Samer, or even employees like Mohsen and Seif, are referred to as "labor leaders," while technically they are not "workers."

Therefore, this oppositional collective identity and "this awareness of a community spirit," to quote Hunt and Benford (2004, 445–46) was forged through a long history of activism, during which the labor movement players entered into confrontation with the regime subplayers (i.e., the government and the company management) in the 1970s and 1980s. It emerged victorious, despite the cost it paid in terms of repression, as the following section will discuss.

"Politicized" Leadership and a Legacy of Victories

The Mahalla labor movement has a long history of activism. First of all, the labor mobilization of 1975 took place in a context of social frustration that worsened because of the policies of economic liberalization under the presidency of Anwar Sadat. The demands of this strike were: the application of the Civil Service Reform Act for all workers in the public sector; (the dissolution of the company's Board of Directors, which they regarded as corrupt; and other claims related to increasing workers' bonuses.

19. For more information about the formation of boundaries and collective identity, see Taylor and Whittier 1992; Hunt and Benford 2004; Melucci 1996; and Diani and Mische 2005.

Sadat's enactment of the Civil Service Reform Act was the main trigger for this mobilization, as it privileged government employees, particularly in terms of promotion. However, this act was not intended to be applied to employees or workers in the public sector (El-Banna 1992, 561). As Fatouh, former labor leader in the Mahalla Company, stated, the act caused resentment among public-sector workers, who began to feel that the Sadat government was opposed to their interests (interview with author, January 31, 2009). Furthermore, just before the outbreak of the strike, the company management had taken hostile measures against company workers, such as the elimination of restaurants that provided workers with quick meals at affordable prices (Abdel 2002, 87).

According to Hassan, one of the leaders of this mobilization, most of the company leaders did not subscribe to any particular political orientation. They were mainly former military personnel returning from the War of 1973, very frustrated because they had not received the honor they felt they deserved (Hassan, interview with author, January 31, 2009). Being deprived of the privileges accorded by the Civil Reform Act was a trigger point for these leaders, who mobilized the workers. The movement engaged in several repertoires of contention, including strikes, sit-ins, and demonstrations in front of the company management's door—actions that were repeated during the 1980s, as well as in the 2006 mobilizations. To this repertoire, the mobilization of 1975 added breaking and entering of company officials' houses. The workers entered just to steal chickens from their refrigerators. Their intent was to display them in front of the company management's door during their demonstration, all the while vocalizing that they indulge in luxurious meals of pigeons and chickens, while the workers subsist on beans ("*Humma yaklu hamam w-firakh w-ehna al-ful dawakhna w-dakh*"; Abdel Latif 2002, 88). This symbolic act was intended to express frustration over the privileges enjoyed by the company employees, who were already better paid than the company workers. The staff, in fact, already had easy access to chickens procured by the company cooperative (*gam'iyat al-sharika al-istihlakiyya*) which the workers did not have access to (88). This slogan would henceforth be the watchword for all future mobilizations of the Mahalla labor movement. White (1992) asserts that social networks are composed and created through narratives and historical references with embedded meaning. In the same vein, I argue that the social networks that were mobilized in 2006 also relied on such meanings that were embedded in their history of contentious interactions with the regime. As Diani and Mische (2015, 317) suggest, the articulation of social ties within a movement comes about as a result of "a cultural and discursive process; it involves the narration of a shared past, present, and future."

In response to these acts of protest in 1975, the security apparatus encircled the company. They intensified their presence in the city's main streets, which led to the transfer of contentious interactions to the street. The security forces entered the company to put an end to the strike by force, using batons and teargas (Abdel Latif 2002, 89–90). The security crackdown outside the company enclosure prompted residents of the city to use violence against the police, throwing stones at them, a scenario that would be repeated approximately thirty years later following the strike of 2008 (88). To put an end to the strike, company management was obliged to maintain negotiations with the labor movement's leaders. The government met all their demands, including the application of the Civil Service Reform Act for all employees and workers in the public sector. As a result, the movement emerged victorious from this episode. The demand for the dissolution of the Board of Directors, however, was denied, because, according to Hassan (2009), agreeing to it would have meant admitting the inability of the government (which supported the management) to contain the workers' protests. This same demand concerning the Board of Directors would be met following the strike of 2007, demonstrating that the strategic players of the Mubarak regime thought and acted differently. The change in stance presented an opening in the arena of labor rights, which the movement's leaders exploited to mobilize and win more concessions from the government (as will be explained later).

The period between 1976 and 1985, although a moment of relative calm within the company, was nevertheless a significant period in its history of activism. As mentioned in chapter 1, these few years saw the birth of multiple forms of activism within the labor community. At the Mahalla Company, labor committees were organized to mobilize workers to claim their rights from a regime that was no longer as favorable to them as President Nasser's had been (Saher, interview with author, April 16, 2010). Among these committees were the Committee for the Defense of Labor and the Public Sector, which put out a publication called *Fajr* (The Dawn), and the Committee for Production, which published *Sawa'id al-intaj* (Hands for Production; Saher April 16, 2010). This activism reflected an even more significant reality: the emergence of new leaders or new strategic players. Labor activists who become militant through these committees (and others) would later organize the workers to strike in 1986. It was also during this period of the 1980s that the political ideologies of the leaders were shaped. A large number of them would join leftist parties such as Al-Tajammu' or even the Communist Party (Hassan January 31, 2009). It should be recalled that, in 1977, President Sadat had taken the initiative to introduce party pluralism in Egypt. Former company leader Fatouh (2009) states that most of the labor movement leaders thus had a political affiliation and defined political views. Within this activist group, they were gradually receiving their "political and organizational education." Their political and party affiliations fed their labor activism (2009). This fact is important because it highlights a key difference between the former and later leaders and their relationships with politics.

Moreover, the Mahalla labor mobilizations of 1986–88 took place in a context where the Mubarak government pursued a policy of economic liberalization favoring the private sector to the detriment of the public sector. On June 8, 1981, the government enacted a new labor law, Act No. 137 for the Organization of Labor Relations. The text of this law stipulated the right of workers to remuneration for their weekly rest days.[20] However, this was never implemented in public-sector companies, under the pretext that they were governed by Act No. 48 of 1978, which covered labor relations in the public sector, and mentioned nothing about this right. To force the government to bend, the labor leaders of the ESCO Spinning and Textile Company in the Shubra al-Khema district of the governorate

20. Salah Shaker, "13 'aman 'ala idrab ESCO" [13 Years since the ESCO Strike], Center for Socialist Studies, https://revsoc.me/workers-farmers/13-man-l-drb-skw-86/ (accessed July 23, 2024).

of Qalyubia decided to confront the government in the legal arena. They filed a lawsuit against the government and won. The latter, however, did not agree to implement the court rule (Shaker n.d.).

This governmental reluctance to implement the court rule incited the "politicized" Mahalla Company leaders to advocate for its implementation. As highlighted by a former leader in the company, this pushed the leaders of the movement to return back to work-related rights, mobilizing the workers in the Mahalla Company to strike until they obtained their rights concerning this remuneration, as stated by Act No. 137 (and the broader labor movement's right to secure it) (Lotfy, interview with author, August 15, 2009). Security agents responded by arresting the movement's leaders. However, the strike continued with renewed vigor as the workers stood in solidarity with their leaders.

Fatouh, one of the strike leaders, explained:

> The workers, in solidarity with us, refused to cancel the strike unless we are released. They chanted the slogan: "No production before liberation [la intag ila baad el ifrag]." (2009)

In order to appease the workers, the government agreed to release the movement's leaders and to implement the act. Thus, the protest movement achieved success.

In 1988, the government decided to cancel the sum allocated to workers in the public sector at the beginning of the school year, which was known as the "school grant" (*minhat al-madaris*). The decision was a provocative one for the workers, who depended on the grant each year. A demonstration was organized once again in front of company management to reclaim the grant. For the first time, the workers demonstrated while carrying a symbolic coffin for Mubarak (*na'sh Mubarak*) as a sign of indignation and resolution.[21] This event ended with the victory of the movement and the cancellation of the decision. The government acted quickly for fear that the situation would escalate, especially if the labor

21. According to Lotfy, this mobilization marked a strengthening of the refusal of the Mubarak regime policies, which appeared to be as hostile toward the workers as those of Sadat.

demonstration moved to the street and were to spill over outside the company door (Saher 2009).

As a result of this protest, the movement experienced a campaign of arrests that targeted all of its leaders, without exception. Organizers of this mobilization were transferred to other factories outside the Mahalla Company (Saher 2009). Toward the end of the 1980s, this situation resulted in the movement being deprived of these leaders who adopted an oppositional political stance vis-à-vis the government's politics. In this way, a gradual depoliticization of the labor movement took place in the larger context of the decline of political parties in Egypt. It would be necessary to wait another decade before witnessing the emergence of a new generation of leaders who would mobilize the movement in 2006. As the next section will discuss, these leaders would maintain a more distant relationship with oppositional political organization during contentious episodes.

The 2006 Trade Union Elections and the Impact of the "New Leaders"

It is difficult to explain the emergence of the Mahalla labor movement in terms of a favorable political opportunity, given that the various players or the movement's leaders did not perceive this to be the case in 2006, as my discussions with them attested to. In contrast, the political opportunity structure approach could serve to explain the frequency of the Mahalla labor movement protests. The movement mobilized three times in three successive years, in 2006, 2007, and 2008, and this had never been the case before. The political opportunities perceived by the movement's leaders following the strike of 2006 served to trigger these subsequent protests in a relatively short period of time. The identification of these opportunities occurred as the result of the contentious interaction between the movement's players and the regime's players in the arena of work-related rights, which had never before taken place. To use the interactive language of players and arenas (Jasper 2014; Jasper and Duyvendak 2015; Jasper 2021), the movement's players discovered an opening in the arena of labor-related rights through their contentious interaction with the regime's subplayers (the government and the company management) that they had not seen before.

Analysis of the emergence of the Mahalla labor movement allows us, therefore, to shed light on the limitations of the political opportunity structure approach in terms of its causalities and to enrich it with other elements. It also shows the relevance of the language of players and arenas in providing a more comprehensive and interactive approach, which also considers cultural dimensions and interpretations of the players, and the effects of these on their actions. A combination of the factors may serve to explain the emergence of the movement.

One factor is the massive electoral fraud in the trade union elections of 2006 that reached the Labor Union Committee of the Mahalla Company. The Mahalla Trade Union Labor Committee is affiliated with the Textile Industry Trade Union (composed of seventy-seven trade union committees), which in turn is affiliated with the Egyptian Federation of Trade Unions.[22]

Mohsen, one of the company's labor leaders, explained the increase in the amount of fraud during the 2006 trade union committee elections as follows: "The 2006 union elections were very blatantly rigged (Bi-sura fajja). The twenty-one members of the Company Labor Trade Union Committee all came fraudulently. This had never been the case before—only five or six candidates earned the elections by fraud" (interview with author, April 14, 2010). This electoral fraud not only closed all channels of communication with the government and the company management; it also prevented the candidates who lost from achieving their ambitions of representing the workers.

Electoral fraud alone does not offer a satisfactory explanation for the emergence of the 2006 Mahalla Labor mobilization, but its concurrence with the nonpayment of the annual bonuses by the government that year does. In fact, in March, prime minister Ahmed Nazif released Act No. 467 of 2006, which stipulated the right of public-sector workers to an increase in their annual bonuses. The decision increased the amount of these bonuses by 100 EGP (specified by the prime minister's Decision No. 122

22. Mostafa Bassiouni, 2009, "Azmat al-tanzim al-niqabi fi Misr" [The Crisis of the Trade Union Organization in Egypt], Center for Socialist Studies, November 2009, https://revsoc.me/workers-farmers/zm-ltnzym-lnqby-fy-msr/ (accessed July 23, 2024).

of 1984), making them worth two months of their initial salaries (Bedir 2006). This decision, made in 2006, was the first of its kind in a decade—more precisely, since 1984 (Saher 2009). It was to be implemented by the company management, which neglected to do so.

The candidates who had been squeezed out of the union elections would jump at the opportunity to mobilize the movement at a time when they already had fresh networks of support inside the factory. The timing itself proves it: the declaration of a strike on December 6, 2006, as a sign of protest against the nonpayment of bonuses, came just a few weeks after the fraudulent trade union elections in mid-November 2006. In this context, CTUWS would provide the necessary legal support to the Mahalla labor leaders.[23] Ashraf, a labor leader in the company, confirmed that the organization's director, a professional lawyer, was the one who clarified to the workers their entitlement to this two-month bonus (interview with author, April 8, 2010). Hence, the strong social networks formed during the election campaign would be a reliable resource and a source of support for the movement's leaders in mobilizing the workers to secure this financial right to their two-month-income bonus in December 2006.

Another factor in the emergence of the movement was the perception of a major chance for its success in spite of the cost of action. Goldstone and Tilly's (2001) reflection on how the perception of opportunities and threats influenced a movement's decision to act seems relevant in this regard. They also criticize the assumption that an increase in risks or threats is directly equal to the reduction of opportunities, and vice versa (183). They propose, therefore, to differentiate analytically between the movement's chances of success and the risks or costs that a movement could suffer if it decided to act, or not to act. Thus, they define opportunities as the chances that the movement's action will allow it to achieve its desired result. Threats are defined as the cost of the movement's inaction (183). This being so, a movement could accept high costs if it believes that the chances of its success are great and could even decide to run the risk of protest, in the absence of opportunities, if the costs of inaction are high.

23. CTUWS endorsed labor protests since 2006 in Mahalla as it provides the labor leaders affiliated with legal and logistics support.

This differentiation is relevant to the emergence of the Mahalla movement, since the decrease in repression and the liberalization of media, while providing arena openings, didn't motivate the movement's leaders to initiate the 2006 protests. At the same time, the threats posed by the 1991 structural adjustment agreements and the intensification of the regime's neoliberal economic policies since 2004 did not prompt this labor movement to mobilize. Instead, the motivating factor for the movement's strategic players to act was their belief in the movement's chance of success, given its history of successful contentious interactions with the regime players, especially in the arena of labor-related rights, and its capacity to face repression. This means that players' actions were based on the meanings they attributed to the world surrounding them (Jasper 2014, 65–66), and that, contrary to the structural theories, the language of players and arenas has the advantage of taking into account the cultural dimensions that acknowledge how strategic players attribute meaning to the world and act accordingly (Jasper and Volpi 2018, 27).

As a result, the union elections provided the leaders with the necessary social resources (networks) for launching a protest, the nonpayment of bonuses provided the ideal opportunity to do so, and the former, successful labor protests in the history of the movement created the perception that the chances of success for this mobilization would be great. The company's activist history, and its success during its contentious interactions with the regime players in the arena of labor-related rights, were especially emphasized by the director of CTUWS during my discussion with him, as he himself had been one of the leaders of the 1986–87 strike (Saher 2009). This means that players' choices are influenced by past interactions, the history of past decisions, accumulations, understandings, and expectations that occurs in the various contentious arenas. Player and arenas thus reflect the weight of history (Jasper 2021, 245).

The Movement's Leadership: Sociological Portrait, Activist Career, and Divergence of Positions

To define the leadership of the Mahalla labor movement, two complementary definitions will be adopted: one used by Jasper (2014, 184), who defines decisive leaders as "those who have either official positions or informal respect that allows them to mobilize resources, demand others' attention, and speak for an organization. Their choices and arguments tend to have more influence than other people's"; and one proposed by Morris and Staggenborg (2004, 171) in which "the movement leaders are the strategic decision-makers who inspire and organize others to participate in social movements."

The Mahalla movement's leadership is divided into two main groups. The first group camp of the movement's leaders/players was positioned around CTUWS, based primarily in Helwan, an industrial working-class suburb of Cairo known for its steel factories. The CTUWS was founded by Kamal Abbas, a leftist trade unionist and former steel worker, who was fired from the iron and steel factory in Tebbine (Helwan), following a labor strike he organized in 1989. As a result, Abbas founded CTUWS.[24] In 1999, he and a dozen or so of his activist colleagues, who were involved in the labor movement of the 1970s and 1980s, decided to base another branch of CTUWS in the city of Al-Mahalla al-Kubra, to assist the workers of that working-class city (Saher 2009).[25] The Ministry of Labor and the chairman of the Egyptian Trade Union Federation (ETUF) have held CTUWS responsible, to some extent, for the labor mobilizations in 2006 and the period that followed.

Among the founders of CTUWS in Mahalla City are two very important figures from the former labor leaders of the Mahalla Company, Saher and Reyad. Despite being one of the high-level employees in the company, Saher decided to join the labor strikers, thus becoming a labor leader in the 1980s. His management of CTUWS came just after his retirement in the 1990s (Saher 2009). The second leader, Reyad, was the figurehead of

24. In 2000, Dar Al-Khadamat received the French Republic's award for human rights. See Dalia Shams, 2008, "Echoes of the Factories," *Al-Ahram*, February 8, 2008.

25. For the organizational structure of Dar Al-Khadamat in Mahalla, I am talking primarily about two councils: the first is a large council consisting of some twenty activists and former labor leaders, which meets every year and a half. Its role is to take initiative in relation to the performance of the activities in the organization and its system. The second is a smaller council consisting of seven persons (among them Saher and Reyad), which meets biweekly. Its role is to execute the ideas and decisions of the larger council.

the Mahalla strikes from 2006 on. He had been a worker in the spinning section of the company since 1964 and later retired in 2009 (Reyad 2009). Saher was a former member of Al-Tajammu' Party (Saher 2009). Reyad does not deny his leftist political orientations, but denies his membership in any political party. The two leaders followed a path that was very rich in activism, and they have much in common. Together, they participated in the strikes of 1975 and were leaders of the 1986 strikes. They were involved in the foundation of the Committee for the Defense of Labor and the Public Sector, formed for the defense of the rights of workers in the 1980s. The foundation of CTUWS was, therefore, the materialization of a long-standing vision. In the 1970s, they participated in writing the "Know Your Rights" section of *Fajr* magazine, published by the leftist party Al-Tajammu', about the news of the workers and their activism (Saher 2009).

The main purpose of CTUWS, as Saher points out, is to assist the workers in the public and private sectors in everything related to the acquisition of their rights when violated. To this end, CTUWS offers workers the training courses required to become senior workers and provides the workers with a place to meet to take important decisions, such as calling for strikes. As an example, during the strike of December 2006, the CTUWS office in Al-Mahalla al-Kubra provided a safe and convenient meeting place for a wider group of worker-leaders. More importantly, CTUS provides legal assistance and support to workers through lawyers working with them (Saher 2009). Thanks to this legal assistance, the leaders who were defeated in the union elections were able to file complaints. They joined CTUWS and became permanent activists within it (Ashraf 2009). Along with Reyad, this group of leaders was composed of four others: Yehia, Ashraf, Yasser, and Samer, all of them nearing forty years of age in 2006. They became affiliated with CTUWS following their eviction from the union elections and formed the first group of leaders to organize the labor strike of 2006.

It should be noted that this group was quite heterogeneous in terms of their education, hierarchy within the company, and paths of activism. Reyad and Yehia had an elementary school education, while Ashraf and Samer had continued their studies at a technical institute. These institutes generally provide four years of technical study after middle school. Yasser was an engineer with a university degree. After finishing his studies at a technical institute, he joined the engineering university and received his diploma. Yehia worked in the company's spinning department since 1964, and Ashraf was a technician in the spinning department since 1993. Yasser was an engineer in the weaving section, and Samer was a technician, also in the weaving department (Saher 2009).

An important note in this context is the positioning of these leaders within the various departments of the company—spinning, weaving, cotton, wool, and clothing—where the majority of the workers were concentrated, providing them with broad social networks. The professional ties maintained between the leaders and workers within these plants explains the social capital that this group of leaders enjoyed among the workers. More importantly, their participation in the union election in November 2006, in contrast to the second group of leaders/players (as will be discussed later), allowed them to rely on even denser social networks. Participation and success in union elections within the Mahalla company depended on a wide network of relationships developed within the factory. This can be attributed to the candidates' networks of representatives (*mandubin*), distributed in the different departments of the factory (*qism*). These representatives kept the leaders/candidates aware of problems and assessed their popularity within the factory (Duboc 2011, 8). This demonstrates the density of the networks that were formed through trade union elections, and that were an asset for one group of leaders over the other.

As regards their political activist backgrounds or their political affiliations, Yehia and Samer had no party affiliations and were never members of a political organization. Although Reyad had leftist orientations, he was not a member of any political party (Saher 2009). Ashraf and Yasser, on the other hand, were members of the National Democratic Party (NDP), the state party. They were leaders at the base of the organizational structure of the party" (Ashraf January 31, 2009). It is worth noting that the internal organization of the NDP was divided into three levels: (the governorate level (*Al-muhafaza*), including a secretary general and an office consisting of fifteen to sixteen members; the centers level, comprised of Several centers (*Al-marakiz*) affiliated with this office, at the governorate level, reflecting the different central divisions of the governorate; and the units level (*Al-wihdat*), made up of several units (either in residential areas or villages) associated with these centers. It was at this last level that Yasser and Ashraf were positioned.

Ashraf did not see the company management's violation of the worker's economic rights as a hostile stance from the Mubarak government concerning the workers. On the contrary, he thought this encouraged the distribution of roles: the government was doing what it could, and the workers in turn should do their work and claim their rights (interview with author, April 15, 2010). For the two leaders to be members of the NDP didn't contradict their willingness to serve the workers; on the contrary, it strengthened it.

As they both explained: "We became members at the NDP with the intention to help and serve. Our aim is only to serve our fellow citizens by providing them with the services that we can make available by being NDP members at the Mahalla City Council, such as city street lights. In any case, we have no choice because there are no other credible alternative ways for providing these services" (Reyad and Ashraf 2009).

It is precisely in this context of providing services, this time at the company level, that the five leaders/players came together for a common purpose. Their diverse political orientations did not divide them because they shared the same concept of how a leader should function within the movement. They believed that labor leaders should aspire to serve the workers by reclaiming their infringed rights, regardless of their political stances.

As a result, Reyad, who perceived that the NDP was hostile to workers' interests, even cooperated with Ashraf, a party member, because they shared a common goal: getting the workers their financial rights. It was for the same objective that these four leaders decided to run in the Company Labor Union Committee elections. As candidates for union elections, they would be able to provide services to workers, such as facilitating access to health care within the company. It is thus clear that for this group of leaders as a whole, their interest in providing services for their colleagues did not necessarily lead to opposition to regime players. Ashraf, one of the members of the NDP, who was also a labor leader, confirmed that his affiliation with the NDP as a social network was advantageous. It provided him with negotiation channels, consequently increasing the likelihood of resolving workers' claims (Ashraf 2009).

It should be noted that this definition of a leader, where the notion of facilitating better access to rights and services takes precedence over political affiliations, appears to be different from the dominant model of twenty or thirty years previous (in the 1970s–1980s). During these years, the labor leader was above all a political activist affiliated with a political party. Unlike the 1980s, when political parties were able to attract workers who had participated in organizing strikes in the factory, the end of the Mubarak regime saw a decline in the influence of partisan structures. For this reason, the forms of activist engagement of the workers changed: workers began to distance themselves from political parties. This change in political context influenced the leadership of the movement in 2006. "Natural leaders" (*Qiyada tabiʿiyyia*) originated from among the ranks of workers, and were able to easily gather their colleagues around them, precisely because they were perceived to be defending their rights.

Ashraf (2010) explained it this way:

> To be a leader-worker is something natural that a man is born with. If a man falls down, the majority pass by and continue as if nothing has happened. Only one or two men will take the initiative to stop and help the man get up, the one who does have the character of a leader. Personally, I've always been a leader because I always tried to claim my rights and help my colleagues to get theirs. Before working at the Mahalla Company, I worked for a few years in a company in Saudi Arabia. I mobilized my colleagues there also to recover our financial rights.

Furthermore, it was through their profiles and functions as natural leaders that they acquired their legitimate authority over the members of the movement. As Reyad (2009) explained very simply: "A labor leader is someone who generates positive results for his colleagues in getting them their rights. That is why they obey him and have confidence in him."

In this camp, there were two women labor leaders/players: Soad and Afaf. They both worked in the company's clothing department, having started at about the same time in February 1984 (Soad 2010). They were not directly connected to CTUWS, but had the same profile of "natural leaders" as the others. They were considered leaders even though, because of their family responsibilities, they did not participate in the decision-making processes, which remained the privilege of male leaders. Their roles were focused instead on mobilizing the clothing department, where most of the women worked, as soon as the decision to organize a strike was relayed to them (Amer, interview with author, January 7, 2009).

The second group of leaders/players was formed within the League of Textile Workers (Rabitat al-'Amilin bi-l-Ghazl wa al-Nasij). The league was founded in 2007 as a result of differences in positions between the leaders of the two groups just after the December 2006 strike. The idea, which never came to fruition, was to form a league that would unite all the textile workers in Egypt, beginning with the Mahalla Company. Its purpose was to form an independent union capable of defending workers' rights and replacing the General Trade Union for Textile Workers that had been co-opted by the regime (Mohsen 2010). Attempts to legalize Al-Rabta took place through the legal support offered by the Center for Socialist Studies, an arm of the Revolutionary Socialists, an unregistered Trotskyist political organization. It emerged at the beginning of the 1990s with the goal of becoming an alternative to the weak leftist parties. These attempts failed, however, because, according to Mohsen (2010), labor leader and principal founder of the league, there weren't sufficient financial resources to open a headquarters for it and complete the legalization procedures. Nevertheless, this argument should be viewed in light of the fact that the league failed to build a base among the working class. The fact that the number of Al-Rabta members did not exceed 300 workers proves this point. According to Fawzy, one of the other labor leaders who founded of Al-Rabta, the league began with fifty workers in 2007 and then managed to grow to approximately three hundred workers in 2008 (interview with author, August 17, 2009).

The founding leaders of this league—Mohsen, Seif, Morad, Fawzy, and Wahid—were also diverse in terms of their positions within the company and paths of activism, but they were more similar in terms of education. It should be noted that Wahid was not a member of Al-Rabta, but was one of its closest supporters and shared the majority of its views. To make the analysis easier, the author categorized him as one of this group of leaders. Mohsen, Wahid, Morad, Fawzy, as a minor employee, technical professor, and technicians, respectively, continued their studies in technical institutes right after finishing middle school (Saher 2009). As an employee in the company, Seif had a university-level education (interview with author, August 10, 2009). Mohsen was a quality control officer. Wahid taught technology to the young workers in the company. Morad and Fawzy were technicians for electrical engines and for company car garages. Seif was a young employee, working in the public relations department of the company (Mohsen 2010; Morad, interview with author, April 14, 2010; Wahid, interview with author, April 11, 2010; Seif 2009; Fawzy 2009).

It is clear from the positions of these five leaders within the company that, unlike the CTUWS group, they were not in the manufacturing departments. This was a disadvantage in terms of their ability to form strong social relationships with the workers, particularly in comparison with the others. The CTUWS leaders had also gained strong social networks during the union elections of November 2006.

Wahid (2010) illustrated this with the following examples:

> Yasser is an engineer in the weaving department, which means that he is already right there in the middle of the workers. This allows him to easily build a social base through his daily contact with them. Reyad is a worker in the spinning department, which is the largest department in the company, and is known by all the workers, thanks to his long history of activism. My position is quite different, now that I'm in the technical school, quite far from the factory workers. Mohsen, as an employee, is located outside of the company manufacturing departments and far away from the workers: he has to go through three doors to get from his office to the factories. Fawzy is located in the garage and Morad in the electricity department, still far from the factories where the majority of workers are located.

Wahid's remarks in 2010 are important, as he sheds light on the relatively limited capacity of this group of leaders/players to interact with the movement's members—a fact that would influence their future choices and decisions.

What also made this group homogeneous was the shared socialist vision that shaped their interpretation of the world around them. This argument is supported by the special relationships that Al-Rabta maintained with the Revolutionary Socialists, who had taken charge of the (uncompleted) task of its legalization. Al-Rabta was in no way an extension of the Organization of the Revolutionary Socialists. Nevertheless, the two organizations were compatible because they shared a similar political orientation. In contrast to the CTUWS group, Al-Rabta was characterized by the political militancy of its members. They also believed that the function of a labor leader was not limited to claiming the rights of workers but extended also to militating against a regime that was generally hostile to workers' interests, as I will discuss later (Morad 2010; Wahid 2010). Moreover, two of this group's leaders were part of the generation of politicized leaders that had experience of activism within the company during the 1970s and 1980s. The first was Mohsen, one of the leaders of the 1986 strike and the initiator of the idea to form a league. He already had a rich activist history. In the 1980s, he was a member of the leftist Al-Tajammu' Party. He left at the end of the 1980s to join the Egyptian Communist Party, which was transformed at the beginning of the 1990s into an organization with a limited number of members. It was at that time that he departed the organization to join the Revolutionary Socialists, toward the beginning of the 1990s. By the end of the 1990s, he left this group as well as a result of internal rifts (Mohsen 2010). The second leader was Wahid, who was also one of the leaders of the 1986 and 1988 strikes. Since 1979, he had been an active member of the Iraqi revolutionary party, the Socialist Baath Party, because he had lived there for three years. In 1984, he joined the Mahalla Company. After 1986, he assumed high-ranking positions in the former Egyptian Communist Party (Wahid, interview with author, July 23, 2010). Toward the end of the 1990s and the party's deterioration, he left and is no longer a member of any party.

Seif, on the other hand, considered Mohsen to be his teacher or his spiritual father in terms of activism (Seif 2010). He was not a member of any political organization, but he identified closely with socialism. Morad and Fawzy sympathized with the Revolutionary Socialists, as was obvious during the time of the foundation of Al-Rabta. It is difficult to know whether they were members or not, since they never openly acknowledged it. The Revolutionary Socialists preferred to work undercover because their organization was not formally legalized. Thus, only a few of these activists were known; the rest were not. In this context, it would be interesting to point out that after the January 25 Revolution, some of the Revolutionary Socialists formed an underground party called the Workers' Party (Hizb al-'umal), and Morad was among them. Kamal Khalil, director of the Center for Socialist Studies, and one of the political figures in the Organization of Revolutionary Socialists, was one of its cofounders.[26]

As has been outlined, there were two groups of leaders with different relationships to politics, and different social networks, both inside and outside the company. These factors are crucial in understanding their choices during protests, as well as the reactions of regime players, and, consequently, the interactional dynamics of contentious episodes in the different contentious arenas. Each of these choices engendered a different reaction on the part of the regime players and, as a result, influenced the movement's outcomes (whether in terms of success or demobilization).

The Dynamics of the Strategic Interaction: Tactics and Framing

With a view to mobilizing the workers, the movement's leaders formulated a "diagnostic frame," identifying the corruption of the company management as the source of their problems. Benford and Snow (2000, 615–16) define the diagnostic frame as being related to "the identification of the problem or the locus of attribution." This framing motivated the workers to act collectively because their factory, their source of livelihood, was on the line. Accordingly, the leaders connected the violation of their rights over their two-months-worth of bonuses with the company management's corruption (Ashraf 2009). This frame became even more resonant among the workers, as Al-Gebally, the company chairman, sold a piece of land of approximately 35 feddans to the Investment Association (*Hay'at*

26. Since its establishment in 2001, this party has not succeeded to collect the five thousand endorsements (*tawkilat*) necessary for its legal foundation.

al-istithmar) for a sum of 650 million EGP (Bedir 2006). This action triggered anger against an administration that was not only corrupt, but was also privatizing "their" company. The leaders circulated this within the movement and began to mobilize the workers to strike.

To start, the leaders disseminated this framing through their support networks, which had already been shaped during the trade union elections in November 2006. These social ties served as the main platforms and channels of communication through which the leaders made the decision to strike. The ex-candidates, who became movement leaders, had representatives (*mandubin*) distributed throughout the different divisions (*aqsam*) of the factory, which enabled them to transmit this framing and to organize the workers. This is how social ties between the leaders (who failed in the elections) and the workers evolved over time, helping to create a new opportunity for the movement's leaders to reinvent themselves and mobilize the workers. Through the flow of discussions, or in other words, through "conversational interactions" with their social networks (Passy and Monsche 2014, 42), (which were strengthened through the electoral process), the leaders worked on shaping workers' convictions and motivation to join the protest.

That is what Ashraf, the labor leader eliminated from the trade union elections, and Reyad, a labor leader affiliated with CTUWS, explained during their interview:

> Each of us identified ten or so workers from his own department that he was confident in, and asked them to organize the workers to strike. Those workers would then explain the importance of the strike in fighting the corruption of the new company directors and getting our rights to the bonuses. They would also ask others from their circle of friends in the company to spread the news. The idea was that all the workers in all the departments would be aware of the violation of their rights and convinced of the need to strike. (2009)

Reyad described these individuals entrusted with spreading the news as the "second layer of leaders," on whom they could always count while mobilizing. It should be noted that Reyad, despite the fact that he was not a candidate for union elections, had informal representatives within the company due to his long history of activism. In other words, he had a social network that had been formed over the years on which he could rely to mobilize the workers (Reyad 2009). Moreover, these "representatives," or "second layers," were also used to transmit workers' enthusiasm or disagreement to take part in strikes, which was often gauged before any official action was taken (Reyad 2009).

In addition, the movement was built by activating the interpersonal networks that already existed though daily interactions at work. An example of this would be the cafeteria (*al-buffet*), where the workers of the Mahalla Company would have a cup of tea or a sandwich during their break. Each production unit or department had its own cafeteria. The workers called it the "mini-Parliament," because that is where they gathered to talk about their work and their personal lives. It was the mini-Parliament where the leaders and their friends would explain issues and convince and organize workers (Reyad 2009). It is a space for dialogue and debates that gave the opportunity for the emergence of a model of democratic leadership (Alexander 2010). It is through these discussions that the leaders would help the workers to develop the cognitive dimensions that would push them to participate in the contentious actions they called for. Social interactions through talks and discussions can "forge a cognition based on injustice and the necessity of action" (Passy and Monsch 2014, 42), thus inciting the workers to join the movement and participate in this contentious action.

Historically, the violation of workers' rights by the company would be enough to trigger a protest. Yet, in 2006, it had been a long time since the last protest in 1988. Aware of this fact, the movement's leaders pursued a flexible strategy (Saher 2009). As mentioned earlier, to better see the interaction between players and arenas, it would be useful to focus on players' actions during their strategic engagement. This includes, according to Jasper (2014, 45; 2015, 17), three basic types of action: persuasion, coercion, and payment. Along these lines, the movement's leaders put forward an evolutionary strategy that began with persuasion (seeking to convince their opponents to fulfill their demands), followed by coercion (organizing a strike including work stoppage and occupying the company) if the government and company management neglected their claims. The rationale behind this strategy was to be able to reverse their decision if the company management agreed to their demands, or if the workers thought to disengage.

This strategy followed three successive stages. The first stage was to present their demand for two months of bonuses to the head of the Trade Union Committee (who had just been fraudulently elected), convincing him of their rights, and asking for his support. In case of his refusal, this would also serve to highlight the official union unresponsiveness, once a strike had been called for (Wahid 2010).

The second stage was to set the scene for the mobilization: encouraging workers to refuse to take their salaries as a sign of protest, and as a first step preceding a strike if the company management still ignored their demands.[27] The movement leaders chose this repertoire of protest to give some time to the company management to change their position and to ensure the movement's cohesion. They were still taking into account that the workers had not called a strike for eighteen years, and that they would need to proceed gradually (Azouz and Dora 2006, 3). The movement leaders wanted to be sure that the workers would not break off the strike once they started. Not collecting their salaries would guarantee their commitment (Reyad 2009; Wahid 2010). I am basically referring here to the leaders affiliated with CTUWS as the second group of leaders/players (mentioned earlier), with the exception of Mohsen and Wahid, who did not appear on the scene until later—mainly during and after the strike (Saher 2009). Mohsen and Wahid were known by the CTUWS leaders because of their long history of activism within the company, which is why they were involved in these decision-making meetings.

It was thus that, on Sunday, December 2, workers in the sectors of engineering, production, and those in the service garage, refused to collect their wages. On Monday, December 3, and Tuesday, December 4, the workers in

27. Mohamed Azouz and Adel Dora, 2006, "27000 ʿamil bi-ghazl al-Mahalla yamtaniʿun ʿan tasalum ujurihum wa yuhadidun bil-iʿtisam" [27,000 Workers at Mahalla Refuse to Take Their Wages and Threaten to Hold a Sit-In], *Al-Masry Al-Youm*, December 4, 2006.

the spinning and textile departments followed suit.[28] This request to not take their salaries materialized thanks to the solidarity among the workers. Ashraf (2009) commented: "The one who had more money gave to the one who was in need, so that that person would not collect his salary."

Labor leader Wahid (2010) gave a concrete example of this solidarity:

> It turns out that a girl needed her salary because she was going to get married in a few days. She asked me to make an exception, but I refused, and told the workers about her situation. A few minutes later, hundreds of workers offered to help so that she wouldn't have to collect her salary.

The third stage was the formal call for a strike and confirmation of the final date, set for December 7, 2006. The workers heard the news by word of mouth, as well as flyers distributed by the leaders specifying the date of the strike (Wahid 2010). The leaders and their representatives in the various departments would take small quantities of leaflets (so as not to attract the attention of the agents) and distribute them in the area where they were working. They were passed quickly from one person to another and within less than a day had spread throughout the entire company. They also left a few flyers in the restrooms, as a way of informing the company management in the hope that they would take action, which would prevent them from having to strike (Wahid 2010).

On Thursday, December 7, the workers were prepared to go on strike. Thousands of workers left their machines and gathered in Talaat Harb Square, just in front of the company management's door. It was the same square where all of the sit-ins since 1975 had taken place. The strike lasted two days before the protestors' demands were met, on the third day.

The first group of workers arrived at 7:30 a.m., among them thousands of women. They were to join a third group of workers, who had worked from 11 p.m. until the next morning, so they had not left the company to start the movement's sit-in (Reyad 2009). It should be stated that the work was usually conducted in shifts by rotation. There were three shifts

28. "Yawmiyat intifadat 'umal al-Mahalla" [The Uprising of the Mahalla Workers from Day to Day], 2006, *Al-Karama*, December 19, 2006, 12.

(*wardiyyat*) of approximately eight thousand workers each, according to their working hours at the company. The first shift of workers (*al-wardiyya al-oula*) was from 7:30 a.m. up until 3:30 p.m. The second shift of workers (*al-wardiyya al-thaniyya*) was from 3:30 p.m. until 11:00 p.m. The third shift was from 11:00 p.m. until 7:30 a.m. the next morning.

The women workers, very enthusiastic and militant, had already gathered and went quickly to the square, scolding, "Where are the men? The women are here!" So the third shift workers quickly left their machines to join the male and female workers who had gathered in the square, chanting, "Two months, two months!," referring to the two months of bonuses they wanted to obtain (Beinin and El-Hamalawy 2007). During the afternoon of the same day, the second shift workers arrived, and so the workers of the three shifts were all assembled. This last group of workers spontaneously took it upon themselves to bring as many snacks as possible for the third shift, which had not left the company since the evening (Reyad 2009). At 11 p.m., the labor leaders convinced the female workers that they already had enough workers in place, and that it would be better for them to go home and return the next day with food (Reyad 2009).

As emphasized by Amer (2009), a correspondent for a prominent privately owned newspaper in Mahalla, the following Friday morning witnessed a gradual decline in the number of workers as the day progressed. Friday being the weekend, and the workers' day off, organizing the sit-in by rotation was more difficult than it had been during the week. The workers were leaving the company either to see their families or to cultivate their lands (a significant number of company workers had small plots of agricultural land, either in Mahalla or in the neighboring villages). Sometimes they returned to the sit-in later, but not in any organized manner, and the continuation of the sit-in to Friday night was more or less symbolic. In such circumstances, the leaders aimed to convey to both the management and the security agents positioned behind the company enclosure that the collective protest action was still ongoing. The tactical repertoire they used to do this was beating barrels like drums to show that the sit-in was not over (Amer 2009). The number of workers remaining during Friday night was approximately seventy, among them the leaders and the more militant workers, according to the labor leaders interviewed (Ashraf 2009; Wahid 2010; Reyad 2009).

As a response to these actions, the government and the company management (as two regime subplayers) started to react. They were followed by the security apparatus (as the third regime subplayer). The government delegates and the company management began to concede by persuasion. However, the movement's refusal to yield pushed security forces to deploy nonviolent coercion embodied by an intimidation strategy. Smithey and Kurtz (2018, 195) define intimidation as "the *threat* of direct violence, which may be physical, verbal, or written, and other subtle efforts to demobilize activists without the use of direct violence." Accordingly, the security agents threatened the workers with violence unless they dispersed, but they didn't succeed in their endeavor (as will be explained).

With the end of the second day of the strike, Abdel Hamid Noweir (then secretary general of the NDP in the governorate of Gharbiya, professor of geology and dean of the Faculty of Science at the University of Tanta), and Ezzat Drag (NDP delegate to the People's Assembly since the parliamentary elections of 2005), a businessman who owned a tourism company in Mahalla, and former technician at the city's phone company, both went to the sit-in. They tried to convince the workers that they didn't have any right to the two-month bonuses, just to receive twenty-one-days' worth of bonuses (Reyad 2009). This statement was the result of discussions undertaken between these two men, the company management, and members of the Trade Union Committee (Amer 2009).

According to labor leaders Reyad and Ashraf (2009), this suggestion was made in order to divide the workers. Nevertheless, it was refused by the workers who had just chased the two government delegates from the sit-in, chanting, "Two months, two months, we only want the two months!" (Reyad 2009). The way the labor leaders had framed the right to two months of bonuses was decisive, and any suggestion of less than this only strengthened the workers' perception of the company management as being corrupt and unfair toward them. As Reyad stated: "Workers were making a 'two' sign with their hands, indicating their request for two months of bonuses, refusing to consider any other proposal. The demand was engraved in their minds this way, and it became very difficult to change" (2009).

The end of the day and the night of the second day was marked by an increase in security pressures on the workers who had not yet left the sit-in, numbering approximately seventy workers. According to Amer (2009), a correspondent for a prominent independent newspaper in Mahalla, state security followed closely what was happening and was in direct contact with the company management. He confirmed that two or three security vehicles met police officers in front of the main door of the company. State security agents were among those police officers. The strategy of the security agents was to send delegates to convince the workers to demobilize. State Security ordered company management to give three days of leave to the workers in order to prevent them from returning to the company the following day (i.e., Saturday). Cars with microphones circulated in the streets of Mahalla and surrounding towns to announce this decision. Police officers stationed outside the company spread rumors in collaboration with company security agents that they were going to enter to end the sit-in, using force against the workers (Wahid 2010), while the security officers pressured the labor leaders to end the strike. At dawn, they sent a delegate to threaten the use of force and try to convince them to demobilize (*Al-Dustur* 2006, 2).

Faced with these pressures, the labor leaders chose to continue their resistance. For the activists who remained, especially those from CTUWS, resistance had become the only remaining option—otherwise they faced "career failure." In other words, if the protest failed, their leadership positions would be called into question. In response, they invited the workers to continue to beat the barrels with all their might to provide an image of unity and persistence (Wahid 2010; Ashraf 2009). The leaders also asked the security agents to give them a period of two hours to exit (*Al-Dustur* 2006, 2). This was the time needed to contact other company workers to come to their rescue by joining the sit-in. The seventy workers at the sit-in phoned all the workers they had numbers for, and asked them to contact others.

The message they spread was: "If you don't return to the sit-in, we will be arrested by the police, who will probably use violence, so come back right away!" (Ashraf 2009). This message was aimed at activating support networks within the movement and "identity boundaries," between the "we" (workers facing the threat of eviction) as distinct from "them" (security agents and company management. "Identity boundaries" defined by Tilly and Tarrow (2015, 36) as "the creation of a new boundary or the crystallization of an existing one between challenging groups and their targets." It had its impact on the workers who responded positively to the call. It was the commitment and solidarity with the community that emerged, especially toward the leaders, to whom they were attached. Conversational interactions appeared once again to be valuable in influencing the movement's members' cognitive toolkits (Passy and Monsch 2014, 31). Hence, on Saturday, at approximately 7 a.m., the workers arrived and occupied the company (Beinin and El-Hamalawy 2007). This incident completely changed the equation for the movement.

As Ashraf, Reyad, and Wahid described the events: "It was thanks to the workers' solidarity with us that we were able to succeed. We all cried with joy at the sight of them coming to our rescue" (Wahid 2010; Ashraf 2009). The incident thus ended with an agreement to meet the workers' demands in order to put an end to the protest. On Saturday, December 9, the third day of labor action, minister of labor Aisha Abdel Hadi, and minister of investment Mahmoud Mohy al-Din, made their appearance on the 9 a.m. news, stating that the workers would have their rights to a month-and-a-half of bonuses before the beginning of February. Moreover, granting these bonuses would be carried out by the management of the other public companies. Similarly, the minister of investment declared the cancellation of company debt with the banks, which amounted to 960 million EGP.[29]

The workers saw this and heard the final decision on a large screen that company management had set up in a well-known place within the company called Talaat Harb Square. At 11 p.m., the company security director sent them a leaflet signed by company management upholding their rights. At that time, they ended their sit-in (Reyad 2009).

29. "Sarf al-arbah bi miqdar shahr wa nisf shahr" [The Payment of Premiums for a Month and a Half before the Beginning of Next February], *Al-Ahram*, December 12, 2006.

Outcomes: Did Players Perceive Arena Openings?

The 2006 strike owes its significance not only to its success in achieving immediate labor demands (the two-month bonuses), but also to the results it produced both within and outside of the movement. Outside the movement, it led to a "spillover effect," leading to a tripling in the number of labor protests just a year later. Within the movement, it led to the formation of a new configuration of leaders who were aware of the nonviolent strategies deployed by the security apparatus and were further encouraged to call for workers' protests in 2007 and 2008.

In fact, the course of the contentious interaction of 2006 led to the expansion of the movement's leadership, as the CTUWS leaders (who called for the strike) would become acquainted with other workers who were involved in it (Fawzy 2009; Morad 2010; Seif 2009).

Saher (2009), director of CTUWS in Mahalla explained it this way: "During the course of this last strike, the CTUWS labor leaders got to know other young leaders whose activism and enthusiasm were visible. Fawzy, for example, was always carried on his colleagues' shoulders to chant the claim of 'two months' during the sit-in. He was thus quite visible and well-known."

Along with the CTUWS leaders, Mohsen and Wahid, these new leaders participated in organizing the 2007 strike and, as a result, were involved in the foundation of Al-Rabta with Mohsen. Their dedication during this strike thus strengthened their cooperation in organizing further labor protests. It was in this way that the movement's leadership began to be configured immediately following the 2006 strike.

The contentious interaction of 2006 between the movement's players on one hand and the security agents as one of the regime's subplayers on the other, in the arena of work-related rights, enabled them to detect a modification in the security strategy deployed. As emphasized by Latif, a journalist in a prominent privately owned newspaper, unlike in the 1970s and 1980s, security forces didn't resort to violence against them. This change of strategy emboldened the former leaders, who still remembered the violent events that took place in the 1970s, 1980s, and 1990s (interview with author, April 9, 2010).

As Mohsen (2010), a leader of the 1986 Mahalla company strike, stated:

> The change in the way the security agents acted with us was amazing. However, this doesn't imply the inability of the regime to exercise violence against us. On the contrary, it shows that it no longer wants to do so because of a change in strategy. The regime clearly opted for negotiation over the use of force.

In reference to the mobilizations of 2007 and 2008, he added:

> Before, during the 1980s and 1990s, we couldn't mobilize as easily as we do now, the more frequent use of force prevented it.

Mohsen interpreted this change as being due to the evolution of the media, and ease of communicating internationally, which pressured the regime to improve its image, at least internationally.

Wahid (2010), leader of the 1986 strike, also shared Mohsen's perception of the change of security strategy with regard to repression, but interpreted it differently:

> The complicity of the security agents is striking. They still surrounded the company as they had done during the previous strikes. What is new is that they didn't use force. The government is now using a new policy with us, a policy of strategic patience (siyasat al-nafas al-tawil). They want us to withdraw without their having recourse to violence against us.

Hence, the leaders' perception of the change in strategy by state security, combined with their success in obtaining their rights, encouraged them to go on and to call for other protests with a perceived lower cost. This means that, through the players' interaction with other players/opponents, they were able to perceive encouraging changes in their approach (Jasper 2015a, 23). It was by entering the arena of collective action, in interacting with their opponents, that political opportunities were perceived and interpreted, and not before.

Conclusion

It has become evident that the leadership of the Mahalla Labor movement was somewhat divided in terms of vision, ambition, and experiences in activism. Understanding this division is crucial for analyzing the strategies and choices made by various players in contentious episodes, and it will continue to be important in the future. One significant conclusion in this regard is the decisive role played by the candidates eliminated from the trade union elections in the emergence of the movement. While the movement already had a substantial history of activism and organizational capacity through robust solidarity networks, it is challenging to envision the initiation or organization of the 2006 strike without the efforts of these leaders in mobilizing their support networks, established during the trade union elections.

Furthermore, the activism of these leaders and the success of their tactics allowed them to navigate security pressures, ultimately leading to the success of the strike. Their achievements in this contentious episode prompted them to identify additional political opportunities following a change in the security forces' strategy in the arena of labor-related rights. This encouragement propelled them to intensify their activism and advocate for other rights that were not previously prioritized. Specifically, their endeavor to withdraw confidence from the trade union committee of the company, which they deemed illegitimate, and their efforts to press for its dissolution, will be discussed in the next chapter.

3

Does "Self-Limitation" Win?

A "Self-Limited" Strategy versus Opposition to the Regime

Introduction

In this chapter, I focus on how the movement's players interacted with the opening in the regime's players strategy in the arena of labor-related rights. Unlike with structural theories, I employ a cultural perspective to analyze the tactics and decisions of key players, examining how their interpretations of regime actions influenced broader dynamics in contentious interactions. I explore the failed attempt by movement players to challenge ETUF by seeking the dissolution of the trade union committee affiliated with it. This episode is pivotal for understanding the dynamics of the movement, revealing divergent strategies within it—specifically, the success of a "self-limiting" strategy over direct opposition to the regime in achieving the movement's financial demands.

Additionally, I delve into the dynamics of the 2007 contentious interaction between regime players and the Mahalla labor movement players. I argue that the movement's organizational resources were necessary but insufficient for success against the Mubarak regime players. Instead, the framing, strategies, and tactics employed by movement leaders determined their capacity to capitalize on the opportunities provided by the regime players' actions, neutralize the security apparatus, and sustain the movement during a six-day strike. Emphasizing the exploitation of the regime's relative media liberalization and the strategic alliance between private press and labor movement players, I examine the dynamics of the movement's players success in their strategic interaction with the regime players.

Choosing Not to Challenge the Regime Players?

The interactive approach adopted in this research does not assume that "each interaction starts from scratch, ready to be defined and negotiated willy-nilly" (Jasper 2021, 245). On the contrary, the players' decisions and actions relied on past experiences, understandings, and interpretations.

Ashraf, company labor leader, confirms this, referring to the trade union committee members: "After the success of our strike in 2006, we felt that it's possible to see our demands met if we continue to exert pressure and to protest. That is why we decided to protest and ask for the replacement of those we don't support" (interview with author, January 31, 2009). Analyzing this contentious episode is important, because it is precisely this moment that prompted the two parties of the contention (the movement's players and the regime players) to establish a certain interpretation of the situation. They then formulated their future strategies vis-à-vis one another based on this interpretation. Thus, a detailed description of the dynamics of the contentious interaction will serve to explain how the movement's leaders identified the opportunities that the government and ETUF actions might provide, or the constraints they may impose. Understanding how they interpreted the actions of their opponents is important for understanding their future choices, and how these choices would influence the movement's outcomes.

Three main motivations are behind the movement leaders' attempts to dissolve the trade union committee: first, not only did it not support the labor demands when the leaders presented them, it also sided with the company management against these demands. Second, the support provided by CTUWS to the workers only exacerbated the hostility of their leaders toward the trade union committee, which had been indifferent to them. Third, there were personal reasons related to the fact that four of the movement's leaders (Ashraf, Samer, Yehia, and Yasser) participated in the trade union committee elections within the company in November 2006 and did not win because of electoral fraud. They felt that they were the legitimate representatives of the workers, whose right to representation had been personally violated.

The labor leaders, primarily those attached to CTUWS, organized the workers to sign a document calling for the dissolution of the union committee. This committee represented the Mahalla Company workers within the Textile Union, affiliated with ETUF, chaired by Hussein Mugawer. According to Act No. 35 of 1976 governing the affairs of unions in Egypt, the Textile Union had to agree to dissolve the trade union committee representing the workers of the Mahalla Company if a simple majority (50 percent + 1) of workers (with the right to vote in the company's General Assembly) approved the dissolution.[1] The CTUWS assumed full responsibility for the writing of this document, particularly from a legal point of view. The leaders were thus able to collect fourteen thousand signatures, the number needed to write it into law, since the number of company workers was approximately twenty-four thousand. In this context, on January 31, 2007, a delegation of one hundred workers went to meet with the president of the Textile Union, Sayed al-Gohary, a former staff member in the Shebin Al-Koum Spinning and Weaving company (located in the governorate of Menufiya), and gave him the signatures that had been collected demanding the dissolution of the company's union committee. The union president avoided the workers so that he would not be obliged to sign the document confirming receipt of the necessary signatures.[2] The workers went directly to ETUF headquarters to inform Federation president Hussein Mugawer and to present their demands.

This shift in contentious arena union from labor-related rights to trade union politics marks a move from simple economic demands to those challenging the regime itself, as this subverts the clientelist pattern

1. Mohamed Azouz, 2007, "'umal al-Mahalla yashabun al-thiqa min al-lajna al-niqabiyya" [Mahalla Workers Withdraw Confidence from the Trade Union Committee], *Al-Masry Al-Youm*, January 28, 2007.

2. Haytham Gabr, 2007, "'umal al-Mahalla yuwasilun al-nidal" [The Mahalla Workers Continue Their Fight], Center for Socialist Studies, February 7, 2007, https://revsoc.me/workers-farmers/ml-lmhl-ywslwn-lndl/ (accessed July 23, 2024).

of state-labor relations established since the postcolonial era. This was confirmed by the president of ETUF, Hussein Mugawer, who accused the labor leaders in his statement to the daily *Al-Masry Al-Youm* newspaper on January 31, 2007, of being driven by forces external to the labor movement and in opposition to the government (referring to political forces).[3]

Nevertheless, there was no evidence to confirm that there was coordination between any political forces and the labor movement. On the contrary, any coordination between them was denied by both parties during my discussions with its leaders (Ashraf 2009; Reyad 2009; Zaki, interview with author, January 24, 2009; Maged, interview with author, January 24, 2009). This accusation of association was intended to achieve two strategic objectives: to delegitimize the labor movement's demands by claiming they were pushed by political organizations who wanted to realize their own agenda, and to signal to the labor leaders that this demand crossed a red line, and that it would be better to think of a compromise during the meeting. The labor leaders got these signals, as will be discussed later.

The demand to dissolve the trade union committee was covered by several newspapers. The front page of the daily *Al-Masry Al-Youm* newspaper, on January 28, 2007, already stated that the Mahalla labor movement was seeking to withdraw confidence from the union committee.[4] What the regime most feared, a spillover effect, was starting to take place. A few days after the Mahalla textile workers presented this demand, the Shebin al-Koum workers followed suit. The textile workers in Shebin al-Koum (in the governorate of Menufiya) reported that, although they put an end to their strike after receiving their financial rights, they would do

3. Mohamed Azouz, 2007, "Mujawir yatahim "anasir mukhriba' bil-wuquf wara' sahb al-thiqa min al-lajna al-niqabiyya bi-ghazl al-Mahalla" [Mugawer Accuses Outside Forces of Being behind the Labor Attempt to Withdraw Confidence from the Union Committee], *Al-Masry Al-Youm*, January 31, 2007.

4. Already, the demand to dissolve the trade union committee had spread in all the newspapers and was even mentioned on the front page of the daily *Al-Masry Al-Youm* newspaper with the date of January 28. See "'umal al-Mahalla yashabun al-thiqa min al-lajna al-niqabiyya" [The Workers of Mahalla Withdraw Confidence from the Trade Union Committee], *Al-Masry Al-Youm*, January 28, 2007.

anything to dissolve the trade union committee in their company (which was also affiliated with the Textile Trade Union).[5] According to Reyad, a company labor leader, this spillover effect was a source of concern in the government and among minsters—namely ,the minister of investment and the minister of labor, who asked the president of the ETUF to provide clarification and suggest rapid solutions (Reyad 2009). Along similar lines, Mugawer called the CTUWS labor leaders back in to negotiate and reach a compromise.[6] He let them know during the meeting that it would be better to accept the concessions and avoid open conflict. Labor leader Ashraf (2009) reported Mugawer's words as follows: "Do not think that we are going to let you do this! How did you dare to believe that what you are doing would be accepted?" (Ashraf 2009).

He proposed an end to the crisis by offering some economic gains to the workers, and, in return, the leaders would back down on their request to withdraw confidence in the trade union committee. His proposal included some concessions: an increase in the meal allowance from 19 to 42 EGP, and an increase in the monthly bonuses, to 7 percent of the base salary (Ashraf 2009). He also proposed replacing the president of the trade union committee, to defuse the crisis. The movement's leaders of CTUWS accepted this compromise. They chose Mosaad al-Feki, a former employee in the Mahalla Company and a member of the trade union committee, as the new president, thus legitimizing, in some ways, the trade union committee.

Against this background, it should be noted that CTUWS leaders managed to identify well with the priorities of their social base, which labor leaders Reyad and Ashraf explained as follows:

5. "Al-'umal yalja'un lil-qada' li-hal al-lajna al-niqabiyya" [Workers Have Recourse to Justice to Dissolve the Trade Union Committee], *Al-Masry Al-Youm*, February 2, 2007.

6. Before this meeting, another had taken place between the labor leaders and the president of the Federation of Trade Unions on Feb 1. On the agenda was the question of the dissolution of the union committee and the economic demands of the workers: increase monthly premiums, increase meal allowances, increase compensation benefits, increase annual premiums, and increase wages and their alignment with the inflation. However, no concrete decision was taken, despite the insistence of the two parties.

> We had to let this matter of the dissolution of the union committee drop, it was not a priority for the workers. They're more interested in having their financial demands met. When the workers saw that they had made a lot of financial gains, they put aside the demand for the dissolution of the union committee (Al-'umal lamma hassit bil-maksab al-madiyya qalit mish mohim). We cannot continue our battle without having the support of the workers, (Maniqdarsh nikamil min ghir sanad), so we decided to give in on this point. (Reyad 2009)

This means that the compromise came about as a result of, on the one hand, the leaders' interpretation of the ETUF president's actions—whereby players act according to the meanings they attribute to the world surrounding them and to the actions of other players (Jasper and Volpi 2018, 27; Jasper 2014, 65–66), and, on the other hand, the internal debate taking place within the movement between its leaders and followers (Flacks 2004, 147).

CTUWS leaders also took a somewhat conciliatory position toward the regime players. Mugawer's offer was seen as an opportunity worth taking advantage of, thus avoiding open conflict and a possible crackdown by the security apparatus. They preferred, on the contrary, to consolidate their internal legitimacy as leaders who dealt with the financial priorities of the movement they represented.

In point of fact, the results of Mugawer's strategy were very well received by the government when they saw that the workers had backed down on their decision to dissolve the committee. The president of the federation even invited the twenty-one members of the trade union committee to the meeting on February 11, 2007, without informing the labor leaders, and took photos of all of them. These photos were sent to the ministers of investment and labor as a show of reconciliation between the workers and their trade union committee. According to Reyad (2009), the president of the federation wanted to prove to the two ministers his success in containing the crisis.

It is clear that the arena of labor-related rights offered more openings to the movement's players in comparison to the arena of union politics. The regime players were ready to present concessions to the movement's leaders in the former, but blocked more fiercely their moves in the latter.

Players attach different meaning to arenas as Jasper (2015a, 23) points out. In that sense, the regime players considered the arena of union politics as being more threatening to power. This was evidenced by the relief of the government after the success of the ETUF president in achieving concessions, as well as by the subsequent crackdown on the CTUWS by security forces and local authorities in Mahalla, following its legal and logistical support for workers who "dared" to seek the dissolution of the union committee.[7] On April 29, 2007—approximately two months after the attempt to dissolve the trade union committee—security agents invaded the main office of the CTUWS in Helwan. Central Security Force vehicles surrounded the building and blocked Mohamed Sayed Ahmed Street, where the organization was located. The manager of the office of the police commissioner in Helwan (*Al-ma'mur*), the district president (*Ra'is al-hay*), the president of the City Council (*Majlis al-madina*), and a representative of state security (*Mufatish mabahith amn al-dawla*) arrived, cut off the electricity, and sealed the premises (*Shamma'uha*).[8] The organization's employees tried to object, but state security agents informed them that they are surrounding their office and asked them to come out peacefully to avoid being humiliated.[9]

Among other things, Al-Rabta leaders did not welcome this decision. Substituting the dissolution of the union committee for the achievement of economic gains meant, for this group of leaders, that the government had succeeded in "co-opting" the CTUWS leaders—not by granting personal privileges, but by persuading them to renounce what was more crucial to their own interests. For Al-Rabta, dissolving the trade union committee would change the balance of power vis-à-vis the government: it would put

7. CTUWS also supervised the union elections from 2006 to 2011 and published reports denouncing the electoral fraud that took place.

8. This security crackdown aroused the solidarity of human rights organizations at national and international levels, notably Human Rights Watch, which described this event as a return to civil society in Egypt. Sixteen Egyptian organizations also expressed their solidarity with CTUWS in a press conference.

9. Ebtisam Taalb and Ahmed Zaki Othman, "Dar al-khadamat al-niqabiyya: 25 'aman min al-nidal al-'umali" [The Center for Trade Unions and Workers' Services: 25 Years of Labor Activism], *Al-Badil*, August 17, 2007.

the workers in a position of strength. Furthermore, in their opinion, it would guarantee the achievement of a wider set of labor claims. Consequently, they interpreted the other leaders' position as a strategic error. As Morad, founding member of Al-Rabta, said:

> The chance to dissolve the trade union committee is dead because of the CTUWS leaders. Now that the government has been able to make us give in on this demand, I wonder why it would get us our financial rights, as long as we've already given in on the most important thing [referring to the dissolution of the union committee]? (Interview with author, April 14, 2010)

This event thus marked the beginning of the split between these two groups, and the faction of leaders who refused to accept the outcome of this meeting decided to build the Textile Workers League (Rabtat al-ghazl w-al-nasij), commonly known as Al-Rabta. As mentioned previously, Al-Rabta was supposed to be the core of a trade union for all workers in the textile industry, independent of the state corporatist Egyptian Trade Union Federation.

Mohsen (2010), labor leader and founder of this league, explained:

> The idea to build Al-Rabta was born after the unsuccessful attempt to dissolve the trade union committee. We thought we would leave the official textile trade union and build an independent trade union capable of representing us. The league should then be the hub for this union.

Morad (2010) added:

> As a result of the disappointing response of the other group of leaders regarding the dissolution of the union committee, we thought of creating this league to regroup us. The idea was to form a union able to represent labor interests. I am convinced that the unity of the workers in every workplace is the only way to succeed.

The foundation of Al-Rabta began with about fifty workers who sought to build an organization that represented the workers after the failed attempt to dissolve the trade union committee. Mohsen, Fawzy, Morad, and Seif were the first to advocate for the foundation of this organization. Despite receiving some assistance from the Revolutionary Socialists, the founders of Al-Rabta failed to obtain headquarters and funding and also to mobilize a social base within the labor movement. Wahid (2010) expressed the problem of the absence of headquarters for this organization:

> You can't really speak of an organization called Al-Rabta (The League) but simply of a group. To put it simply, "Tell me where you are, and I'll tell you who you are."

As previously mentioned, Al-Rabta's membership did not exceed three hundred in 2008 (Fawzy 2009). The reason for this was that it was unattractive to workers, because building an independent trade union was not their top priority, as the failed attempt to dissolve the union committee demonstrated. Nevertheless, it gained a degree of visibility in political circles in Cairo, and the idea of establishing a new union garnered some attention. Hence, on May 1, 2007, during the Labor Day celebrations (Eid El-Omal), which were held at the headquarters of the leftist El-Tajammu' Party, one of the hot topics was the obstacles to building independent labor organizations.[10]

In fact, the relevance of Al-Rabta as a group of workers comes from the fact that it gathered a number of workers and labor leaders who shared the same views on the diagnostic and prognostic framings of workers' problem and claims, and on the strategies to be pursued. Benford and Snow (2000, 615–16) define the prognostic frame as being related to "proposing solution to the problem, a plan of attack, and the strategies for carrying out the plan." Al-Rabta leaders managed to publish an internal, nonperiodic publication, *Sawt al-'Umal* (The Voice of the Workers), in which they tried to advocate for their opinions, interpretations of the situation, and plans to be adopted. This was even more evident as they prepared for the strike on April 6, 2008, when the minimum wage demand appeared in the March edition of the magazine (as will be discussed later).

In sum, this contentious episode helped to, on the one hand, clarify the priorities of both parties of the contention—the regime players and the

10. "Ishtirakiyun: al-quwwa al-'umaliyya 'ajiza 'an insha' itihadat mustaqilla" [Socialists: The Labor Forces Build Trade Union Federations], *Al-Masry Al-Youm*, May 3, 2007.

movement's players (of CTUWS)—based on their interpretations of each other's actions. This also impacted their strategies in future contentious interactions. On the other hand, it also differentiated between the priorities of each group of the movement's leaders. These differing positions materialized in varying interpretations by each camp, both during and after their interactions, and has been evident in the dynamics of subsequent protests. This reflects Jasper's (2014, 65–66) interactive and cultural understanding of actions and strategies as being based on the interpretation and meaning attributed by the players to other players' actions: an "action may be physical but it is also based on meanings: we understand what we are doing, and we attribute meaning to what others do as well. These meanings emerge during the actions themselves, and there are conflicts over what those meanings are." This leads us to the next section, where the different framings and strategies of Al-Rabta and the CTUWS leaders will become even clearer.

The Victory of a "Self-Limited" Framing of Demands?

The ETUF president's promises relating to monthly premiums and meal allowances were not carried out until July 2007. Consequently, the leaders decided to call a new strike at the end of July. To resolve the problem, Aisha Abdel Hadi, the minister of manpower, summoned the leaders of CTUWS on July 15 to negotiate with them (Amer 2009). In this meeting, she promised to meet all their demands. She even issued an immediate decision to increase their annual bonuses to 130 days as a pledge of good will. Nevertheless, as of the beginning of September, this pledge still had not seen the light of day—hence the decision of the leaders to call the workers to strike on September 23, 2007.[11]

The decision to strike on the 23rd of September ensured that all workers had received their salaries, the 20th of the month being the last day for salary distribution. Choosing September, coinciding with the Islamic month of Ramadan that year, would guarantee the sympathy of the general

11. Tamer Hindawy and Khaled El-Adi, 2007, "Wa 'umal al-Mahalla uhadidun bil-i'tisam ba'd khitat al-idara" [The Mahalla Workers Threaten to Strike Again], *El Karama*, January 23, 2007.

public and the media for the workers, who remained in the sit-in, despite fasting, to claim their rights (Wahid 2010).

It is clear that the earlier contentious interaction (the attempt to dissolve the trade union committee) pushed the movement's players to formulate a strategy of limiting pressure on the regime players and remaining within the margin of action they would tolerate. Furthermore, their reading of the workers' priorities led them to adopt the same approach. They diagnosed their problems as resulting from the neglect of the government and company management, in order to achieve their immediate financial rights. Therefore, their prognosis for this problem was to continue to exert pressure on the government and company management within the arena of labor-related rights, so that they might fulfill their demands without moving to any arenas that the regime players might have perceived as threatening (i.e., syndical or political arenas). The CTUWS leaders thus remained within the framework of reactive demands, seeking only to regain their financial rights, which the government had neglected. They adopted what I call a "self-limiting strategy," in which the CTUWS camp would present the six demands that were concrete and easy for the government to achieve. The objective was that the government would agree to at least the first three, which they considered priority areas (Amer 2009).

The six claims were as follows: (1) an increase in the meal allowance; (2) an increase in the risk allowance to 37 percent of base salary; (3) an increase in the monthly bonus of at least two months (i.e., approximately 130 days) of the initial salary for the year 2006–7; (4) alignment of the monthly premiums with the original salary; (5) bus transportation for workers living outside the city; and (6) a housing allowance for the workers with no housing, and the construction of houses with several floors for workers rather than single-floor dwellings (Reyad 2009).

Al-Rabta camp, on the other hand, wanted to present a list of fourteen demands, including economic claims, such as: (1) an increase in the meal allowance; (2) an increase in the risk allowance to 37 percent of base salary; (3) payment of a month and a half of the bonus as it had been decided following the December 2006 strike; (4) an increase in the monthly bonus to at least 20 percent of the basic salary; (5) a development bonus of 50 pounds; (6) the application of Article 85 of the Labor Code of 2003, which states that a worker is entitled to a day of leave in addition to the salary for the day worked on public holidays; (7) the application of Article 78 of the Social Protection Code, which states that sick days must not be deducted from the payment of bonuses; (8) a housing allowance for the workers with no housing; (9) a promotion schedule for company workers; (10) implementation of a training program to develop the skills and qualifications of each worker, and (11) putting in place a timetable for payment of annual bonuses (Wahid 2010). These claims were accompanied by three more contentious demands: (12) holding management accountable for the company's financial situation; (13) alignment of wages with inflation for all workers in the textile industry; and (14) the establishment of a framework agreement for textile workers in Egypt, aligning wages with prices (Wahid 2010). These last two claims reflect one of the main objectives of Al-Rabta, which saw itself as the protector of the rights of all workers in the textile industry, as mentioned previously.

Al-Rabta camp thus took a more proactive approach, which was to not only respond to the workers' immediate claims, but also to push the regime to revise its policies regarding the workers. They diagnosed the problem as being related to the overall policies pursued by the regime vis-à-vis the workers in the different arenas (labor, syndical, and political); thus, their prognosis was to advance claims that pushed for more structural changes in the regime's relation with the workers. This explains their anger at the failed attempt to dissolve the trade union committee. It is thus clear that, unlike with the first camp of leaders, their activism was based on opposition to the regime players they considered hostile to workers' interests, a position that was influenced by their socialist political stance.

In this context, it is worth noting that the CTUWS leaders' demand for acquisition of the 130-day bonus was the motivation for this strike. In contrast, the demand for an agreement pegging wages to inflation for textile workers in Egypt didn't get enough support from rank-and-file workers. This fact signals the victory of the CTUWS leaders' "self-limited framing" and demonstrates the social base they had within the company. Furthermore, the movement's players' prioritizing of limited financial demands signaled to the regime players that their actions and claims remained in the arena of labor-related rights and didn't move to the arena of "politics," which the regime players considered to be more threatening.

The 2007 Strike: Dynamics of the Strategic Interaction

In an almost similar way to the mobilization in 2006, on Sunday, September 23, night-shift workers left their machines and headed toward Talaat Harb Square in the company. At 7:30 a.m., the second shift workers arrived and joined them, until the arrival of their colleagues from the third shift at 3:30 p.m. The unity of the movement was guaranteed by the slogans formulated. During the whole day, up until *iftar* (the meal breaking the fast), they chanted these slogans, denouncing the company's management. Their primary demand was an increase in the monthly bonus of at least two months (i.e., approximately 130 days) of the initial salary for the year 2006–7.

The slogans were also directed at the company's chairman of the board, Abdel Fattah al-Gebally, whom workers accused of being a "corrupt thief." Remember that the company had only started to show losses with the advent of al-Gebally as head of the administration in 2006, and the workers blamed the losses on the administration, which they saw as corrupt. Labor leader Soad stated:

> If workers are working and the company is showing only losses, it is the company management that must be held accountable, not us. It's not up to us to assume responsibility for a corrupt administration. (Interview with author, February 7, 2010)

The workers' frustrations were expressed in various ways: a sign was posted in front of the door of the company, with the inscription "al-Gilani [the chairman of the board of the Public Company for Spinning and Weaving] and al-Gebally [the company's chairman of the board] have eaten my children's food" (*Al-Gilany w-al-Gebally akalu akl 'iyaly*).[12] One

12. Karim Al Beheiry, 2007d, "Istmirar i'tisam 27 alf 'amil min 'umal ghazl al-Mahalla lil-yawm al-thani 'ala al-tawali" [The Sit-In of 27,000 Workers in Mahalla for the Second Day], Egy Workers, September 24, 2007, http://egyworkers.blogspot.com/2007_09_01_archive.html.

of the best-known slogans they launched was "They eat pigeons and chickens and we're eating beans. We're tired of eating beans, and the beans are tired of us" (*Humma yaklu hamam w-firakh w-ehna al-ful dawakhna w-dakh*). Recall that this slogan was transmitted from one generation to another within the company since the strike of 1975. They even installed gallows (*mashnaqa*), where they hung an effigy of al-Gebally, then built a coffin (*na'sh*) for it and carried it around the company.[13]

The labor leaders, in concert with the workers, formulated a "motivational frame" for protesting and striking—rights that the company management had violated. The violation became the rationale behind their mobilization. Benford and Snow (2000, 617–18) define a motivational frame as "the rational for engaging in ameliorative collective action including the construction of appropriate vocabularies of motive." It was the notion of "rights" in particular that they advocated for. It is worth noting that the routinization of workers' strikes—which multiplied by the hundreds during 2007—reinforced this framing. Striking became, in a sense, the effort needed for putting pressure on the government and obtaining their rights. This framing was even transmitted from father to son during the sit-in. A ten-year-old son of a company worker participating in the sit-in shared that his mother had informed him that they were present to demand the rights that had been taken away by the company management, whom he referred to as "thieves." He further mentioned that he accompanied his mother to ensure she wasn't left alone with the "thieves" (Amer 2009).

By the end of the first day of the strike (Sunday, September 23), there were reactions from two regime subplayers, government representatives, who had tried to persuade the workers that they had no rights to ask for, and security agents, who used coercive, nonviolent methods to oblige the labor leaders to concede.

The government action aimed to persuade the workers to renounce their claim and to simultaneously delegitimize the strikers in the eyes of

13. "'umal al-Mahalla yarfudun al-hizb al-watani wa al-ikhwan" [The Mahalla Workers Refuse the NDP and the Muslim Brotherhood], 2007, *Al-Ahaly*, July 26, 2007.

the media and the public. The ministers of labor and investment stated on the popular television program *El-Beit Beitak* that the workers were not entitled to these bonuses. They even added that the workers had received their rights and that there was no legitimate reason for them to strike.[14] These ministerial statements immediately radicalized the slogans of the protesters. The target of the workers was now no longer the company management, but the government that plainly supported it. Among the slogans that surfaced was "There is no God but God, the government is the enemy of God" (*La illah illa Allah al-hukuma 'aduw Allah*; Al-Beheiry 2007c). By the phrase "enemy of God," the workers meant "the enemy of justice," which they upheld as one of the main values of any religion. This turnaround generated more media interest and at the same time opened the door gradually for political organizations to enter the scene, as I will argue later.

A few hours after these government statements, security forces arrested five labor leaders: Yehia, Samer, Ashraf, Raed, and Fawzy. The previous ministerial statements had given the green light for these arrests, on the pretext that they had cut off the electricity in the company and forced the workers to strike: this was the complaint that al-Gebally, the company's chairman of the board, brought to the office of the police commissioner (Al-Beheiry 2007c). The labor leaders were transferred to the Mahalla police's second commissioner's office and were not released until the evening of the third day of the strike, Tuesday, September 25 (Al-Beheiry 2007c). A few hours later, they were transferred to the State Security office in Mahalla, where negotiations took place. In fact, this arrest had the implicit purpose of negotiating with the leaders under pressure, so that they would accept a compromise (Amer 2009). Ezzat Drag, a Mahalla member of parliament (and member of the NPD), was present at this meeting. He even stated that he had already held negotiations with the

14. Karim Al-Beheiry, 2007c, "Infijar fi wadi al-Mahalla bi-sabab tasrihat al-wazira Aisha Abdel-Hadi" [The Situation Broke out at Mahalla as a Result of the Declaration of Aisha Abdel Hadi], Egy Workers, September 24, 2007, http://egyworkers.blogspot.com/2007/09/blog-post_4647.html.

Ministry of Investment in their name, and that the Ministry had agreed to only forty days of bonuses.[15]

However, the leaders refused to concede. They were released without making any commitments to the security agents, stating that they could not do so without the agreement of the strikers. The workers held on to this notion of claiming their rights and refused to demobilize without receiving their full right to the 130-day bonus. In fact, the previous contentious interaction in 2006 encouraged the workers to form their own interpretation of the government's position: to acquire their rights, they must persevere and continue to protest. This vision was reinforced by the concessions that the government had previously made as a result of the strike. Players' actions are thus influenced by the interpretation and meanings that emerge during the contentious action itself (Jasper 2014, 65–66).

The movement's leaders also estimated that the cost of action at this moment was low, considering that, from the first day of the strike, the attitude of security officers had been peaceful. This is how labor leader Wahid (2010) explained it:

> The complicity of the security agents before and during this strike was striking: the State Security knew all about our initiatives. However, no reaction. This may have been the case during the strike of 2006, but it has never happened in Mahalla. It was clear that the security strategy had changed. The security officers even allowed the media to enter the company to speak with us and take pictures. Three whole days without any reaction on the part of the state, but also without any intention of negotiating.

This change in security strategy was interpreted as an opportunity that must be seized upon.[16] Moreover, the insistence of the labor leaders on

15. Mohamed Abul Dahab, 2007, "idrab al-mahalla yastamir le al-youm al-rabei'" [The Mahalla Workers' Strike Continues for the Fourth Day], *Al-Dustur*, September 27, 2007.

16. During the first four days of the strike, the security vehicles were placed just in front of the entrance of the city of Mahalla, near the train station, but never surrounded the company as they did during the strike of 2008.

organizing a demonstration on July 1 in front of the company office, calling for the resolution of labor demands, despite the State Security officers' request not to do so, confirms this interpretation of the security force's actions. During the last week of June, State Security agents from the Mahalla commissioner's office summoned Reyad. They ordered him to cancel the demonstration and threatened to arrest him if he refused to execute this order. To force him to give in, they reaffirmed that the government would never yield to their undue pressure.

Reyad, however, did not back down on his position and stated that, on the contrary, the government would give in:

> Teachers protested to demand "special consideration" for a wage increase, and the government complied. The Al-Azhar Mosque preachers did the same thing, and the government again gave in. Why wouldn't it do the same for workers with similar demands? (2009)

This position and actions of the labor leaders means that, through their interactions with the regime players (during the strike of 2006), and their interpretation of its subplayers' (government and security forces') positions and actions, they formulated a strategy based on continuing to further pressure the government to fulfill their financial demands. This means that the meaning the players attributed to the other players' actions determined their choices and strategies. According to Jasper (2014, 238), "Players constantly monitor and interpret what all the players are doing in the relevant arena." They and act and promote their goals based upon that interpretation.

The arrest of some of the movement's leaders and the negotiations that followed had alerted the workers that this strike would likely be much longer than the previous one (Reyad 2009). Consequently, they put in place a protest survival strategy, ensuring the movement's flexibility, while displaying its worthiness, commitment, and visibility. They also ensured that this mobilization would be perceived as being legitimate, both by the authorities and the media.

As an example of flexibility, workers were encouraged to return home from time to time, so they wouldn't get exhausted, before returning to the sit-in. The labor leaders also encouraged the workers to monitor their farmland during the evenings, without being obliged to remain at the sit-in (Amer 2009). Some workers brought their children if they couldn't leave them at home, which completely transformed the atmosphere of the sit-in to become more friendly and helped it survive longer. Each cluster of workers that returned home brought back food and necessary items for their colleagues. Organizing these tasks also happened spontaneously among groups of friends, who divided the work of bringing the two essential meals in the month of Ramadan: the iftar evening meal (breaking the fast), and suhur (a small meal before dawn in preparation for fasting the next day; Reyad 2009). Similarly, the women workers shouldered the responsibility of providing for the basic needs of their colleagues.

As labor leader Soad (2010) stated, female workers participated in the sit-in for a certain period of time and then returned home to cook and bring food as close as possible to the time of iftar:

> We were concerned that the workers wouldn't be able to continue the strike because of the harsh conditions of the fast. We had to take charge of the food as much as we could to help the men continue protesting. So, we would all return home to cook and bring food to our colleagues, instead of maintaining a passive presence at the sit-in.

This solidarity among the workers also furthered the protest's survival by decreasing the likelihood of free riders. As labor leader Afaf recounted:

> One of the workers was crying during the sit-in because his house was empty and he didn't have a penny. So, we collected money from our colleagues and brought him sugar, bread, a bit of food, and "thamr" [a kind of date juice which is traditionally enjoyed during Ramadan]. We gave him everything and asked him to go give it to his wife for the iftar and come back later. (Interview with author, February 7, 2010)

To ensure the worthiness, commitment, and visibility of the movement, labor leaders had recourse to two tactics: one tactic was to form what Seif called the "strike orchestra" teams (interview with author, August 10, 2009). Workers were organized to beat barrels continuously, one team after another, day and night. Beating the barrels not only built enthusiasm and courage among the strikers; it also signaled to the security officers the commitment of the workers, who were staying alert and not sleeping, meaning they were ready to resist if at any time the security forces decided to enter the company (2009). The other tactic was to organize several events within the company during the day, increasing the workers' worthiness, enthusiasm, and visibility. Usually, two events were organized: the first during the day, and the second after iftar. Among the slogans they chanted during their demonstrations were "Shame, shame, the thieves go free, while the honest are behind bars" (*Yady al-hasra w-yadi al-'ar, al-lusus ahrar 'ayshin w-al ashraf khalf al-aswar*). By thieves, the workers were referring to company management, and by behind bars (walls), they meant the imprisoning walls of the company. Other slogans were also launched: "You have no right, Aisha [referring to the minister of labor], where are you, Mubarak (the president of the Republic)?" (*La ya 'Aysha, la, la, malkish haq, finak, finak ya Mubarak*; Al-Beheiry 2007i).[17]

These slogans, while exhibiting confrontation between the movement and the government, also demonstrated the strategy of restraint that the CTUWS leaders advocated for. They did not directly challenge the head of the regime, they and never framed the protest as open conflict with regime players. The idea was to appear nonthreatening to regime players and to remain in the arena of labor-related rights, rather than give the impression of moving to the arena of politics. The workers were even asking the president of the republic to intervene on their behalf to procure their rights, as the slogans show. In addition, a few tents were set up for napping, relaxing, and entertaining the children. They were providing for a long-term sit-in and sending a message to the government and to the security forces that they were there to stay (Seif 2009).

As emphasized by Latif, a journalist in one of the prominent private newspapers, the labor leaders, in order to safeguard the legitimacy of the protest, periodically visited the plants to ensure that the machines remained in good condition; they were afraid that the government would

17. Karim Al-Beheiry, 2007i, "Istimrar idrab ghazl al-Mahalla lil-yawm al-khamis" [The Mahalla Workers' Strike Continues for the Fifth Day], Egy Workers, September 27, 2007, https://egyworkers.blogspot.com/2007/09/blog-post_7069.html.

take the pretext of possible damage to machines to delegitimize their sit-in (interview with author, April 9, 2010). Morad and Fawzy, workers in the department of electricity and in the garages, respectively, took it upon themselves to be sure the technicians and drivers didn't strike. It is important to note that one of the tasks of the department of electricity was to send water through the pipes to the homes of the company workers and staff members (Latif 2010). They also had ambulances ready in the garages. It was important to maintain this image of responsible workers asking for their legitimate rights. This image not only deprived the government of its weapon of delegitimization, but also garnered the sympathy of potential allies, particularly the media.

As the protests continued, security forces began to use coercion as a reaction to the movement's perseverance. This was succeeded by the unsuccessful persuasive efforts of the government (and its allies). The security forces thus employed a policy of intimidation, which was followed by the government decision to negotiate during the fourth and the fifth days, after intimidation did not bear fruit. By the end of the sixth day (specifically, the dawn of the seventh day), the government yielded to the demands of the workers.

To intimidate the workers, the security officers began to circulate rumors stating that they were going to break into the company and put an end to the strike by force (Latif 2010). However, this rumor appeared to the movement's leaders as inconsistent with the generally peaceful attitude of the security agents, so they responded by threatening to escalate, spreading rumors that the workers were going to leave the company grounds to demonstrate with the Mahalla city residents (Reyad 2009). Moving the contention to the street arena was the scenario that the regime players feared the most. Here, I recall the history of the contentious interactions between both players, as well as the legacy of the Mahalla labor movement, and the support it enjoyed from Mahalla city residents. This doesn't mean that the security forces wouldn't have repressed the workers if they had demonstrated outside of the company. The cost of this action, however, was higher for the government, as it affected its image. The workers' threats had a somewhat stabilizing effect by balancing the power between the two players, thus thwarting the security forces' intimidation tactics.

In this context, the government (and its allies at the trade union level, in the Parliament and at the local level) decided to hold negotiations with the labor leaders in order to persuade them to accept a partial fulfillment of the workers' demands. Ezzat Drag, a member of the Mahalla Parliament (NDP), and Hussein Mugawer, the president of ETUF, phoned Ashraf and Yasser, as members of the NDP, and proposed that they agree to receive 40 days of bonuses instead of 130 days (Wael 2009). Aisha Abdel Hadi, the minister of labor, called Reyad and Yasser to propose this partial fulfillment of the demands, but to no avail (Reyad 2009). The last attempt was them going in person to the sit-in to convince the workers to accept the 40 days of bonuses. Abdel Hamid Noweir, the president of the NDP in Mahalla City, and Ezzat Drag went to the company to personally convey this compromise. Their attempt, however, was not successful. On the contrary, the workers chanted all the more loudly, refusing partial fulfillment of their demands and chasing the two officials out of the company.[18]

There remained a final step: to send government delegates to negotiate and hopefully arrive at a solution to this conflict, as well as to fulfill the workers' demands.

The Media and the Private Press: Influential Allies?

Since the success of the 2006 strike, the workers' cause received more coverage in Egyptian media. The privately owned press in particular devoted entire pages and extensive reporting to the issue, validating the movement as well as forming a type of implicit solidarity with it. A survey of the coverage of the Mahalla labor movement protests during 2007 and 2008 by the three main privately owned daily newspapers (*Al-Masry Al-Youm*, *Al-Badil*, and *Al-Dustur*) shows that these three newspapers accounted for nearly 50 percent of the journalistic coverage of the Mahalla protests, whereas the three government-owned dailies (*Al-Ahram*, *Al-Akhbar*, and *Al-Jumhuriyya*) provided only 15 percent of the total media coverage of

18. Karim Al-Beheiry, 2007a, "'umal ghazl al-Mahalla yatrudun mas'uli al-hizb al-watani al-muwafidin min al-hukuma lil-tafawud wa tawaghulat amniyya dakhil al-masani'" [The Mahalla Workers Chased out the Representatives of the NDP], Egy Workers, July 28, 2007, http://egyworkers.blogspot.com/2007/09/blog-post_3533.html.

these protests (Abdel Ghafar 2009). In other words, of the 901 articles covering the Mahalla strikes in 2007 and 2008, *Al-Masry Al-Youm* published 87 articles, *Al-Badil* 160, and *Al-Dustur* 178, making a total of 425 articles, while *Al-Ahram* published only 45 articles, *Al-Akhbar* 28, and *Al-Jumhuriyya* 40, forming a total of 113 articles (2009).

Not only were the Mahalla labor movement, with its successful strike in 2006 and its successive protests, an interesting topic for the media; they were also an indispensable tool for the labor movement. Broadly speaking, the regime's strategy of relative liberalization of the media, particularly the margin of autonomy it conferred on the privately owned daily newspapers at the time, presented the movement's players with an opening and an opportunity, which they sought to exploit.

The private press validated the significance of the movement and its leaders (Gamson and Wolfsfeld 1993, 116). By disseminating information on the national level, the media gave the labor claims substantial visibility. Media coverage provides movements with a measure of discursive presence or influence as it helps it to gain recognition and visibility (Amenta et al. 2015a, 302).

The labor leaders' strategy, therefore, was to exploit as much as possible the opportunity to generate the movement's visibility in the media. They would rely on the media to pressure the company management and political decision-makers to respond to labor claims. The movement's leaders perceived the media to be an influential ally that was able—to some extent—to change the balance of power in favor of the labor movement. In other words, they believed that the security forces would renounce resorting to violence if the media increased the movement's visibility. It is important to note, however, that the leaders asked for the support of workers and nongovernmental organizations, but never from political opposition.

In this context, it is worth mentioning an event that confirms that the movement's leaders perceived the press to be their allies and were seeking to use them in their contentious interactions with regime players. Following the 2007 strike, the Mahalla City Council secretary and the president of the ETUF refused to allow coverage in privately owned newspapers of the negotiations taking place at the City Council (Majlis al-madina) between the movement's leaders and the government and its allies. However, the labor leaders refused, even threatening to withdraw from negotiations, if journalists were not given the right to cover the event. Labor leader Reyad (2009) explained: "If the government ever fails to keep its promises, these journalists will be our witnesses."

Amenta and colleagues (2015b, 233) assert that the press plays the role of referee, as "journalists decide which players are going to be taken most seriously and receive the most playing time. That is, they decide whose voices will be heard most prominently, whose understandings of an issue are to be presented, and which issues will be deemed as representing the main lines of conflict." This is especially the case with the private press coverage of the Mahalla labor movement's contentious actions. The privately owned Egyptian media places significant importance on its statements and actions. To understand the reasons for this, one should consider the activism that lies behind these positions, and that also motivates them. Journalists are activists in the field and are engaged in a struggle for the production of social meaning (Duboc 2009a). An article written by sociologist Marie Duboc in 2009 on the forms of commitment in the coverage of workers' strikes in Egypt is interesting in this regard. Duboc explains that journalists with privately owned daily newspapers cover social news due to a bias (*inhiyaz*) in favor of labor rights (*Al-qa'ida al-'umaliyya*), or, more precisely, working-class issues. The political leanings or the markedly leftist political activism of many such newspapers at the time motivated their decision to work on social issues (2009a).

For example, some of the journalists working on labor issues for *Al-Badil* and *Al-Dustur* newspapers were also members of the Revolutionary Socialists organization.[19] The most obvious manifestation of this alignment was the degree of their support for workers, particularly during strikes. In addition to the telephone contacts that the journalists provided to the labor leaders, journalists from *Al-Badil*, *Al-Dustur*, and *Al-Masry Al-Youm* remained day and night in the Mahalla factory during the September 2007 strike—a rather intense form of embedding in the heart of the protests (Duboc 2009a). This was confirmed by labor leader Mohsen (2010):

19. Field observation.

> We are extremely grateful to the journalists of the "independent" press [in reference to privately owned media, which is more independent of the regime and its stances than state-owned media]. They stayed with us night and day during our 2007 strike. We felt sorry for them staying with us, and asked them to return home to rest a little, but they always refused.

Furthermore, these social ties bolstered the support of some journalists and activists to the extent that they became extensions of family circles and friends, which often proved to be critical in establishing trust with the workers. This was the case for the Dustur correspondent in Mahalla, an activist in CTUWS and a very well-known figure among the Mahalla workers, since his father had participated in labor strikes during the 1980s and 1990s. During the 2006 strike, before receiving a lot of media attention and building connections with journalists, the labor leaders used to send this *Al-Dustur* journalist the information first, so they could be sure the first information published about their strike would be correct (Duboc 2009a).

The private press has also broadened up the scope of the movement (Gamson and Wolfsfeld 1993, 116)—that is to say, the effect it could produce in terms of solidarity or sympathy (Koopmans 2004, 367). The media was also useful in establishing broader circles of support for the labor cause inside and outside of Egypt. Declarations of solidarity were made by workers, activists, and the political opposition organizations in Egypt, as well as by a few labor unions outside of Egypt. Kafr al-Dawar labor movement leaders (in the governorate of Beheira), for example, were the first to express their solidarity with the Mahalla workers. They published their news release on July 22, 2007, the eve of the declared Mahalla Company labor strike. In it, they insisted on the legitimacy of the labor strike, since the workers were demanding their financial rights, which had been violated.[20] On September 26, 2007—the third day of the strike—the National Education, Health, and

20. Karim Al-Beheiry, 2007e, "Qiyadat ghazl al-Dawar yu'linun al-idrab al-tadamuni al-thulatha' al-qadim" [The Leaders of Kafr al-Dawar Declare a Strike Next Tuesday in Solidarity with the Workers of Mahalla], Egy Workers, September 24, 2007, http://egyworkers.blogspot.de/2007/09/blog-post_5665.html.

Allied Workers' Union, one of the largest unions in South Africa, issued a press release in solidarity with the Mahalla workers. They described the Mahalla strike as activism, in a similar fashion to their own, and in a context of increasing neoliberal policies.[21] Note that CTUWS had exchanged experience and expertise with this union. This type of statement not only increased the visibility of the movement, but also raised the morale of the strikers. These statements were reported by the privately owned press. The labor leaders and members of the movement also distributed them during the sit-in to encourage each other (Seif 2009).

Similarly, the media attention received by the workers at Mahalla echoed in the political arena in the city of Mahalla, as well as in Cairo. It was thus that the Kifaya (Enough) movement and the Center for Socialist Studies, attached to the organization of Revolutionary Socialists, released two communiqués in which they affirmed their solidarity with the workers. They said that their demands were legitimate, and that the strike had become the only way to obtain them. Solidarity was represented within the communiqué as a shared objective of the two parties.[22]

With the advent of the sixth day of the strike and the shifting tone of the workers' slogans, which had begun to target the government directly, the Kifaya movement and other political parties decided to show even more solidarity by organizing a demonstration in Talaat Harb Square in the center of Cairo. This would gradually lead to their emergence, as players, during the strike of 2008. The security forces deployed a preventive strategy vis-à-vis these solidarity protests. A preventive strategy consists of dispersing people before too large a crowd gathered (Uysal 2006, 274). The security forces thus closed all the streets leading to the city center in

21. Karim Al-Beheiry, 2007g, "Al-niqaba al-wataniyya lil-ta'lim wa al-'umal al-mutahidun akbar niqabat janub afriqia wa al-'alam tu'lin tadamunha ma' 'umal ghazl al-Mahalla" [The National Union of Education and United Workers, One of the Largest Unions in South Africa, Declares Its Solidarity with the Workers of Mahalla], Egy Workers, September 26, 2007, http://egyworkers.blogspot.de/2007/09/blog-post_26.html.

22. Karim Al-Beheiry, 2007b, "Bayanat tadamuniyya ma' 'umal al-Mahalla" [Declaration of Solidarity with the Mahalla Workers], Egy Workers, September 24, 2007, http://egyworkers.blogspot.de/2007/09/blog-post_330.html.

order to prevent them from organizing the demonstration.[23] The Kifaya activists were therefore pushed to demonstrate in front of the Journalists' Union building (not far from the city center), where their presence was less visible and less threatening to the regime players.[24]

The reaction of security agents to this event revealed their strategy: they would be more open if the mobilization occurred either in the arena of labor-related rights, or in the arena of politics. Having players connected across both arenas appeared to be threatening. In other words, they would be more tolerant if the labor leaders organized a protest with strictly economic claims, as in the case of the Mahalla labor strike in 2006 and 2007, or if the political players organized a strictly political demonstration, as had been the case with dozens of events organized in front of the syndicates of lawyers or journalists in Cairo since 2005. The security apparatus players were on high alert as soon as the political players went beyond simply declaring their verbal solidarity with the labor movement's players and undertook contentious action in solidarity with them.

The Political Parties Committee in Mahalla also stated its support and solidarity with the workers on the eve of the first day of the strike. Since 2005, the committee had been well known by the Mahalla workers. It consisted of the main political opposition parties (Al-Amal, Al-Tajammu', Al-Nasseri, Al-Ghad, Al-Wafd, and Al-Jabha), the Kifaya movement, and the Muslim Brotherhood. The reason for its foundation in 2005 was to coordinate the opposition among the different political forces at the local level. This type of committee was formed in many governorates, but the Mahalla City committee was one of the most active.

Each year, one of the political parties had the role of coordinating the committee's actions and meetings. Their tasks consisted largely of organizing symposia, to exchange various points of view concerning political news and, most importantly, to organize demonstrations. Since 2006,

23. Note that this event was organized at the time in solidarity with the Mahalla workers, and with a few journalists arrested by security agents a few days before.

24. Ahmed Rabie, 2007, "Tazahurat tadamun li-Kefaya ma' al-sahafiyin wa 'umal al-Mahalla" [Manifestations of Kefaya in Solidarity with the Journalists and the Workers of Mahalla], *Al-Itihad*, September 29, 2007.

these demonstrations were held each month in protest over the deterioration of socioeconomic conditions and inflation. As emphasized by Maged (2009), a prominent member of the Political Parties Committee in Mahalla, the demonstrations occasionally served the purpose of expressing disapproval of external events, with the siege of Gaza being a primary concern. He also added that these demonstrations were organized in the afternoon, most frequently in Al-Shoun Place (in Mahalla city center), just after work hours. This encouraged workers, employees, and students to join in on their way home from work or university. It was in this way that the number of participants in these events increased from one month to the next, with thousands of workers and employees joining a few dozen political activists in protesting for sociopolitical causes. As I will discuss in the next chapter, during the demonstration leading up to April 6, 2008, the number of protesters reached seven thousand. This doesn't mean that there was any coordination between the players of the labor movement and those of the political opposition. While the labor leaders welcomed the political parties' expression of solidarity with them, they (especially those affiliated with CTUWS) totally refused the organization of any joint action with the opposition.

As Zaki (2009), member of the Mahalla City Political Parties Committee explained:

> There is no coordination between us and the Mahalla Company workers. They only campaign for their strictly economic claims (Al-matalib al-madiya al-dayiqa). We are always careful not to cause division in the rank of the workers. That's why we decided to distinguish between political activity and labor activity, so that the workers won't accuse us of exploiting their movement (Yatahimuna birukub al-haraka al-'umaliya). . . . Of course there are informal connections between some of us and some of the labor leaders. Certainly, we know each other and we speak often, but we never coordinate our activities.

These statements were confirmed by Reyad (2009), a labor worker leader connected with CTUWS:

> Our demands differ from those of the political parties. We're not interested in whether a government remains in power or it leaves, this is

not our problem. We're protesting for the satisfaction of our financial demands.

These statements are important for this analysis. As in the next chapter, one of the main reasons behind the decision of the CTUWS leaders to demobilize is that the labor issue had become politicized. As confirmed by Reyad's testimony, the CTUWS leaders refused to allow their economic objectives to be diverted to other political issues, particularly since this entailed threatening regime players, which they refused.

Outcomes of the 2007 Contentious Interaction: Success and Reinforcement of Internal Divisions

This contentious episode ended with the success of the movement's players and a decision by the regime players to make concessions. This very likely seemed a less costly option than intervention by force, which could have been detrimental in terms of the regime's image. Hence, the State Security office phoned labor leader Reyad and informed him that a delegation consisting of the president of the ETUF, delegates from the Department of Labor in the Ministry of Labor, and members of Parliament would travel to Mahalla from Cairo to negotiate with the workers. He requested that they form a delegation representing the labor movement in these negotiations (Ashraf 2009). Two microbuses were dispatched to take them to the Mahalla City Council (Majlis al-madina), at city hall, where the negotiations were held.[25]

The government delegation promised to fulfill the workers' demand for 130-day bonuses, with the increase divided across three instalments, the first being a bonus of 70 days. The promise of an increase in the meal allowance from 42 to 90 EGP, one of the movement's other priorities, was also granted. The negotiations ended with an agreement to remove the company's chairman of the board, Abdel Fatah al-Gebally, from office, as he had been widely accused of corruption by the workers (Reyad 2009).

25. The delegation of leaders is not formed by voting or a similar procedure within the movement. According to Reyad, agreeing on the members of the delegation was no problem as long as the labor leaders were already known and accepted within the movement, they only needed to be regrouped.

Finally, the president of ETUF (the de jure labor representative) promised the Mahalla labor delegation (the de facto labor representative) that he would negotiate the other demands with them later.

Gamson (2015, 383) states that "it is useful to think of success as a set of outcomes that fall into two basic clusters: one concerned with the fate of the challenging group as an organization, and one with the distribution of new advantages to the group's beneficiary. The central issue in the first cluster focuses on the *acceptance* of a challenging group by its antagonists as a valid spokesman for a legitimate set of interests. The central issue in the second cluster focuses on whether the group's beneficiary gains *new advantages* during the challenge and its aftermath." According to this framing, the movement leaders' negotiations not only brought about success in achieving their financial demands, but also in acquiring, once again, the government's recognition of the movement's leaders as its legitimate representatives.

It is interesting, however, to consider how the two camps of leaders interpreted this success, as differences in perception and positioning would profoundly influence the future choices of the movement and its evolution. The CTUWS leaders saw this result as a great victory, given that their top priority demands were granted. In contrast, the leaders of the other camp considered the victory to be only partial, given that the demand for price-wage alignment for textile workers was not granted. As labor leader Wahid (2010) stated:

> This is a victory with the taste of defeat. The real demands have not been met, especially the alignment of salary with prices. . . . Al-Gebally's dismissal was the bone the government threw us to pull out of the game and stop the protests. And the proof is that the one who replaced him is no less corrupt. On the contrary, during his tenure, the company has sustained large losses that exceed those that took place when Al-Gebally was in office.

Conclusion

In conclusion, the movement made use of organizational and situational aspects to exert pressure on the regime players and obtain a positive outcome concerning at least a portion of its main claims: the formulation of a resonant motivational framing and tactics leading to the movement's mobilization, as well as to its persistence throughout this contentious episode; the ongoing agency of the movement's players; and the choice of the CTUWS leaders to adopt a position rejecting open confrontation with the regime players.

These last two factors infer that the Mahalla labor movement's organizational resources were a necessary but insufficient condition for its success in challenging the players of the authoritarian regime of Mubarak. In contrast, the way in which movement leaders/players interpreted regime players' actions—as providing an opening in the arena of labor-related rights—in addition to the framing and strategies that they put in place during their contentious interactions with regime players, determined the capacity of the movement to take advantage of these openings, "neutralize" the security apparatus and succeed in achieving workers financial claims (even if partially).

Finally, the differences in perception (and priorities) between the two groups of leaders—as demonstrated in this chapter—are relevant to an analysis of the evolution of their choices, and, consequently, of the outcomes that the movement might generate in future contentious interactions. It will not be surprising to see that the leaders of Al-Rabta pushed for wage-price alignment, and later on also for the minimum wage, which completely changed the stakes and the repertoires of action of the movement, thereby opening the door to its demobilization in 2008.

4

From Hero to Zero?

Contesting Authoritarian Rules and Demobilization of the Mahalla Labor Movement

Introduction

This chapter focuses on the Mahalla labor movement's decision to initiate a new strike in April 2008, centering on a broader socioeconomic demand: the establishment of a minimum wage for all Egyptian workers. This marked a significant shift from narrow economic claims to nationwide demands, challenging the policies framing the regime's relations with workers. I explore internal dynamics within the movement that led to prioritizing the minimum wage demand on a national scale. The growing influence of Al-Rabta group leaders advocating for a confrontational stance against regime players played a crucial role.

Additionally, I delve into the entry of political organizations on the scene after the movement adopted a national demand. Media relayed this demand, attracting political solidarity and politicizing the labor issue. The media's discursive opportunities transformed into a threat for the movement, amplifying political framing over its initial economic framing. I also analyze the strategic interaction between regime and movement players in the context of labor demand politicization, revealing strategic trade-offs, dilemmas, and cognitive visions that shaped leaders' decisions.

Crucially, I emphasize the contrasting outcomes resulting from leaders' choices—the compromising stance of CTUWS leaders led to demobilization, while the confrontational approach of Al-Rabta leaders resulted in repression. Unlike previous strikes, the state security apparatus coerced labor leaders into demobilizing workers. I conclude by detailing the repertoire of repression employed by the security apparatus and the outcomes of contentious interactions at the Misr Company and Mahalla al-Kubra, shedding light on the complete demobilization of the labor movement after the strike on April 6, 2008.

The Dynamics of Transposition to the National Level

The labor leaders of the two camps met in January 2008 because the government had failed to fulfill its promise to increase the meal allowance. It was at this meeting that they decided to strike on April 6, 2008, since their aim was to pressure the government to act on this demand, as well as the other claims that had lain dormant since 2007.[1] April 6 was chosen by the leaders for two reasons: on the one hand, to be sure that all the workers would have received their wages before calling for the sit-in, the 5th of the month being the deadline for salary payments, and, on the other hand, to put the security agents in an embarrassing situation, since the local elections (*Intikhabat al-majalis al-mahaliya*) were to take place on April 6 (Wahid, interview with author, August 15, 2009). This date was subsequently postponed to April 8, in light of the Mahalla city protest developments.

For the first time, the two groups of leaders agreed on the fact that wage-price alignment for all workers in the textile industry should be the priority. Since the government had neglected their demands, the CTUWS leaders decided to abandon the "self-limiting framing" they had previously followed and to adopt Al-Rabta's position. In fact, CTUWS's reorientation largely reflected a position of escalation toward the government. Tilly and Tarrow (2008, 216) define escalation as a change of objectives and tactics to others that are more radical. A combination of factors explains their change in stance.

To begin with, the CTUWS leaders' assessment of the movement's potential led them to evaluate the balance of power as being in their favor. Therefore, they felt that they were able to get more benefits from

1. The movement's decision to strike was relayed by Egyptian dailies. See, for example, "'umal al-Mahalla ya'udu lil-i'tisam fi April" [The Mahalla Workers Will Strike in April], *Al-Masry Al-Youm*, 3.

a government they perceived as being susceptible to pressure, in light of the concessions it had made in the past. Players thus reflect the weight of past interactions, accumulations, understandings, and expectations, in line with Jasper's frame of analysis. Each interaction does not start from scratch, but is rather based on the dynamics and outcomes of the previous ones (Jasper 2021, 245).

Moreover, their internal reputation within the movement pushed them to reevaluate. The nonachievement of the labor demands (especially those related to the meal allowance increase) placed the CTUWS leaders in a fragile position in the eyes of the workers (Morad, interview with author, April 14, 2010). As a matter of fact, their credibility was questioned. Adopting this radical position toward the regime players thus reflected their desire to preserve their authority within the movement.

As emphasized by Amer, correspondent of *Al-Dustur* newspaper in Al-Mahalla city, CTUWS's repositioning was confirmed by the leaflet that its leaders distributed in the company at the beginning of February 2008, referring to the increase in the price of food and to the workers' declining standard of living (interview with author, August 9, 2009). In the leaflet, it was also mentioned that previously, workers accepted appeasements and consensual solutions while waiting for a final response from the authorities. However, since the labor requests have been rejected, the workers would declare a strike on April 6 (2009).

The demands that propelled the movement included demands that had not been previously met, such as the increase in the meal allowance. Other demands concerned the workers' new claims, such as having points of sale for bread in front of the company, and augmentation in the allocated funds for the Transportation Association (Amer 2009). The need for points of sale for bread was due to the shortage of bread in the country. Government-subsidized bread was not in sufficient quantity in the city's bakeries, and sometimes there was none at all. Regarding the Transportation Association, it was in charge of transporting the company workers from the towns outside of the city of Mahalla. Overarching both of these categories was the demand to peg wages to inflation.

Al-Rabta players/leaders would quickly seize the opportunity presented by the internal consensus on wage-price alignment to step up their oppositional strategy toward the regime players. Beginning in mid-February 2008, instead of claiming only this alignment, they demanded a minimum wage for all Egyptian workers. As Rabab al-Mahdi has stated (2011), this constituted a change in the type of labor demands the movement put forward; it was a break with the prevailing concept of the moral economy. In other words, this demand demonstrated that the labor movement had dropped its previous attempts to pressure the government for its financial rights in favor of direct opposition to government policies. Labor leader Wahid (2009) explained the movement's evolution in this way:

> Mohsen [founder of Al-Rabta] and I had always insisted on the minimum wage, but there was no internal agreement on this issue within the movement. The workers and the other leaders [i.e., the CTUWS leaders] saw it as an unattainable dream. Now is the time to demand it unequivocally.

Similarly, Al-Rabta labor leader Morad (2010) indicated:

> Wage-price alignment was just a thought, an alternative to the minimum wage, because the workers were divided on this subject. But this framework agreement divides the workers and scatters their efforts in their fight against the government. The time has come to close ranks.

Accordingly, on the eve of the National Council for Wages meeting (*Al-majlis al-qawmi lil-ujur*), Al-Rabta leaders organized a demonstration demanding a minimum wage of 1,200 EGP.[2] It should be noted that Labor Law No. 12 of 2003 stipulates that the National Wage Council was supposed to meet periodically to clarify and recommend the minimum wage as a function of price increases. Nevertheless, the council had not met since the early 2000s (Bassiouni 2008b, 4). The demonstration organized by Al-Rabta leaders took place in Talaat Harb Square, which was located opposite the company management's door, in front of the enclosure. It

2. Mostafa Bassiouni, 2008b, "Qiyadat niqabiyya wa 'umaliyya tutalib bi-iqrar al-had al-adna lil-ujur bi-1200 junayh shahriyyan liyatasawa ma' khat al-faqr al-'alami" [Labor Leaders Demand a Minimum Wage Equal to LE1,200, Compatible with the Poverty Line], *Al-Dustur*, February 10, 2008.

began at 3.30 p.m., the time the first shift of workers would be leaving and the second shift entering, so that both shifts would be present.[3] According to Morad, Seif, and Wahid, almost ten thousand workers participated (Morad 2010).[4]

In fact, Al-Rabta set the amount at 1,200 EGP based on the United Nations criteria, which placed the poverty line at $2 dollars per day. They calculated that a family of four needed $5 per day to live, which would be 40 EGP per day, and 1,200 EGP per month (Wahid 2009). However, during its February 18 meeting in 2008, the National Wage Council recommended a minimum wage increase of 135 EGP to only 300 EGP.[5] The average Mahalla worker's salary varied from 200–500 EGP after about ten years of work.[6] As a result of these disappointing statements, Al-Rabta leaders used their periodical magazine, *Sawt 'umal al-Mahalla* (Voice of the Mahalla Workers) to threaten a strike. In the March 2008 edition, they also stated that if the government maintained its position and rejected their demands, chief of which was the minimum wage, their response—referring to the April 6 strike—would be scathing.[7]

The minimum wage demand in itself represented a challenge to the Mubarak regime and its main players. More importantly, it led to the

3. Mostafa Bassiouni, 2008c, "24 'amil bi-ghazl al-Mahalla ya'tasimun al-yawm lil-mutalaba bi-ajr 'adil li-muwajahat irtifa' al-as'ar wa takalif al-ma'isha" [Twenty-Four Thousand Workers at the Mahalla Company Stage a Sit-In to Demand a Salary Increase Just to Confront the Increase in Prices], *Al-Dustur*, February 17, 2008.

4. The same number was confirmed during my interviews with Seif and Wahid, on January 13, 2009, and September 23, 2010, respectively.

5. "Al-qawmi yawsi bi-raf' al-had al-adna lil-ujur bi-300 junayh shahriyyan" [The National Wage Council Recommends Increase in the Minimum Wage by 300 EGP Per Month], 2008, *Masrawy*, February 18, 2008, http://www.masrawy.com/News/Egypt/Economy/2008/february/18/minmum_salry.aspx.

6. Mostafa Bassiouni, 2008a, "Al-had al-adna lil-ujur bayn al-matalib al-sha'biyya wa tala'ub al-hukuma" [The Minimum Wage: The People's Demands and Government Tricks], *Al-Akhbar*, January 31, 2008.

7. *Sawt 'umal al-Mahalla* [The Voice of the Mahalla Workers], 2008, non-periodic magazine issued by Al-Rabta informal organization in Al-Mahalla company, March 2008, 2–3.

creation of new repertoires of action and framing, which increased the regime players' mistrust. Furthermore, this new approach aroused the attention of political actors and the media and contributed to a gradual transposition of the movement's demands to a national scale, as this chapter will show.

While the CTUWS leaders confined themselves to a few statements indicating that the minimum wage would be the rallying cry of the strike, they never really intended to act on it. The escalation of their position with the regime players was never meant to lead to open conflict.[8] The main purpose was to pressure the government to meet their strictly economic demands.

Conversely, the Al-Rabta group would unambiguously express its opposition to the regime players and, as a result, contributed to the escalation of the conflict. For the first time during this protest, which they organized, the movement players would appear in a kind of political confrontation with the regime players for a cause that went beyond the labor movement's narrowly framed demands. This was reflected by the slogans used during this demonstration directly challenged the head of the regime. They referred not only to the government—as had been the case at the time of the strike in 2007—but also to the president of the Republic, who until then had not been the subject of any criticism. Some of the slogans chanted were: "Down with Hosni Mubarak!" (*Yasqut, yasqut Hosni Mubarak*), "You who govern us from Abdeen, such bad government we've never seen!" (referring to Abdeen Palace where the President resided; *Ya hakimna min 'Abdin hukmak zift w zay al-tin*). Some chants revealed their sense of frustration with a president who was perceived as being indifferent to the raging battle: "Gamal [referring to Gamal Mubarak, the president's son], tell your father Mahalla hates you!" (*Ya Gamal, qul l-'abuk f-al-Mahalla biyikrahuk*), and, as before: "They eat pigeons and chickens

8. In an interview with the newspaper *Al-Badil* on February 22, Ashraf and Yehia reported that the watchword of April 6 would be the minimum wage increase. See: "'umal al-Mahalla: la taraju' 'an idrab 6 April" [The Mahalla Workers: No Backing Down on the April 6 Strike], *Al-Badil*, February 22, 2008.

and we're eating beans. We're tired of beans, and the beans are tired of us!" (*Humma yaklu hamam w-firakh w-ehna al-ful dawakhna w-dakh*).[9]

In addition, the repertoire of the demonstration and the arena of contention changed. One hour after its start, enthusiastic workers exited the company enclosure, which had never happened since 2006. The arena of contention thus switched to street politics. Morad (2010) explains:

> The minimum wage issue concerns all Egyptian workers, not only those in Mahalla. There's no question of staying inside the company.

Morad also recognized the national and wide-ranging scope of the movement's demands. Since all actions are reactions as interaction unfolds over time (Jabola-Carolus et al. 2020, 640); the demonstrators' change of repertoire of action, and this switch toward the arena of street politics, resulted in a change in the security forces' repertoire of contention. Police officers surrounded the demonstrators, and, for the first time, they resorted to repression. They prevented the demonstrators from moving toward Al-Bahr Street, the main street in front of the company (Wahid 2009). The shopkeepers (*dakakin*) near the company had already begun to join in (2009). According to Wahid, the police threatened to use force and even commit a "massacre" (*Mathbaha*) if the demonstration spread any further (2009). This reaction shows that the security agents were well aware of the risk involved if the labor protesters and the Mahalla residents joined forces.

With the new national dimension to the movement players' demands, the Mahalla political parties committee was encouraged to seize this opportunity and demonstrate its solidarity with the cause. On March 6, 2008, the committee organized a demonstration in Al-Shoun Square in the city center of Mahalla, taking up the same demands as the labor movement.[10]

9. Karim Al-Beheiry, 2008a, "'umal al-Mahalla yakhtariqun al-hajiz al-amni wa yahtifun yasqut yasqut Hosni Mubarak" [The Mahalla Workers Breach the Security Cordon and Chant "Down with Mubarak!"], Egy Workers, February 17, 2008, http://egyworkers.blogspot.de/2008_02_01_archive.html.

10. This fact would mark the beginning of the political interest aroused by the Mahalla labor movement at the national level just a few days later.

The theme of this demonstration was protesting the alarming increase in the price of food, and the demand for wage-price alignment. The choice of the iconic Al-Shoun Square was due to the fact that most of the public transportation stops were there, and workers and city employees would pass by on their return home from work. The demonstration was held in the afternoon to encourage the other workers and employees to participate. To organize this event, the committee members divided up the neighborhoods among them, with the representatives of all parties in the committee responsible for distributing leaflets to inform residents about the demonstration (Zaki, interview with author, January 24, 2009).

At around 4 p.m., thousands of workers and employees joined the few hundred activists who had already gathered in the square. The demonstrators' slogans bemoaning the price increases and the shortage of bread prompted the city residents to join in, because they could easily identify with these demands. Maged, a leading member of Mahalla committee of political parties, stated that this event had been the most successful since 2005–6 in terms of popular participation. According to Maged, nearly seven thousand people participated (interview with author, January 24, 2009). Zaki (2009), another leading member of the Mahalla political parties committee, commented that this high rate of participation had not been seen since 2006 when the number of demonstrators did not exceed three thousand. As explained by Della Porta and Atak (2015), in the street politics and the policing arenas, interactions between both sides of the contention leads to moves and countermoves as the police adapt their strategies to moves by demonstrators. Therefore, the increase in the number of demonstrators, which alarmed the police, pushed them to change their behavior and strategies. Central Security Forces surrounded the demonstrators with a security cordon, and, for the first time since 2006, they used force (batons) against the demonstrators. Seventeen activists were arrested, but they were released at the end of the day (Zaki 2009).

These two contentious episodes attracted the interest of political organizations outside the city of Mahalla. These organizations would base their appeal for political protest on the labor movement. Hence, the next section deals with an analysis of the dynamics of politicization of the labor issue.

Discursive Opportunities and Dynamics of Politicization

Up until the demonstration on February 17, 2008, the complaints still centered around specific, financial demands at the Mahalla factory, as they had been during the strikes of 2006 and 2007. This was characteristic of all the strikes and protests that took place in Egypt since 2004. The February 17 labor demonstration was based on the demand for a wage increase, which added a national dimension to the workers' grievances.

Actually, the media coverage of the event fostered certain kinds of "discursive opportunities" for the labor movement (Koopmans 2004, 2005). Koopmans uses this term to refer to the chance that a divisive message will be disseminated in the public sphere. Koopmans identifies three mechanisms as discursive opportunities, likely to affect the chances of the message's transmission: visibility, which concerns the scope of media coverage of the message; resonance, as in the echo the message produces in terms of the reaction of third-parties—allies or the authorities to which the movement is opposed; and legitimacy, as in the degree of support the message acquires from third parties. I argue that these three mechanisms, which might mean an increase in opportunities for the players of any other movement, were instead transformed into threats for the players of the Mahalla labor movement.

The privately owned press had given substantial visibility to the February 17 labor demonstration by publishing the information. The February 17 issue of *Al-Dustur*, for example, announced on the front page that twenty-four thousand workers at the Mahalla Company held a sit-in to demand wage increases equal to the rise in prices (Bassiouni 2008c, 1). This message, once relayed and therefore made visible, reverberated among Cairo's political circles, where it was considered a significant development. Duboc (2009b, 64–65) explains that in an article published by *Al-Dustur* on February 27, Kamal Khalil, a member of the Kifaya movement, and director of the Center for Socialist Studies of the Revolutionary Socialists organization, was the first to express this vision of the February 17 demonstration as indicative of an evolution toward action on a national scale. For Khalil, this event was the sign of a new orientation (*Masira jadida*) for the labor protests, which, until then, had been dominated by demands specific to each factory.

In his opinion, the scope of the Mahalla workers' demonstration lay not only in the pressure it put on the government, but also in its ability to forge a national movement. The cooperation between workers of different industrial sectors and the other socioprofessional categories that had already organized demonstrations and strikes (e.g., doctors, teachers, journalists, judges) was therefore conceived as a mark of success. This interpretation of events conferred legitimacy on the movement players' demands, spurring them on to further action. This was followed by two political initiatives aimed at transforming the call to a labor strike into a national protest. These initiatives would later cooperate, generating increased media attention.

The first initiative took the form of an appeal launched by political forces in Cairo in March 2008 (particularly the Karama, Wasat, Al-Ghad, and Al-Jabha al-Dimuqratiya parties, Al-A'mal Party, and the Kifaya movement). They had decided to organize demonstrations in solidarity with the workers and to protest price increases. The Kifaya movement, we should remember, held a similar demonstration in front of the Journalists' Syndicate in Cairo in solidarity with the Mahalla workers in 2007. What was new this time was the decision to broaden the scope or scale of events so that April 6 would be a "Day of Rage," mainly against inflation. The broad success of the Mahalla political party committee's most recent demonstration, in terms of popular participation, strongly encouraged this initiative.

The second initiative took form on March 22, 2008, with a call to a general strike in solidarity with the labor movement, launched by two young activists: Israa Abdel Fatah member of Al-Ghad Party and Ahmed Maher member of Al-Jabha al-Dimuqratiya Party. These two activists learned of the Mahalla movement's claims and followed the course of events in the privately owned press without having any direct relationship or ties to the movement. They interpreted events similarly to Kamal Khalil. However, they would go much further: they would call for a national strike using a group they created on Facebook.

The online call for a general strike consisted of ten broad demands relating to the improvement of the quality of life and public services (health, justice, security, public transport, education, housing for young people, and access to medicines). Economic demands were linked to political demands, such as the protests against price increases, nepotism, police violence, torture in police stations, corruption, imprisonment, and arbitrary trials (Duboc 2009b, 66). The messages posted on the site indicate that members of this electronic group intended to identify and perform rather passive individual actions, consisting mainly of staying home that day: "You're not going to go to work, you're not going to go to the university, you're not going to go to school, you're not going to open the store, you're not going to open the pharmacy" (67). The emphasis was on tackling the problems suffered by many Egyptians: "We want livable wages, work, education for our children, hospitals for our care, medicines, security, freedom and dignity, housing for young couples (*Shuqaq lil-ʿirsan*). We reject nepotism, police who violate our rights (*Mish ʿawzin dubat baltagiya*), torture in police stations."[11]

This online appeal, with all the novelty that it represented, aroused substantial media interest. Once again, the privately owned media played a major role in transmitting the news that an online general strike was being organized. The political forces that launched this first call noticed the media interest aroused by the young activists' initiative. They then decided to coordinate their action with them. As a result, their proactive vision for the day was incorporated into the online calls. Kamal Khalil mentioned that workers intended to strike at their workplaces, and political groups would stand in solidarity with them. They planned to show their support through demonstrations, viewing it as a more active mode of protest and the most effective means to convey solidarity.[12]

11. Roshdi Al-Desouki, 2008, "Al-daʿwa li-idrab 6 April bil-telephone al-ardi wa-email-at wa rasa'il al-chat wa al-kitaba ʿala hitan al-shawariʿ" [The Call to Strike on April 6 through the Phone, E-mails, and Writing on Street Walls], *Al-Dustur*, April 5, 2008.

12. Rasha Reda, 2008, "Al-tazahur wa al-idrab laysa al-shakl al-wahid aladhi tahtaj min khilalahu" [Demonstrating and Striking Are Not the Only Ways to Protest], *Al-Badil*, April 6, 2008.

This aspect is key to understanding how the events unfolded during the day of April 6. In reality, the forms of protest suggested on the flyers, and those disseminated online and by text message, expressed a form of conflict between the two modes of contradictory action: the mode of proactive action preferred by the political forces, and the more passive mode advocated by the cyberactivists. This conflict was reflected by the call to four repertoires of action, both passive and active:

1. Wear a black jacket when walking in the street and preferably carry a sign about the strike.
2. Refuse to go to work, to the university, or to school.
3. Refuse to buy any product whatsoever, in protest against the merchants and the government, who have increased the prices.
4. Join one of the events organized by the political opposition, at the head of which was the Kifaya movement[13]—in one of the well-known squares in the various governorates—such as Tahrir Square in Cairo, Hakneya Square in Alexandria, Al-Mahata Square in the governorate of Sharqia, Al-Saa Square in the governorate of Damanhour, and finally Al-Shoun Square in Mahalla.[14]

Abdel Halim Kandil, leader of the Kifaya movement, also said in the newspaper *Al-Badil*, on April 6, that, according to the information he possessed, more than twenty-one demonstrations would take place in twenty-one different places. According to Maher, the slogans of these events would be about striking as a legitimate right against poverty and hunger, and bringing everyone together against corruption (Reda 2008, 7).

The traditional parties, such as the Nasserist Al-Wafd Party and the leftist Al-Tajammu‘ Party, refused to join this call to strike. Refaat al-Said, president of Al-Tajammu‘, justified his party's position by explaining that the instigators of the general strike had not been clearly identified (Duboc

13. "Idrab 6 April . . . lih?" [The April 6 Strike . . . Why?], *Nahdet Masr*, April 4, 2008.

14. "Qiyadi fi idrab 6 April yatawaqa‘ musharakat 150 alf muwatin" [A Leader of the April 6 Strike Expects the Participation of 150,000 Citizens], *Al-Masry Al-Youm*, April 6, 2008.

2009b, 66). Toward the beginning of the month of April, the Muslim Brotherhood also refused to join this strike, maintaining a rather nuanced position. They declared their support for the right to strike as a means for Egyptians to express themselves and to protest against the authoritarian practices and repressive measures of the executive power that had corrupted Egyptian political life and failed to provide a response to the problems suffered by Egyptian citizens. However, the communiqué expressed the need for a coordination of protest actions in order to maximize the movement's effectiveness and its chance of success (66-67).[15]

The same divisions emerged at the level of the political parties committee in Mahalla. In fact, unlike the more traditional parties (Wafd, Nasserite, and Tajammuʿ), which were categorically opposed to participating in this call to strike, the Kifaya movement, as well as the new parties with young members in their ranks (e.g. Al-Jabha and Al-Ghad), were in favor of the action (Shawky, interview with author, April 14, 2010). Furthermore, many young members of the traditional political parties, including Al-Wafd and Al-Tajammuʿ, announced their participation in this call, despite their parties' official refusal.[16] According to Nader, member of the political parties committee in Mahalla, the conservative position of the old guard leaders was fully rejected by those of the younger generation (interview with author, August 11, 2009).

The participation of Kifaya in this call at the level of Mahalla City was not only due to the movement's known orientation and position on protest, but also to the activist career of Bassem, its representative in the Mahalla political parties committee, and his personal relationship with the company labor leaders. Bassem had been a long-standing member of

15. See also Elhamy Al-Mirghani, 2008, "Ru'ya li-ma hadath fi 6 Abril" [An Analysis of What Occurred during the April 6 Strike], Hisham Mubarak Law Center, September 25, 2008, http://www.hmlc-egy.org/node/850.

16. It should be noted that this committee had already decided to have a truce following the security crackdown during its last protest on March 6, 2008 (i.e., a month before the strike). However, this decision was rejected by the Kifaya movement, as well as by a number of political parties like Al-Ghad and Al-Jabha.

the Communist Party and maintained a friendly relationship with Kamal Khalil, a former party executive and member of the Kifaya movement. More importantly, as Bassem himself stated, he maintained his friendship with Wahid and Mohsen, former party executives and the leaders of Al-Rabta in the company (interview with author, January 24, 2009).

In Mahalla City, Bassem and a few young activists would thus decide to actively participate in this call for a "Day of Rage," taking the initiative to distribute leaflets inviting citizens to demonstrate. As emphasized by Shawki, a prominent young member of the Political Party Committee in Mahalla, Al-Shoun Square had already gained recognition among the city residents as the primary assembly point due to the committee's past organization of demonstrations in that location. The leaflet invited the citizens of Mahalla to demonstrate in solidarity with the company's labor strike, against price increases, and the unjust policies of the government. The political forces engaged in these contentious actions took precautions while distributing leaflets, to avoid being caught by the security agents. This is what Shawky (2010), who was among the young people who distributed leaflets in the working-class districts of Mahalla, had to say:

> We always moved in groups of at least three: one of us was distributing the leaflets and the other two walked twenty to thirty meters in front of and behind him to surveil the surroundings. If one of us had been observed doing this by the security agents, he would have been arrested on the spot.

From this time forward, the politicization of the labor issue had become obvious. However, the call for a general strike was never mentioned in the economic demands of the Mahalla labor movement. This call, presented by cyberactivists and political forces as a kind of generalized anger against socioeconomic and political conditions, transformed the framing of economic labor claims—although national in scope—into a different, more political framing. This is what Jasper (2014, 196) calls the "strategic dilemma of powerful allies," in which allies to the movement, while providing it with useful resources, seek, on the contrary, to pursue their own goals by reinterpreting, for instance, the movement's initial cause. In the case of the Mahalla labor movement, however, it didn't seek to establish any alliances or coalitions with the political opposition for the sake of resources. It is the political opposition, rather, that, as explained above, decided to ally with the movement. Therefore, it initiated a general strike that advocated for claims that differed from the labor movement's proclaimed demands.

The dynamics of this general strike, and its aim to challenge government policies, was fodder for the media. It has been noted that journalists can often act as purveyors of meaning, gatekeepers, and debate moderators between the different players involved in discursive struggles or contention (Amenta et al. 2015b). Indeed, the interaction between a movement's players and media is usually characterized by a struggle over framing (Gamson and Wolfsfeld 1993, 118; Vliegenthart and Walgrave 2012, 12). In the case of Mahalla, this again highlighted the same "strategic dilemma of powerful allies" (Jasper 2014, 196), but this time it was the media (not the political opposition) that was de facto (and contrary to the opposition) a strong ally to the movement. By focusing their coverage on the demands of this "general" strike, the media reinforced the new political framing of demands, and amplified them at the expense of the economic framing initially proposed by the Mahalla movement's leaders. The now visible political dimension of the strike greatly increased the distrust of the regime players, which led to a toughening of security procedures.

The Dynamics of the Strategic and Contentious Interaction

Perceiving a political escalation of the labor issue, the government reacted by enacting a preventive strategy at the national level, as well as on the scale of the Mahalla Company. On April 5, the Interior Ministry issued a press release concerning the political forces' call to strike on April 6, in which it warned that the security apparatus would take all necessary measures against those who would dare to block traffic, demonstrate, or prevent work (referring to the general strike).[17] A campaign of arrests targeting Kifaya activists had already started in the week preceding April 6.

17. "Al-dakhliyya tahzur min ay muhawala lil-tazahur aw i'aqat 'amal al-yawm . . . wa tatawa'ad bi-ijra'at fawriyya hazima" [The Ministry of the Interior Denounces Any Attempt at Protest or Stoppage of Work], *Al-Masry Al-Youm*, April 6, 2008.

In addition, government and public-sector institutions threatened severe administrative punishments in the case of a work shutdown.[18]

The appearance of political forces on the scene put the regime players on their guard with respect to a possible resurgence. According to Davenport (2005, 10), regimes will resort to the use of repression in response to political threats, which they perceive as likely to transform the politico-economic system they have maintained. Hence, contrary to what happened during the previous strikes, the regime players, feeling politically threatened, reacted both more rapidly and more harshly to these actions. The regime thus put in place a strategy of concessions and repression aimed at completely suppressing this strike.[19]

As early as March 29, exactly one week after the virtual call for a national strike, the regime presented a list of economic concessions to the workers at the Mahalla Company. The Public Spinning and Weaving Company (Al-Sharika al-qabida lil-ghazl w-al-nasij) with which the Mahalla Company is affiliated, presented these concessions in a press release, stating that bread would be distributed to the workers in bakeries located in front of the company, so that they wouldn't have to stand in line in front of bakeries in the city.[20] As we recall, this had been one of the fundamental demands expressed by the labor movement's leaders. The Textile Union was also involved in preventing this strike by putting pressure on the minister of investment, calling for more concessions. On March 30, the minister announced in a news release that the meal allowance would increase from 42 to 90 EGP, as the movement had demanded, but not before the following April 15.[21]

18. "Al-wizarat wa al-hay'at al-hukumiyya ta'mal bi-kamil taqatuha al-yawm bi-ta'limat mushadada" [Ministries and Governmental Institutions Are Working under Close Monitoring Today], *Al-Masry Al-Youm*, April 6, 2008.

19. For more information on authoritarian regimes using strategies of repression and concession, see Bronstein 1995; Caraway 2009; Rasler 1996; and Cai 2008.

20. Mostafa Bassiouni and Mohamed Abul Dahab, 2008a, "Al-sharika al-qabida tawzi' al-khubz 'ala al-'umal dakhil aswar ghazl al-Mahalla" [The Holding Company Decides to Purchase the Bread within the Company], *Al-Dustur*, March 20, 2008.

21. Mostafa Bassiouni and Mohamed Abul Dahab, 2008b, "Qiyadat 'umaliyya: ziyadat wazir al-istithmar la takfi wa hadafuha tafwit maw'id al-idrab" [Labor Leaders: The

In this contentious episode, the government's strategy consisted of mixing concessions with a persuasive, demobilizing counterframing.[22] This counterframing found a degree of resonance in the ranks of the CTUWS leaders. Benford and Snow (2000, 619) define the concept of resonance as being "relevant to the issue of effectiveness or mobilizing potency of the proffered framing. Two sets of interacting factors account for variation in degree of frame resonance: credibility of the proffered frame and its relative salience." This counterframing shed light on the risks that the labor movement would encounter because of its politicization, putting the initial framing of the movement in a vulnerable position. The movement's players were thus confronted by a situation of "frame vulnerability," to quote Almaida (2019), who suggests that a frame is made vulnerable because of an assault from a countermovement and its own opposing frame (132). The regime transmitted information primarily through the Textile Union, but also through the intermediaries of former members of the Mahalla Company trade union committee, in concert with state security agents. They sought to persuade the workers that their insistence on holding this strike would impact their movement negatively, in multiple ways.

The Textile Union leaders warned that the ongoing politicization delegitimized the labor cause and gave a strong pretext for the security forces to use force against the workers. The Mahalla State Security Office convened some of the movement's leaders to threaten them with a violent crackdown and a campaign of mass arrests if the labor strike took place.[23] According to Seif, some leaders received phone calls from the State Security office, accusing them of making illegitimate demands and plotting the fall of the political regime (interview with author, August 10, 2009).

Ministry of Investment's Increase Is Not Sufficient and Their Intention Is to Cancel the Strike], *Al-Dustur*, March 31, 2008.

22. For more information on counterframing, see Benford and Snow 2000, 625–26.

23. Mostafa Bassiouni and Mohamed Abul Dahab, 2008d, "Al-sa'at al-akhira qabl idrab al-Mahalla, al-idara wa al-amn wa al-tanzim al-niqabi yuhawilun tahdi'at al-'umal, wa al-'umal sawfa nudrib" [The Final Hours before the Mahalla Company Strike: The Administration, Security, and Union Organization Are Trying to Shout down the Workers . . . the Workers Say: We Are Going to Do the Strike], *Al-Dustur*, April 5, 2008.

Moreover, some Textile Union leaders spread a rumor among the leaders that the security agents were planning to bring in thugs to start a fire in the company and then accuse the leaders of arson. Their arguments were based on the fact that the government wanted to prime public opinion to favor the company's privatization and, as a result, its division (Ashraf, interview with author, August 11, 2009). This counterframing resonated well because it was credible. In fact, it played on a threat already perceived by the workers; the company leaders always shared a fear that it would one day be privatized by the Nazif government. This counterframing also played on the close relationship that the workers retained with the factory. On March 30, a leaflet of unknown origin noted that no one should respond to the April 6 strike call, as it could potentially harm the factory. It cautioned workers against aligning with political movements such as Kifaya, which might exploit the efforts of the Mahalla workers to fulfill their own goals. The advice extended to workers was to be cautious, as these forces were absent during their strike efforts in 2006 and 2007. The leaflet thus sought to send a clear message: that the labor movement's demands had taken a different turn from those of previous years and would likely result in a different reaction from the regime players.

The textile union also invented a new way to spread its counterframing within the company, offering a paid training day to workers in the week before April 6 (Bassiouni and Abul Dahab 2008d, 1). According to Wahid, the company's labor leader, between March 31 and April 5 some five hundred workers attended these training programs daily, making a total of six thousand workers. All in attendance were given a bottle of Pepsi, 20 EGP, and a pack of cookies (Wahid 2009). According to Wahid (2009), alongside the technical training, an important message was delivered to the workers: "If you participate in the April 6 strike, the company—your livelihood—will be destroyed."

Faced with this strategy of concessions and repression implemented by the regime players, the leaders of the two groups were presented with tough choices. As Jasper (2015a, 20) notes, in a strategic interaction between players each option carries risks. This brings us to the "strategic dilemma and decisions" that movement players face in strategic interactions, as Jasper explains. These dilemmas have to do with risk-taking (pitting safe against risky options) and trade-offs between short-term and long-term goals (2014, 196). Given their different biographies, objectives, and strategies, I show that the two groups of leaders performed a different interpretation and calculation of the cost-benefit ratio that involved the regime players' actions, and the opportunities and threats those actions provided or imposed.

On March 30, the CTUWS leaders gathered at the organization's headquarters in Helwan (Saher, interview with author, August 4, 2009). In this meeting, which was never reported by the Egyptian press, the labor leaders interpreted the actions taken by the regime subplayers (textile union, security agents, and government) as threats to the movement, which it anticipated it couldn't overcome, at least under the current circumstances. Two factors guided this new decision: on the one hand, their perception of the threats or risks the movement would face in the event of a strike; and, on the other hand, their perception of the partial benefits or concessions if they decided to cancel the strike.

Saher, director of CTUWS, stated that the leaders were all convinced that their case had been politicized to the benefit of political organizations, and that the politicization of their issues would entail both the repression of the movement and the closure of the company (Saher 2009). Ashraf (2009) confirmed this:

> We are against the politicization of our requests (Ihna did ta'sis matalibna). Our economic demands (matalibna al-madiya) are clear. The political parties have exploited the labor cause and diverted it from its objectives (Al-ahzab al-siyasiya rikbitha). We had to put an immediate end to the strike to save the company. Otherwise, the regime would take advantage of the situation to dismantle it (yifakikha).

For these leaders, the cohesion of the movement and the future of the company were at stake if they were to go ahead with the April 6 strike. Opting for the safest option, while partially declining the short-term objective of the movement for the sake of its long-term cohesion, was thus their choice. Hence, they decided to accept the government's concessions and cancel the strike.

The next day, March 31, 2008, Hussein Mugawer, president of the ETUF, convened a meeting of five CTUWS leaders at the Cairo office. These leaders were selected based on their restraint with regards the government, as well as the strictly financial nature of their demands (as demonstrated during the 2007 contentious episode). More importantly, this choice reflected the government's confidence in the strength of their social base within the company and, as a result, their ability to mobilize or demobilize their colleagues. Those present at the ETUF office were Aisha Abdel Hadi, minister of manpower; Hussein Mugawer, president of the federation; Sayed al-Gohary, president of the Textile Union; Mosaad al-Feki, director of the Trade Union Committee within the company; Ibrahim al-Ramadi, former member of the Mahalla Company trade union committee, and a dozen state security agents (Ashraf 2009).[24] Ashraf and Reyad explained that it was the first time that Mugawer's office was so impressive for them as movement leaders, because of the presence of the security men in the midst of all the trade unionists (Reyad 2009). Labor leaders Fawzy (2009) and Morad (2010), who accompanied them to the ETUF office, reported Mugawer's words to the five leaders: "I have called you here to discuss the strike on April 6. . . . I don't want to hear anything but these three sentences: 'We are sorry. We are not going to strike. We are going to work and increase production.'" He went so far as to point at the photo of Mubarak hanging on the wall behind his desk, and told them: "This man has done so much for this country. He doesn't deserve the chaos that you're causing."

He threatened them with arrest if they refused to sign the document he gave them, in which they had to commit to canceling the April 6 strike,[25] and to distance themselves from the appeal launched by political forces.[26]

24. Mostafa Bassiouni and Mohamed Abul Dahab, 2008c, "'umal al-Mahalla yarfudun nata'ij Mujawir mah qiyadatahum ba'd ijbar khamsa minhum 'ala al-tawqi' 'ala al-ta'ahud bi-'adam al-idrab" [The Mahalla Workers Reject the Results of the Mugawer Meeting with Their Leaders after Pressure Was Exerted on Five of Them to Rescind the April 6 Strike], *Al-Dustur*, April 4, 2008.

25. The document included two main points: rejecting the exploitation of the labor movement by political forces; and canceling the April 6 strike and calling on workers to increase production that day.

26. Bassiouni and Abul Dahab, "'umal al-Mahalla yarfudun nata'ij Mujawir mah qiyadatahum" [The Mahalla Workers Reject the Results of the Mugawer Meeting with Their Leaders], 5.

The CTUWS leaders, however, refused to sign the document without receiving concessions in return. Reyad's response to the federation president's threats was: "We did not come to discuss the cancellation of the April 6 strike. We are here to discuss our demands. We must return to the workers ranks with concrete gains before cancelling the strike (*Lazim nirga' lil-'umal bi-haga malmusa 'ashan nifud al-idrab*)" (Reyad 2009).

Negotiations between the two parties finally resulted in the signing of this document in return for an increase in the meal allowance, and in the quantity of flour distributed to factory bakeries to respond to the workers' need for bread (Ashraf, 2010). The minimum wage demand was postponed to future negotiations. The next day, flour trucks arrived, and a leaflet announcing the increase in meal allowances was distributed throughout the company. Reyad said this was the best they could get because it met some of their short-term labor demands and allowed them to save the movement and company in the long term. As a reminder, Reyad (2010) declared that the increase in the meal allowance had been a critical demand of the movement since the 2007 strike:

> A good leader is one who obtains favorable outcomes for his colleagues. The political parties had already used our strike to maneuver for political purposes (Al-ahzab al-siyasiya rikbit al-idrab). It was no good stubbornly continuing to strike and putting the company at risk.

After signing the document, the CTUWS leaders set out to mobilize consensus (Klandermans 1984, 586) within the company on the cancellation of the April 6 strike. They worked on persuading the workers that the decision was fair. Their arguments were based on the politicization of the labor cause and risks related to the company's security in this new context, and on the partial achievement of their labor demands just one day after the meeting with Mugawer. According to the leaders, this second reason was approved by the workers because of the concrete benefit they had obtained. The CTUWS leaders returned back to their consensual position with the regime players. They gave up their confrontational stance in this contentious episode in exchange for partial fulfillment of their economic demands.

Al-Rabta leaders, on the other hand, did not waver in their position. Their decision to refuse to cancel the strike was informed by their history of political activism, as well as their opposition to the regime players. For them, the April 6 strike had become an objective in itself: they believed that it would alter the balance of power between the movement and the regime. As such, they established a different interpretation of the regime players' actions, and a different cost-benefit calculation from that of the CTUWS leaders. They considered the rapid granting of concessions, immediately followed by threats, to be a sign of the regime's players weakness. Morad (2010) explained:

> The rapid concessions mean that the regime is afraid of this strike, so we should not give in. On the contrary, we need to keep going until all our demands are fulfilled.

Al-Rabta leaders calculated that, in spite of the threats or the risk that the movement was likely to face in terms of repression, it still had a chance to force the regime players to give up if the workers persisted with the strike. This would help to achieve their long-term objective of amending power relations between the regime players and the movement's players.

To mobilize the workers, they distributed leaflets asking the workers not to accept the government's concessions and to stand firm in their decision to strike. Through these leaflets, Al-Rabta sought to persuade the workers to rebut both the government's counterframing and the framing the CTUWS leaders presented in favor of canceling the strike. One of the leaflets emphasized that the regime used the politicization of labor concerns as an excuse to undermine the strike. The leaflet clarified that their demands were solely economic, and, despite the regime's claims linking political forces and the Kifaya movement to the protest, this connection didn't hold true. The leaflet encouraged workers to disregard security threats and to remain resolute in their determination to carry out the strike.[27]

27. Karim Al-Beheiry, 2008d, "Mudawanat 'Umal Misr takshif al-sir al-khafi wara' ziyarat muhafiz al-Gharbia" [The Workers of Egypt Blog Discovers the Secret behind the Visit of the Governor of Gharbia], Egy Workers, April 4, 2008, http://egyworkers.blogspot.de/2008/04/blog-post_3394.html.

It should be noted here that Al-Rabta leaders had chosen Fawzy and Morad (committed Al-Rabta leaders) to accompany the Dar Al-Khadamat representatives to the meeting with the president of the ETUF (as previously described). Both refused to sign Mugawer's document, arguing that they had not been summoned and that they were therefore not required to sign (Fawzy 2009). Mugawer responded that they would both be arrested.

Al-Rabta leaders also used the media as a weapon—especially the privately owned daily newspapers. The leaflets that Al-Rabta distributed created divisions in the ranks of the movement. They wanted to take advantage of the movement's visibility in the private press to exert pressure on the regime players. Al-Rabta even urged the private press to boycott the statements of those who had signed Mugawer's document. In that regard, Seif confirmed that the private press was the most influential on the subject of labor and were the ones providing the most coverage, unlike mainstream television (Seif 2009).

These privately owned daily newspapers—mainly *Al-Badil* and *Al-Dustur*—responded more or less positively to the appeal, albeit implicitly. Their coverage of events focused on the statements that rejected the cancellation of the strike, highlighting the position of Al-Rabta leaders. For example, the CTUWS decision at the March 30 meeting to cancel the strike was never raised by the private press. Their point of view on this decision was not mentioned either. As a result, the private press created an image of the movement as being at the forefront of a national challenge and refusing to cancel the strike despite the pressure to do so. However, the CTUWS position accepting governmental concessions was not covered. Journalists of the private press thus acted as referees who chose to give voice to a certain side of the contention (the labor movement players) and to specific players within it (Al-Rabta players). In speaking about journalists as referees between strategic players in the various contentious arenas, Amenta and colleagues (2015b, 233) surmise, "Journalists decide whether public actors or political contenders get to participate in public debates and, once that is decided, which players are going to be taken most seriously and receive the most playing time. That is, they decide whose voices will be heard most prominently, whose understandings of an issue are to be presented, and which issues will be deemed as representing the main lines of conflict."[28] Here are a few examples of newspaper coverage that illustrate this pattern:

On March 31, with the headline "The Increase in the Meal Allowance for the Mahalla Workers Is an Attempt to Prevent the Strike," *Al-Badil* gave front-page coverage to the message on Al-Rabta's leaflet, which was distributed in the company, refusing the government concession, and reaffirming that the strike would take place:

> The increase in the meal allowance to 90 Egyptian pounds is meaningless given the "insane" price increases. . . . We must guard against rumors spread by security officers or company trade union committee members that the strike will be canceled, because that will not happen until after we achieve our demands.[29]

On April 4, *Al-Badil* and *Al-Dustur* reported on the contents of the leaflets distributed by Al-Rabta in refusal of canceling the strike as if that were the unanimous position of the movement. *Al-Dustur*, for example, headlined: "The Mahalla Workers Reject the Results of Mugawer's Meeting with Their Leaders after Pressure Exerted on Five of Them to Renounce the April 6 Strike." *Al-Badil* confirmed this position by covering only the message of the leaflet distributed by Al-Rabta, who still claimed that the five leaders who had signed Mugawer's document only represented themselves, and that the April 6 strike would take place all the same.[30] On April

28. Amenta and colleagues (2005) see that journalists who act as referees in contention usually choose state players and politicians and give voice to them at the expense of the movement's voice (for reasons related to funding and management direction). However, in the case of the private press coverage of the contention between the Mahalla labor movement players and the regime players, the journalists who also acted as referees—as Amenta et al. assert—chose to give voice to the movement and specifically to Al-Rabta group of players.

29. "Raf' badal al-wajbah al-ghiza'iyya fi muhawala li-man' idrab al-ahad" [The Increase in the Meal Allowance for the Mahalla Workers Is an Attempt to Prevent the Strike on Sunday], 2008, *Al-Badil*, March 31, 2008.

30. "Harb al-manshurat tashta'il fi ghazl al-Mahalla" [The War of the Leaflets Breaks out at the Mahalla Company], 2008, *Al-Badil*, April 4, 2008.

5, the eve of the day scheduled for the strike, *Al-Dustur* reaffirmed that the entire movement remained favorable to the strike. On the first page, it repeated the message of the last leaflet distributed by Al-Rabta: "The strike's main objective was the wage increase, therefore the concession granted on bread does not meet the labor demands. We must strike, and not accept crumbs." The article was headlined: "The Final Hours before the Mahalla Company Strike: Management, Security, and Trade Union Organization Attempt to Calm the Workers . . . the Workers Say, 'We Are Going To Strike!'" (Bassiouni and Abul Dahab 2008d, 1).

As mentioned earlier, the position of the privately owned newspapers might be attributed to the social activism of the journalists who worked for them, many of them being leftist-oriented political activists with a bias toward the labor cause—or, more precisely, toward the working class. It is in this context that the journalistic image of the labor movement should be understood.

On the eve of the strike, headlines in the privately owned press—at least *Al-Dustur* and *Al-Badil*—announced that the labor strike would take place despite pressure from the government and security forces. Leaflets distributed by Al-Rabta leaders encouraging workers to stand firm and not abandon the strike, along with considerable media coverage, helped ramp up the pressure on the regime players. Media coverage of Al-Rabta's position, refusing any concessions, thus lent a political undertone to the entire movement. The press articles confirming the labor strike also encouraged political forces to protest on the same day.

The Repertoires of Repression

When it finally arrived, the day of April 6 across Egypt was a day "to strike without striking." Office employees went to work in a context where government organizations had warned against any absences on that day.[31] Almost no strike was registered in public or private factories. Two exceptions were the Wabariyat Samanoud company in the governorate of Gharbiya,

31. "Al-wizarat wa al-hay'at al-hukumiyya ta'mal bi-kamil taqatuha al-yawm bi-ta'limat mushadada" [Ministries and Governmental Institutions Are Working under Close Monitoring Today], 2008, *Al-Masry Al-Youm*, April 6, 2008.

where three thousand workers stopped work, and the Torah Cement company, in the governorate of Suez, where 60 percent of the labor force did not show up for work (Duboc, 2009, 68). A press release issued on April 3 stated: "The labor leaders at the Kafr al-Dawar spinning factory expressed their support for the Mahalla workers and indicated their intention to strike on April 6 to obtain a minimum wage for all workers, but especially those in the textile sector" (Al-Beheiry 2007e). There were no strikes, however, in Kafr al-Dawar, nor in the other textile firms. Seeing that the Mahalla workers had renounced their strike, the textile workers did the same (Wahid 2009). The transport sector—railways, metro, and bus—was not affected by work stoppages. Traffic, however, was less heavy that day. Some stores did not open for business, fearing clashes with security agents, but the call for a general strike was not followed.[32]

The only protests were a few events organized by about a hundred students and activists in Cairo and in Helwan. The students protested at the universities of Cairo and Helwan, while the activists, including members of the Kifaya movement, organized a demonstration in front of the Lawyers' Syndicate ("Idrab" 2008).[33] Security forces, in turn, resorted to characteristically repressive tactics.

Repression, in this sense, generally seeks to achieve two objectives: what it achieves in itself, and what it communicates concerning that achievement. Repression seeks not only to eliminate its target, but also to communicate capacity, stability, resolve, and a sense of social order (Boudreau 2015, 191). Regime players that feel they are dealing with an existential threat to their power will be prompt to communicate and draw an image of themselves as being strong enough to overcome it (189). Security forces, therefore, commonly resort to repression by relying on a strategy of mixing prevention and deterrence. Uysal (2006) defines a preventive security strategy as consisting largely of dispersing a crowd before it becomes a

32. "Idrab. . yurdi jami' al-atraf" [A Strike That Pleases All], 2008, *Al-Masry Al-Youm*, April 7, 2008.

33. "Waqafat ihtijajiyya lil-tulab al-ishtirakiyyin bi-Helwan wa al-Qahera" [A Demonstration Organized by Socialist Students in Helwan and Cairo], 2008, *Al-Masry Al-Youm*, April 6, 2008.

crowd (274), and deterrence based on a massive, armed presence in order to discourage participation in the street (267). The goal is to prevent demonstrations or crowd formation, a strategy that was operationalized on this occasion in 2008 by the arrest of several cyberactivists, including those who called for the strike on Facebook, and the arrest of political activists before they could even go to the planned gathering places (the public squares and roundabouts mentioned previously), to keep them from garnering other participants.[34] According to *Al-Masry Al-Youm*, approximately thirty-five members of the Al-Ghad Party were arrested in Cairo and in the governorates (Azouz 2008). This was also the fate of approximately twenty-five members of the Kifaya movement, according to Georges Ishak, one of its main leaders.[35]

Moreover, the armed security encircled all of the public squares where demonstrations might be possible, such as Tahrir Square and Mostafa Mahmoud Square in Cairo, Giza Square, and the city council or town halls in Port Said, Mansoura, Daqhliya, and Menufiya.[36] At the Mahalla City level, the security strategy of deterrence was even more visible. As in the other cities, security agents sealed off Al-Shoun Square, where political forces usually demonstrated.[37] Meanwhile, several central security vehicles closed off the entry and exit to the city and all its major arteries

34. Mohamed Azouz, "Al-amn ya'taqil al-'asharat wa yuhasir al-shawari' wa al-mayadin" [Security Agents Arrest Dozens of People and Block Streets and Traffic Circles], 2008, *Al-Masry Al-Youm*, April 7, 2008.

35. "Taqrir markaz sawasiya li huquq al-insan w munahadat al tamayuz hawl nata'ig ba'that taqasi al-haqa'iq alati arsalha ila al-Mahalla fi 6–7 Abril 2008" [The Report Published by the Sawaseya Center for Human Rights and Activism against Discrimination about the Results of Its Truth Commission Sent to the City of Mahalla on April 6 and 7, 2008], 2008, Markaz sawaseya li huquq al-insan we munahadit al-tami'z [Sawaseya Center for Human Rights and Activism Against Discrimination], April 2008, 9.

36. "Al-Mahalla adrabat wa ba'd al-muhafazat tajahalat al-musharaka" [The City of Mahalla is on Strike While the Other Governorates Have Not Participated], 2008, *Al-Masry Al-Youm*, April 7, 2008.

37. "10 alaf muwatin yunazimun muzahara hashida fi al-Mahalla" [Ten Thousand Citizens Organize a Large Demonstration in Mahalla], 2008, *Al-Masry Al-Youm*, April 7, 2008.

as attested by Latif, journalist for a prominent privately owned newspaper (Latif, interview with author, April 9, 2010).[38] This was also the case with the Mahalla Company, which, for the first time since 2006, was transformed, metaphorically speaking, into a military barracks, as Latif (2010) and Morad (2010), a company labor leader, noted.

Although Al-Rabta leaders were incapable of mobilizing the workers and inciting them to strike (following CTUWS's decision to cancel), State Security took preventive measures in order to avoid any possibility of a sit-in or strike at the company. These measures emerged as a reaction to public discourse on the strike of April 6 as reported in the media, particularly in the private press. Certainly, it is not possible to establish a causal relationship between the media framing and repressive behavior of the security forces, but it is difficult to deny that the visibility conferred on the movement in favor of the strike by the private press increased the regime players' mistrust.

Security agents in plain clothes surrounded the company on April 6 and encouraged journalists to enter the company enclosure to photograph the workers as they went to their work. The media thus emerged as a strategic tool that both conflicting parties sought to manipulate in their favor. Ramy, photographer and journalist whose photos of the popular uprising in the city were published by most of the press agencies, testified:

> I saw about a hundred police in plain clothes (Mukhbirin) dispersed throughout the company to ensure that the work was carried out as normal. They made us enter, we journalists, so that we would photograph the workers working under their supervision. I refused to do so and I left because I was against this police control. (Interview with author, June 7, 2012)

In addition to the presence of security agents within the company—which had never happened during previous strikes—security officers also prevented workers from gathering as the shifts changed. Morad (2010) and

38. According to Latif, security officers were present at the main entrance of the city, in the street from the train station, parallel to one of the Mahalla Company entrances. Remember that the company has multiple entrances.

Latif (2010) also claimed that company management, under orders from State Security, released workers from the third shift (who had worked since the eve of April 6) before the scheduled departure time, to prevent them from meeting the workers on the first shift, who were to arrive at 7 a.m. Similarly, under orders from management, the security officers employed directly by the company closed all the doors during work hours to prevent the workers from leaving before the specified time. They also prevented most of Al-Rabta's leaders from entering—in particular Morad, Fawzy, and Seif (Morad 2010).

Due to this intense security presence, events took a different turn in the city of Mahalla than in the other cities. Everything happened quite peacefully and normally up until the end of the first shift at the Mahalla Company, at 3:30 p.m. (also the end of the working day for city employees). However, at Al-Shoun Square, a demonstration of an estimated several thousand participants erupted at around 4 p.m. This was followed by a popular uprising, the largest in thirty years. Although this uprising, as well as the repressive response by the security forces, are outside the scope of this book, I will describe them briefly. This description is important for understanding the entire dynamic of the movement's demobilization.

Using a similar security strategy to the one deployed in other Egyptian cities, police officers tried to prevent any assembly in Al-Shoun Square. The security agents, who were deployed in large numbers and dispersed throughout this central location, encouraged citizens to quickly take transportation home. The city residents, however, didn't leave quickly because they were expecting to attend a demonstration. As a reminder, young activists had distributed leaflets calling for a demonstration that day, and the call to make April 6 a "Day of Rage" had been covered in the media. It was the police checks, along with verbal and physical attacks, that caused the situation to degenerate. These attacks had a provocative effect and led to the spontaneous outbreak of a demonstration in Al-Shoun Square.

While regime authorities seek to shape the intensity of violence, the reality is that a great many acts of violence are shaped by interactions between players. The production of violence is an interactive process, and many acts of repression and coercion are unplanned escalations of what was initially intended to be a more measured response (Boudreau 2015, 189). One scene in particular has been mentioned frequently in discussions with Amer (2009), the correspondent of one of the prominent private newspapers in Mahalla city and a Shawky (2010), young member of the political parties committee as a precipitating factor in this incident: the violent police response to the spontaneous shouts of an old woman from the working-class neighborhood of Mansehya. As she was heading toward the square, she shouted: "Where are the workers? (*Fin al-'umal*?); We don't have anything to eat, we want to live! (*Mish la'yin nakul, 'awzin n'ish*!); We don't want more of Mubarak (*Mish 'awzin Mubarak*)," thus revealing her frustration that the labor strike had been canceled. This can only be understood in the framework of the emotional and social relationship between the Mahalla residents and the company. Hassan (2009), one of the leaders of the 1975 strike, explained:

> In most of the city's families, there are at least one or two people who work in this company, given its size, the social services it provides for the workers, and the working-class nature of the city itself. The Mahalla Company influences the character of the entire city. Its confrontation with the regime over workers' rights goes back to the 1970s, and has created a social and emotional bond between it and the city residents.

We should remember that, since 1975, the company has been central in the collective memory of Mahalla inhabitants as ground zero for activism and the defense of rights that have been violated. Confronted with this woman screaming in anger, Central Security Forces surrounding the square did not hesitate to use force. One of the security agents put his hand over the woman's mouth to prevent her from speaking and pushed her violently. This reaction provoked the people around her and led to a spontaneous demonstration in the square. The demonstrators shouted hostile slogans (and even insults) about the president, his son, and the government: "Gamal (the president's son), tell your father the people of Mahalla hate you! (*Ya Gamal, qul l-'abuk f-al-Mahalla biyikrahuk!*)." Remember that some of the Mahalla residents were already in the habit of demonstrating, thanks to the fairly regular demonstrations organized by the political parties committee in this square.

In order to disperse the crowd, the central security agents were brutal. According to Della Porta and Reiter (1998, 4), "brutality" refers to the degree of force used by the force of order or police. They used their batons to violently disperse the demonstrators. This dynamic, even for maintaining order, led to an escalation of violence (Amer 2009). Young people and adolescents came out of the working-class neighborhoods in the vicinity of Al-Shoun Square to throw stones at the police, reminiscent of similar scenes during the 1975 strike that were registered in the collective memory of the city's residents (Hassan 2009). The police started to run after them, throwing tear gas to break them up, but with no success. Violent confrontations then broke out between the residents and the police in working-class districts near Al-Shoun Square, such as Al-Sweika, Seket Tanta, Al-Gomhoreya, and Al-Mansheya. These neighborhoods were made up of small alleys, where a single tear-gas cannister was likely to reach all of the buildings. The effects of this particular terrain in terms of a crackdown encouraged people to go out and participate in the battle with the police officers (Ramy 2012; Amer 2009). As night approached, the police surrounded these narrow streets. To try to regain control of the situation, they called for assistance from the Central Security Forces posted in the neighboring governorates. The police also recruited hired thugs (*baltagiya*) to help (Shawky 2010). Shops, homes, and schools were ransacked during the clashes. According to the Sawaseya Center for Human Rights report, approximately thirteen stores were destroyed or mobbed ("Taqrir" 2008, 10). Campaign posters of NDP candidates were torn up, and railroad tracks were blocked by the demonstrators (29).

At the end of the day, the attorney general held a press conference in one of the Mahalla schools that had been burned. He stated that the security agents had arrested 157 individuals, including young people under the age of twenty.[39] Furthermore, in addition to the political activists who were detained—like Bassem of the Kifaya movement, three company workers who were Al-Rabta members were arrested and held for fifty-four

39. "Tajadud a'mal al-'unf fi al-Mahalla wa mutaradat bayn al-shurta wa al-mutazahirun" [Resumption of the Violence and Confrontation between the Police and the Protesters], *Al-Masry Al-Youm*, April 8, 2008.

days: Morad, Tarik Amin Al-Sinoussi, and Seif. As a reminder, when they refused to sign the document canceling the strike, Morad and Fawzy were threatened by the president of the ETUF. Security officers had attempted to invade Fawzy's house on the eve of April 6, but he was not there at the time. The press conference report also indicated that sixty-five people—of whom about half were civilians—were injured during the day's events ("Tajadud" 2008).

On April 7, a spontaneous demonstration took place on Al-Abassi Street in a business district located in the city center. The people wanted to send a signal that they were still contending with the regime, represented in this instance by the police. However, they also wanted to press for the release of their relatives and friends who had been arrested the previous day. The demonstrators headed to the police commissioner's office (Qism shurta tani al-Mahalla) chanting: "We want our children (*'awzin wiladna*)!"; "Bring us our brothers from the prison (*Hatu ikhwatna min al-zinzana*)!" (Shawky 2010). Other protests erupted in an equally spontaneous manner in Al-Bahr Street in the center of the city, and Al-Shoun Square. Once again, violent clashes took place between demonstrators and the police. This was a result of the tear gas and rubber bullets used on the protesters. That day, police even resorted to the use of live bullets, causing the death of a young man aged twenty-four, and a fifteen-year-old who was not in the streets but watching from the balcony of his home ("Taqrir" 2008, 12). The demonstrators tore up Mubarak posters that they found along the way. A photo taken by a prominent newspaper journalist perfectly captured the essence of the day: it showed a dozen demonstrators putting a large portrait of President Mubarak on the ground and stomping on it. In doing so, the demonstrators directly attacked the head of state and showed symbolically that April 6 and 7 were indeed "Days of Rage" against the regime in the city of Mahalla. The protests resulted in more concessions being granted to the workers by the government, but also by an increase in repression, until the movement was fully demobilized.

On April 8, a ministerial delegation visited the Mahalla Company. The delegation consisted of the prime minister, the minister of labor, the minister of investment, the governor of Gharbiya, the minister of education, and the minister of local development. Prime minister Ahmad Nazif announced that a US$400 million subsidy would be granted to the company to improve production lines. The minister of labor promised a bonus equal to a month's salary (*mukafa'a*) for company workers, and fifteen days for the rest of the workers in the textile sector. On the occasion of May 1, President Mubarak, while ignoring the minimum wage demand, announced a 30 percent wage increase for public-sector employees, at a cost of 7–8 billion EGP. However, this decision was immediately followed by the announcement of an approximately 50 percent tax increase on gasoline and natural gas, and 10 percent on the price of cigarettes, thereby voiding the president's initiative of any meaning.[40]

The change in security strategy with regard the company was visible in the aftermath of the events of April 6 and 7. Unlike the strikes of 2006 and 2007, but similar to that of April 6, 2008, the security apparatus intervened to totally prevent any protest from being organized within the company. In addition, protest attempts made by the leaders following this strike, including the call for a demonstration in October 2008, and the call for a strike in December 2009, were immediately followed by either the dismissal of the leaders involved or their transfer outside the company, by orders of the management. This was the case with the majority of the labor movement leaders.

As a result of a demonstration of a few hundred workers, organized on October 30, 2008, in front of the administrative offices of the company, Yehia, Fawzy, Seif, Afaf, and Soad were transferred to either the Alexandria office, the Cairo office, or the company daycare center. Their status accordingly changed from that of production worker (*'amil intaj*) to casual worker (*'amil bil-yawmiyya*), which meant a decrease of approximately half their salaries (Saher 2009). The demonstration they had organized was in protest of the company management's corruption, which was blamed for its financial losses.

40. Mostafa Bassiouni and Mohamed Abul Dahab, 2008e, "30% 'ilawa urs Aspirin li-marad al-saratan" [The 30 Percent Bonus Increase Is an Aspirin for Cancer], 2008, *Al-Dustur*, May 1, 2008.

Similarly, when he attempted to organize a strike on December 7, 2009, to demand an increase in bonuses (from 145 days to 228 days of the initial salary), equal pay for workers (150 EGP for all), and a minimum wage, Wahid was summarily dismissed from the company the next day (Wahid 2009). As with the 2008 strike, security officers in civilian clothes entered the company to deter and prevent the workers from participating in the strike (Wahid 2009). Ashraf and Yasser organized a protest of about one hundred workers in solidarity with Wahid on December 21, 2009, inside the company, which resulted in their transfer to the Cairo and Alexandria offices (Saher 2009).

This explains why the Mahalla labor movement was not visible during the revolutionary dynamics of January 25, 2011. The workers participated in several demonstrations in Al-Shoun Square in Mahalla City on January 25 and afterward, but purely as citizens, not as part of a movement, since the latter had already been demobilized after the April 6, 2008, contentious episode. Nevertheless, the demand for the minimum wage also became the leitmotif for workers' demands after 2011.

Conclusion

The movement's decision to challenge the Mubarak regime was influenced by a combination of factors: the presence of leaders within the movement, particularly those from Al-Rabta, who were politically opposed to the regime; the interpretation of regime players' actions as giving opportunities for labor action; and the perception of an "internal opportunity" to promote their oppositional framing within the movement. The policy of escalation by CTUWS leaders provided Al-Rabta with an opportunity to raise the threshold of the movement's demands.

Conversely, the movement's inability to oppose or challenge regime players can be attributed to two factors: the presence of leaders advocating a consensual stance and prioritizing strictly financial demands; and their possession of a broad social base within the movement, preventing mobilization in a threatening manner to the regime players. In contrast to CTUWS leaders, Al-Rabta politicized and oppositional leaders lacked a broad enough social base to mobilize the entire movement. This stands in sharp contrast to the of the Real Estate Tax Collector movement, to be discussed in subsequent chapters. Led by politicized leaders who capitalized on their robust social base, the movement's players successfully contested regime players, challenging the corporatist system and persuading the movement to establish a new independent trade union—a historic development in Egypt since 1957.

5

The Monster Is Coming!

The Emergence of the Real Estate Tax Collectors' Social Movement

Introduction

In this chapter, I delve into a series of events that trace the gradual expansion of contention, marking the emergence of the Real Estate Tax Collector (RETA) movement as a national player. Commencing with a demonstration on September 10, 2007, in front of the Giza governorate's Property Tax Foundation, the movement's momentum continued with demonstrations in Daqhliya and Beni Suef governorates on September 24 and 30, respectively. A significant milestone unfolded on October 21, 2007, with a demonstration in front of the Ministry of Finance in Cairo's Medinat Nasr neighborhood, drawing participants from various governorates. Subsequently, on November 13–14, a sit-in transpired in front of ETUF on Al-Galaa Street in Cairo, featuring participation from RETA employees across the nation.

In this chapter, I examine the motivations and frustrations driving RETA employees to mobilize. I also scrutinize the intricate trade union structure to which they belonged, offering glimpses into the leaders' backgrounds, political trajectories, and social resources within the movement. These factors significantly influenced leaders' choices, decisions during contentious episodes, and their ability to mobilize colleagues. Moreover, I delve into the contentious interaction between Giza's RETA employees and security forces, unraveling the mechanisms that propagated this contention to Daqhliya and Beni Suef. The agency of the movement's leaders takes precedence in this examination. Further, I explore the dynamics and strategic interactions during the October 21, 2007, protest in front of the Ministry of Finance, a pivotal moment leading to the establishment of the Strike Coordinating Committee (SCC). This intergovernorate committee played a crucial role in coordinating national-level actions among RETA employees from various governorates.

Finally, I investigate the dynamics of the November 13 sit-in in front of the ETUF headquarters, analyzing the strategic interaction between movement players and the ETUF as a regime subplayer in the arena of street politics. This contentious episode marked the inception of a distinct collective identity for the movement, adding a crucial dimension to the analysis.

Emergence of the RETA Movement: What Motivations?

During the period of the study, the number of RETA employees was approximately fifty-five thousand, spread out in more than 140 branches throughout Egypt. They are tasked with determining the value of real estate properties and entertainment venues (*malahi*) and maintaining the land register of agricultural properties in order to collect taxes on them. Across the governorates, there is an issue that dates back to the year 1960, when local government Law No. 124 was issued, followed by a decree from the Ministerial Commission for Local Government in 1973. This decree approved the decentralization of the employees of the RETA—that is, the transfer of staff working in central Real Estate Tax Foundations, where they had been working since its creation in 1883, to local councils. At the same time, the central budget was dispersed in separate governorate budgets.[1] Thus, the decentralization of the employees of the RETA took place through Ministerial Decrees 137 and 136 of 1974, which mandated the administrative transfer of the employees of the RETA to the governorates and granted the governorates the right to collect a portion of the real estate tax revenues. More precisely, Decree 136 stipulated that the Real Estate Foundation in Cairo would have the role of technical oversight over The Real Estate Tax Foundations in the governorates, while Decree

1. Gihan Shaaban, "Qisat idrab" [The Story of a Strike], *Socialist Papers* 35, http://www.e-socialists.net/node/868 (accessed August 21, 2024).

137 delegated the supervision of the employees of the RETA to the governors of each governorate, with the aim of increasing the administrative capacity of local government.[2]

These two resolutions led to the deterioration of the socioeconomic and professional conditions of the employees of the RETA. They duplicated accountability, since, on the one hand, they were under the technical supervision of the Ministry of Finance through The Real Estate Tax Foundation in Cairo, and, on the other hand, they were under administrative supervision at the governorate level. This placed them in a lower position professionally to that of their fellow tax collectors in the other areas of tax collection within the Ministry of Finance.[3]

As a consequence of this diffusion of supervisory authority, the collection of real estate taxes saw a decrease in income. The governorate RETA employees were thus deprived of the bonuses and rewards that their colleagues at the Cairo Real Estate Tax Foundation received (30 percent distinctive service rewards, incentives of four-month bonuses each year, 60 percent in exchange for extraordinary efforts, a bonus of one-and-a-half months' salary in return for the process of collecting tax, and 25 percent of their income as a special bonus).[4] As a result, the employees of the RETA in the governorates (fifty-five thousand employees) saw their living conditions deteriorate in comparison with those of the employees of the RETA in Cairo (five hundred employees), who worked directly for the Ministry of Finance. Hence, the income of those in the governorates only averaged between 200 EGP and 400 EGP per month (approximately \$28.8 to \$57.7). After thirty years, it reached 600 EGP (\$86.5; Eweida 2008, 14).

2. Mahmoud Gomaa, 2007, "I'tisam muwazafi al-dara'ib al-'aqariyya bi misr li-su' awda'ihim" [Egyptian Real Estate Tax Collectors Strike Due to Poor Working Conditions], *Al-Jazeera*, November 14, 2007.

3. Gamal Eweida, 2008, "Malhamat al-dara'ib al-'aqariyya" [The Strike of the Property Tax Workers], Center for Socialist Studies, http://www.e-socialists.net/node/1332 (accessed August 21, 2024).

4. Mohamed Azouz, 2007b, "Muwazafu al-dara'ib al-'aqariyya yusa'idun ihtijajihim wa yuhadidun bi-masira li-majlis al-wuzara'" [The RETC Escalate and Threaten to March against the Cabinet], *Al-Masry Al-Youm*, November 15, 2007.

There are other possible explanations for the socioeconomic deterioration of the RETA employees. In 2005, the government decided to merge the three tax sectors into a single foundation for Egyptian tax collectors. This merger took place for all tax employees except the employees of the RETA. The pretext was that the government was waiting for the new law on the real estate tax collection to be enacted, which has still not taken place before 2011. According to Kamal Abu Eita, the NDP businessmen feared that such a law could endanger their property, because it would highlight the privileges they enjoyed. The result of this situation was the evolution of the bonus system for all tax collector employees, except for the employees of the RETA. According to an official in Beni Suef and a member of the strike committee, the bonuses that the employees of the RETA received remain at 50 percent, while the other tax collector employees received increases of 350 to 650 percent, and then to 1, 100 percent in 2007–8 (Shaaban 2008, 36).

Thus, parity with the employees hired by the Ministry of Finance would be at the forefront of the RETA employees' demands. All the RETA employees interviewed from different governorates expressed frustration over the injustice they suffered in comparison with the tax collector employees in Cairo. According to Magdy, a leading member in the RETA movement, this frustration was accentuated by the very sensitive nature of the profession, which many say should have been taken into consideration by the state (interview with author, October 10, 2011).[5]

The Syndical Framework and the Movement Leadership: Political Activism and Social Resources

The Finance, Banking, and Insurance Employees Union, affiliated with ETUF, was the union in which the RETA employees were automatically members. Unlike the other unions affiliated with the federation, the bank and insurance employee union bring together various professional groups of employees working in the field of public finance, such as those in public

5. He expressed his frustration during the interview by saying, "This point really stands out for me—our work finances the state, so is it logical for the state to neglect our rights?"

banks, customs, and those who collect general taxes and real estate taxes. This heterogeneous structure contributed to an underestimation of the employees of the RETA's main problem. Their induction/inclusion within the banking and insurance syndicate with the employees of the other groups served the regime's interests. In its efforts to prevent the creation of a new union representing the employees of the RETA independently of ETUF, the government proposed the creation of a twenty-fourth union to a group of movement leaders, solely for the employees of the RETA within ETUF. As emphasized by Nasser, a leading member of the RETA movement, founding the union committees (*lijan niqabiyya*) representing the employees of the RETA in the banking and insurance syndicate was left to the discretion of the employees. This was different from the case with other unions within the federation, for which trade union committees were always present representing the different governorates (Nasser, interview with author, October 5, 2011). Furthermore, before 1995, there was only one union committee for the banking and insurance syndicate: that of the employees of the RETA in Giza. As time passed, other union committees were formed in different governorates. They reached as many as nine committees in nine governorates (Giza, Daqhliya, Sharqiya, Gharbiya, Kafr al-Sheikh, Ismailiya, Beni Suef, and Baheira) in 2007 (Nasser 2011). As a rule, requests for the formation of new trade union committees were not very well received by the Banking and Insurance Union and the Ministry of Labor. The Banking and Insurance Union even refused to accept application papers for these committees (Shaaban 2008, 35). This reluctance reflects the regime's policy of weakening the capacity of employees of the RETA to organize locally (i.e., in each governorate) in a fixed structure, representing their common demand to return to the Ministry of Finance (Nasser 2011).

As previously mentioned, the 2006–11 union elections were marked by fraud, the purpose of which was to place leaders at all levels of the federation. This approach was quite different from the Mubarak regime's usual policy of rigging elections at the top of the union hierarchy, while the base was generally excluded. In other words, before 2006, the union committees were usually elected without fraud. As a result of this change in policy, the trade union committee elections in Giza and Beni Suef were rigged to remove two leaders known for their activism: Kamal Abu Eita in Giza, and Moheb in Beni Suef.

Moheb, a candidate for Beni Suef's union committee elections in 2006, was threatened with arrest by State Security if he did not withdraw (interview with author, October 22, 2011). According to Moheb, the approval of State Security agents became an essential condition for candidacy in union elections (Moheb 2011). As a result, after 2006, the employees of the RETA in the various governorates were faced with one of two options: either they were deprived of union committees (e.g., as in Qalyubiya, Menufiya, Minya), or they were represented by union committees directly co-opted by the government through fraudulent trade union elections (as was the case in Giza and Beni Suef). One of the rare exceptions was the situation in the Daqhliya governorate, where no union election has been held since 1996. As a result, members of the Daqhliya Trade Union Committee have seen no change since that year (Said, interview with author, October 19, 2011). The committee members had credibility in the eyes of their colleagues because they were chosen by acclamation (*Tadhkiya*), without elections taking place.

In this context, it is apt to adopt the definitions that I used for leaders (or *decisive leaders*) of the Mahalla labor movement for employees of the RETA movement. Decisive leaders, as defined by Jasper (2014), are those who have either official positions or informal respect that allows them to mobilize resources, demand others' attention, and speak for an organization. Their choices and arguments tend to have more influence than other people's (184). As with the Mahalla labor movement, I focus on analysis of the actions of the leaders, whom I consider—in the tradition of Morris and Staggenborg (2004), Robnett (2013), and Ganz and McKenna (2019)—to be key strategic players. Their actions, choices, and decisions influenced the movement's dynamics and outcomes.

When I speak of "movement leaders," I refer to members of the Strike Coordinating Committee (SCC), which was composed of the employees of the RETA from different governorates, and was responsible for intergovernorate coordination. Moreover, the leaders forming this committee had participated in planning and mobilization during different phases of the movement's history: some of them called for the initial protests leading to the movement's foundation and expansion to a national scale, such as Kamal Abu Eita and Hamdy (Giza), Said and Emad (Daqhliya), and Moheb (Beni Suef). Others participated in the movement's last general protest (the December 2007 sit-in in front of the Council of Ministers), as well as the foundation of the independent union. Some, like Nasser (Qalyubiya), would later be part of the Strike Coordinating Committee (SCC). The female employees of the RETA participated in protests from the very beginning. They marched in the streets with their colleagues and helped provide food and other practical needs. However, none of them were members of the Strike Coordinating Committee (SCC). Two distinguishing characteristics of the RETA movement leaders are evident:

The Possession of a Political Career

At the head of the movement was Kamal Abu Eita, the first to call the RETA employees in Giza to protest and to suggest the idea of creating a trade union that would represent the employees of the RETA independently of ETUF. Eita, a former trade unionist, was also a leader of the Nasserist Club at Cairo University in the 1970s. The club was a forum for the intellectual training of activists who adhered to this political orientation. In the 1990s, the lack of internal democracy within the Nasserist Party, which he supported, prompted him to leave the party and found the Karama Party, with a base of young Nasserist militants. Eita was also a founding member of the Kifaya movement.[6] Emad, leading member of the Daqhliya (Official) Trade Union Committee, had an activist career similar to that of Eita, with whom he participated in the founding of the Nasserist Karama Party. Said, another leading member of the Daqhliya Trade Union (Official) Committee, was a leader in the leftist Al-Tajammu‘ Party in Daqhliya. Said was born into a "politicized" family and had been a member of the party, along with fellow family members, since the age of eighteen (interview with author, August 22, 2009). Nasser, an employee of the RETA in Qalyubiya, was also secretary general of Al-Tajammu‘

6. Amr Badr, 2008, "Kamal Abu Eita . . . Al-istiqlal al-tam" [Kamal Abu Eita . . . Total Independence], *Al-Dustur*, December 23, 2008.

Party in Qalyubiya (Nasser 2011). The political activism of these leaders impacted their behavior, in that it motivated them to not only take oppositional positions to the regime, but also to defend the financial rights of their colleagues. As Nasser (2011) said:

> Certainly, being in a political party brings nothing new to society as long as the regime prevents us from acting outside the red lines it draws for any partisan action. However, my membership in Al-Tajammu' Party taught me one thing: you must campaign and persevere as much as possible to obtain your rights. Watching how Khaled Mohie Al-Din (an important party symbol) defended the rights of the poor was always very inspiring for me. This principle of advocacy has always been rooted in me. I was just waiting for an opportunity to emulate my political guide. The RETA protests gave me that opportunity.

Similar to the Mahalla labor movement, there were NDP leaders such as Hamdy, an employee of the RETA in Giza, and Moneim, an employee of the RETA in Menufiya. Moneim had been a member of the NDP since 2005, and a member of the Menufiya local council representing the NDP in 2008. Like Ashraf, NDP member and leader of the Mahalla labor movement, he confirmed that he saw the NDP as the only official channel that provided an opportunity to serve:

> If we wanted to provide services to our colleagues, and if we wanted to have a societal impact, there is no other way than to be a member of the NDP. (Moneim, interview with author, October 19, 2011)

Thus, membership in the NDP reaffirmed the motivation for RETA members to serve their colleagues by trying to help them claim their rights. Contrary to the situation with the Mahalla labor movement players, where the NDP leaders made the strategic decision not to oppose the regime players, some of the RETA members who were also members of the NDP (namely, Moneim) didn't share this stance. Membership of the NDP for them was more reflective of their desire to serve colleagues than of a specific political position.

Moreover, their political careers consolidated their ability to predict the actions of the government and security agents, and, consequently, to enact appropriate strategies to them (Moneim 2011). As Said (2011) explained:

> Abu Eita's career in political activism has been important to us. The security guards didn't manage to shut us down because of the strategies he put in place. Also, during the negotiations, the government couldn't corner us, because most of us knew how to react. To summarize the situation, our political experience provided us with the necessary skills to successfully mobilize our colleagues and negotiate with the government. In short, we drew upon our political experience to successfully force the government to respond to our "un-politicized" and strictly financial and sector-specific demands.

A Syndicalist Career

Participating in trade union elections earlier than those of 2006 (as was the case with Abu Eita in Giza), or becoming a trade unionist by acclamation (as was the case with Emad and Said in Daqhliya), provided these leaders with social resources in terms of support networks. These networks impacted their ability to mobilize their colleagues. As a result of its credible leaders with social networks, the Daqhliya Trade Union Committee played a key role in organizing and mobilizing the employees of the RETA. This was also the case with the Giza trade union committee which, prior to 2006, enjoyed relative independence under the presidency of Abu Eita, who assumed the role in 1995. The credibility enjoyed by Abu Eita and his support networks made it easier to mobilize the Giza employees of the RETA. Sabah, a member of the organizing committee for the Giza strike, commented:

> We always saw Abu Eita protesting against the administration [in reference to the RETA] when it violated our rights. We admired him, we trusted him to look out for our interests, and that's why we were always ready to obey him, so to speak. It was foolish to refuse to answer his call for protest. (Interview with author, October 10, 2011)

The capacity of leaders/trade unionists in Giza and Daqhliya to mobilize their colleagues had already enabled the emergence of some protests before 2006, demanding to annex the RETA employees to the Ministry of

Finance. An example is the March 1999 protest, where a demonstration of two hundred employees was organized in front of the People's Assembly. This protest resulted in the acquisition of some rights but never that of joining the Ministry of Finance. The employees/protestors managed to obtain a bonus of 50 percent of their salaries in exchange for extraordinary efforts, and a 25 percent special bonus. In 2006, a protest was also held in front of the Ministry of Finance, but it had no demonstrable effect because none of the authorities went out to meet the protesters (Shaaban 2008, 35).

Thus, the partial independence of the Daqhliya and Giza trade union committees before 2006 brought to the forefront such union leaders as Emad, the chairman of the trade union committee in Daqhliya since 1996, and Kamal Abu Eita, president of the Giza Trade Union Committee since 1995, and provided them with credibility as well as social support networks. Their position as trade unionists had previously helped them to mobilize their colleagues, and, after 2007, it enabled them to become the decisive leaders of the RETA movement.

The Call for Protest in Giza: Identification of Changing Regime Strategies and Diffusion of Contention

The RETA Protest in Giza

The combination of evicting Abu Eita from the 2006 union elections despite his popularity on the one hand, and the growing frustration of the employees of the RETA because of their mediocre salary in comparison to those in the Department of Finance on the other, are not sufficient to explain their mobilization. The concurrence of these two factors with the victory of the Mahalla workers at the end of 2006—which lasted several days without any crackdown—encouraged the employees of the RETA to act. The victory inspired "admiration and emotional inspiration" (Jasper 2014, 261); it also produced a type of "cognitive liberation" (McAdam 1995, 227–28). The RETA movement's leaders understood that the regime players had changed their strategies and responses to protests, and that, as a result, mobilizing could put pressure on the government (i.e., regime subplayers) and would likely force it to meet their demands, as had been the case with the Mahalla workers. This is what Abu Eita meant when he said that the Mahalla workers taught the RETA employees that there is another way to obtain their rights than to futilely appeal to the government: protesting (Shaaban 2008, 35).

This interpretation was also shared by other movement leaders, such as Nasser (2011), a movement leader in Qalyubiya:

> The political environment is important. I was aware that the security agents are acting otherwise, and that the political scene had shifted. The emergence of the Kifaya movement was proof of that. On the societal level, I also sensed a certain dynamism that became evident with the emergence of the Mahalla workers' movement. I kept track of what was happening through the media. I admired them, I wanted to be in their place and advocate for the acquisition of my rights as well as those of my colleagues.

This highlights the importance of the RETA movement leaders' interpretation and perception of opportunities, and the influence this had on their actions. The language of players and arenas—which I adopt—has the advantage of including cultural dimensions that acknowledge how strategic players attribute meaning to the world and thus act accordingly (Jasper and Volpi 2018, 27). The RETA movement ultimately used the same repertoire of actions as the Mahalla labor movement: strike and sit-in. Adopting these forms of action reflects the movement leaders' conviction of the need for persistence.

During the month of August 2007, Abu Eita met with colleagues in his support network whom he knew personally within the Real Estate Tax Foundation. They would later be the members of the organizing committee of the RETA protest in Giza. He suggested that they take all their days off as a sign of protest against the degradation of their salaries. This suggestion was inspired by the "Stay at Home" campaign (*Khalik fi bitak*), which the political opposition had launched in June 2007. At the head of this campaign were the Karama Party and the Kifaya movement, of which Abu Eita was a member (Shaaban 2008, 36). The purpose of the campaign was to ask people to stay at home on July 23, 2007—a national holiday commemorating the July 23, 1952 revolution—as a sign of protest against the regime.[7] Abu Eita chose to implement the idea of "phased protest" to test the security response with the possibility of turning back and to integrate the employees of the RETA gradually into the protest process in such a way as to achieve gradual buy-in. However, after a lively debate, they all agreed to also organize a demonstration as a sign of protest. The credibility of Abu Eita in their eyes fueled their enthusiasm. As Sabah, Magdy, and Ramadan, members of the Giza protest organizing committee, explained:

> Kamal Abu Eita is known as an honest trade unionist who always fights for our rights. Our confidence in him led us to respond to his call, to rally around him, and to spread this appeal. (Magdy 2011; Ramadan, interview with author, October 10, 2011; Sabah 2011)

They were not concerned that their political activities would lead to a security crackdown because Abu Eita, according to Ramadan, differentiated between political activism (*Al-siyasi*) and sector-based labor disputes (*Al-fi'awi*; Ramadan 2011). Additionally, the interpretation provided by Abu Eita resonated with their perception of the sociopolitical changes surrounding them. The Mahalla labor protest had also led some of the activists among the RETA to believe that it was possible to obtain their financial rights if they made the effort to mobilize and build a social movement capable of exerting pressure on the government (Magdy 2011). Abu Eita's initiative was very well received as the employees realized that protest is the only way to obtain their rights, which they have been calling for in vain for the past three decades (Shaaban 2008, 36).

As a result, a strike organization committee was formed, consisting of approximately a dozen employees of the RETA from all the branch offices in Giza. The committee's mission was to publicize this call to strike in all the branches by sending text messages to RETA employees' cell phones and distributing leaflets urging them to strike (Magdy 2011). On September 11, 2007, the day set for the strike and demonstration, most of the employees went to work, ignoring the call to strike. The event was to begin at

7. "Tagawub mahdud ma' da'wat khalik fi-biytak" [A Mediocre Reaction to the Stay-at-Home Campaign], 2007, *Al-Masry Al-Youm*, July 24, 2007.

10 a.m., but the number of demonstrators was no more than two hundred employees (Ramadan 2011). They demanded parity with their colleagues, as well as their transfer from local administration (in the governorates) to the Department of Finance.[8] They chanted: "Our colleagues earn ten times more, and I can't even buy bread!", "Our wages no longer cover the water and electric bills!", and "Why are the RETA forgotten, why are they neglected?" ("5000 muwazafi" 2007, 49).

The security strategy might be described as being mostly preventive. The intention was to contain the mobilization and to limit, as much as possible, the number of protesters without resorting to violence. Accordingly, central security forces surrounded the Giza Administrative Services Center (Mujjama' al-masalih), where the Giza employees were supposed to gather to demonstrate. They installed a security wall leading to the building and locked the doors to prevent employees from joining their colleagues at the demonstration site ("5000 muwazafi" 2007, 49). This strategy was fruitful only at the beginning of the protest; by the end of the workday, at around 2 to 3 p.m., hundreds of employees had joined their colleagues because of the security agents' tolerant response. They began to break through the security cordon to leave the building and join the demonstration (Ramadan 2011). The number of participants gradually increased, as others were encouraged to join. The daily *Al-Dustur* newspaper confirmed that the number of demonstrators had reached approximately 1,000.[9] This figure was also confirmed by Ramadan, who estimated the Giza employee protesters numbered 1,600 (Ramadan 2011). And so the Giza RETA protest was carried out with considerable success in terms of participation.

8. Mona Yasin, 2007, "5000 muwazaf fi al-dara'ib al-'aqariyya yatazaharun wa yuhadidun bi idrab 'am" [5,000 RETA Employees Demonstrate and Threaten with a General Strike], *Al-Masry Al-Youm*, September 11, 2007.

9. Tamer Abu Arab, 2007, "Muzahara li-alf muwazaf bil-dara'ib al-'aqariyya amam mujjama' al-Jiza lil-mutalaba bi-tahsin ahwalihum wa rabtuhum bil-maliyya" [Demonstration of 1,000 Property RETC in Front of the Mugamma' of Giza to Demand Improvement of Their Work Conditions and Their Annexation to the Department of Finance], *Al-Dustur*, September 7, 2007.

RETA Protest in Daqhliya

The effect of the RETA demonstration was greater than its immediate outcome; it managed to trigger a wave of successive protests. Using McAdam's terminology (1995), the Giza RETA movement could be considered to be an "initiator movement," generating a cycle of identifiable protests and "spin-off movements," which extended beyond the geographical border of the Giza protest. The first spin-off movement was carried out by the RETA in Daqhliya. The spread of contention toward this governorate took place through the mechanism of "brokerage," which included the production of a new connection between previously unconnected sites (Tilly and Tarrow 2015, 31)—in this case, between the protests of Giza and Daqhliya. This brokerage was embodied through a "direct diffusion" route that passed through individuals whose previous contacts help to spread the mobilization as noted by Lachapelle (2011, 54–56).

In fact, Emad, leading member at the Daqhliya trade union committee, had attended the Giza demonstration by pure coincidence. He had gone that day to see Abu Eita to pass along some papers and was surprised by the demonstration. He joined in immediately (Lachapelle 2011, 56). The two leaders already knew each other from the trade union meetings in different governorates. Additionally, they were both founding members of the Karama party. We should also remember that the members of the Daqhliya trade union committee had been in contact with those in Giza since the end of the 1990s, particularly when they tried to mobilize in 1999. The spread of the contention to the Daqhliya employees of the RETA occurred via preexisting personal relationships between the leaders of the two movements, many of whom had fought together as trade unionists in the two governorates (Lachapelle 2011, 54–57).

Said (2009), leading member of the Daqhliya trade union committee, explained the close connection between the groups:

> We've known each other for a long time. Kamal Abu Eita is a friend. We met often as trade unionists to discuss the problem of wage inequality that we were suffering from. The 1990 protest was the first fruit of our meetings.

Abu Eita and Emad met following the RETA demonstration in Giza and decided to put in place a strategy of upward action to claim their rights. They would begin with a demonstration on September 24 in front of the Real Estate Tax foundation offices in Daqhliya (Shaaban 2008, 37). Despite the threats made by Farouk Shehata, president of the Banks and Insurance Union, to members of the trade union committees, the members insisted on mobilizing their colleagues (37). Similarly to Abu Eita, they noted the changes in the regime players' behavior. In this context, the dynamics of the contentious interactions between security agents and the demonstrators in Giza—when security players remained peaceful despite the relatively high number of protesters—gave the green light to the Daqhliya trade union movement leaders to progress in organizing a similar demonstration. As Jabola-Carolus and colleagues (2020) describe, every action is a reaction in strategic contentious interactions. The movement players' actions can thus be understood as a reaction to the peaceful strategy/actions of the security players. Similarly, Said, leading member of the Daqhliya trade union committee, went himself to the security agents' office to warn them straight out that the RETA would demonstrate (2009). The security agents neglected this warning, an action that was interpreted by the movement leaders as another positive sign, and an indication that the security apparatus strategy had shifted in the protesters' favor. It is through the movement players' interactions with the other players/opponents that they were able to perceive the encouraging changes in the latter's strategies (Jasper 2015a, 23).

The Daqhliya trade union committee members already had substantial support networks among the employees of the RETA, and the relative independence of the committee made it easier to initiate collective action. They followed the same techniques their colleagues had used in Giza, but in a more organized manner, because the leaders, as members of the trade union committee, already had social networks and established channels of communications. Thus, each member of the committee assumed responsibility for organizing employees in their own department. The credibility of these trade union leaders led the public servants to respond positively to their appeal.

As confirmed by Said (2009),

> We were credible in the eyes of our colleagues, who had known us for years and years, and had confidence in us. Convincing them to respond positively to our call was not too difficult, although it certainly took effort on our part.

When September 24 arrived, 1,000 employees in Daqhliya, out of a total of 2,700, gathered in front of the local RETA head office. The employees of the RETA demanded their right to parity with the Department of Finance. They chanted Arabic rhymes such as "Wahid, ithnayn, wazir al-maliyya fin?" ("1, 2, where is the Minister of Finance?"), and, in an ironic play on words, ("Ya Nazif, ya Nazif, 'aizin na'mal fi makan Nazif!" ("Nazif, Nazif, we want to work in a clean place!")—the name Nazif means "clean" in colloquial Egyptian Arabic ("Muwazafi" 2007).

The security agents surrounded the demonstration but remained peaceful and made no arrests. And so the protest transpired with the participation of quite a considerable number of employees from Daqhliya, and without any repressive acts carried out against them.

RETA Protests in Beni Suef

There is a notable *diffusion* process that took place in Beni Suef as a result of previous action. "Diffusion" is defined as the spread of contention, an issue, or a way of framing it from one site to another (Tilly and Tarrow, 2015, 31). The diffusion of contention to the governorate of Beni Suef took place through a "mediated route," via brokers who connected actors/players who otherwise had no previous contacts (LaChapelle 2011, 54). In this case, the private media took on the role, publicizing the actions of the two previous protests and connecting actors who were not previously in touch (58). By reporting the comments of employees who were dissatisfied with their daily lives and shining a light on their miserable living conditions, the privately owned newspapers encouraged the "attribution of similarities" among the employees (Tilly and Tarrow, 2015, 126). They also prompted the employees of the RETA in other governorates to protest and to coordinate their actions with colleagues who had already protested.

Moheb, an employee of the RETA who was evicted from the trade union elections in Beni Suef and who would later become a leader of the

RETA movement, heard about the demonstrations in Giza and Daqhliya in the media and decided to go to Giza to meet with Kamal Abu Eita. Friends in Giza arranged this meeting, following which Moheb organized the RETA in his governorate to demonstrate on September 30, 2007. He (2011) explains: "I read about Kamal Abu Eita in the newspapers. I wanted to meet and get to know this man who advocates for our rights. That's why I decided to join his team." Moheb formed a small committee from the members who supported him in the 2006 union elections. These members of the Beni Suef committee undertook the task of organizing their colleagues. They explained the importance of protesting to pressure the government to respond to their demands for parity.

The fraudulently elected official trade union committee threatened the protest organizers with reporting them to the security agents and imposing administrative penalties. They even circulated rumors that the employees who joined the protest would be arrested (Moheb 2011). The movement leaders in Beni Suef met with more difficulties than their colleagues in Giza or Daqhliya because they did not have dense support networks like Abu Eita, who had been a trade unionist for several years, or Emad, who was a leading member of the trade union committee. Despite committee members' efforts at coordination, only a limited number—thirty-three—of the Beni Suef branches was covered (2011). Nevertheless, they succeeded in gathering about a hundred employees to demonstrate on the morning of September 30. They assembled in front of the Beni Suef Real Estate Tax Foundation's administration office and carried banners that read: "Matalibna shari'iyya . . . al-'awda al-maliyya" (Our demands are legitimate. We want to return to the Department of Finance; "Muwazafi" 2007).

This means that the expansion of the movement came about as a result of two factors: first, the leaders' decision to mobilize given their interpretation of the situation as being favorable to their protest and their perception of the change in strategy of the regime players; and, second, the leaders' capacity for taking advantage of their social resources and networks, transforming the latter into protest action and playing an important role in movement building. In this context, the security forces' tolerant behavior toward these three protests encouraged the movement leaders to continue their activism, proving that political opportunities would continue to crystallize during interactions between the movement players and the regime players.

The leaders of the three movements also decided to give the government an ultimatum and announced that, in the absence of a satisfactory reply from the minister of finance, they would call for a protest uniting the employees of other governorates after the month of Ramadan, the first day after the Eid al-Fitr holiday: October 21, 2007.

October 21 Demonstration and the Emergence of a Social Movement (Player)

Up until that time, the movement lacked the organizational structures necessary to coordinate such collective action. In addition to the security pressures that this nascent movement was likely to encounter, it lacked the logistical capacity to disseminate information and coordinate action on a national scale. To mobilize for this protest, Kamal Abu Eita, the movement leader in Giza, and Emad, the movement leader in Daqhliya, began the process of recruitment by contacting former executives of local trade union committees, those whom they already knew as former trade unionists.

In addition, the media coverage of these three successive protests in Giza, Daqhliya, and Beni Suef supported the process of the *attribution of similarities* among employees in other governorates, thus ensuring that they were well informed and prepared. Some of them even contacted the newspapers to take Abu Eita's phone number and contact him directly.

The leaders' role and practice of establishing relationships, building a movement, and mobilizing its members is crucial in determining the way the movement evolved over time (Ganz and McKenna 2019). By relying on their old networks, activating current ones, and building new relationships, Abu Eita, as well as the leaders of the Daqhliya protests, played a role in recruiting new members and mobilizing them against the government. This allowed the formation of the intergovernmental coordinating committee: the Strike Coordinating Committee (SCC). Abu Eita used its connections with active employees in the different governorates, such as Moneim, an employee of the RETA in the Menufiya Real Estate

Tax Foundation. Abu Eita and Moneim had known one another for several years, since Moneim was an activist during the RETA protest in 1999. Several meetings had been held in Cairo, and the committee agreed to organize a demonstration bringing together the governorate employees in front of the Ministry of Finance building on October 21, 2007 (Said 2011). In so doing, the committee members assumed the responsibility for coordinating protest action and trying to mobilize the greatest possible number of employees of the RETA in the different governorates. Additionally, Abu Eita and Emad were in contact, and together met and built relationships with trade unionists who had a reputation for activism. They both worked on activating the network of trade unionists who had not been coopted by the government. This was only the case with the Daqhliya trade union committee, which worked on recruiting and mobilizing the RETA employees of Daqhliya.

The ability to mobilize differed according to the social networks and organizational structures of the leaders in each governorate, and their geographical position. The situation was easier in Giza and Daqhliya because of their organizational structures. In a few governorates, such as Menufiya, nonformal structures existed, such as the "RETA League of Menufiya": a social system that the RETA founded to protect their rights and to help each other financially. The thirteen centers of the Real Estate Tax foundation in Menufiya were represented in this league. The ability to organize was greatly simplified by the presence of this league, as Moneim (2011), leader of the Menufiya movement, emphasized. The governorates of Giza, Daqhliya, and Menufiya thus had some preestablished structures and, consequently, were able to organize more easily and to find a few buses to transport employees. However, most of the governorates did not have such structures, which made initial intergovernorate organization difficult. They were unable to penetrate all the branches of the Real Estate Foundations in the different governorates, or to provide transportation for their colleagues. This was particularly true in the case of the RETA in Upper Egypt, where employees had to take public transport, either trains or microbuses, agreeing to meet at noon in front of the Ministry of Finance in the Madinet Nasr district in Cairo (2011). As a result, the RETA in the governorates that were geographically distant from Cairo, like Upper Egypt or northern Sinai, were only able to participate in the protest symbolically. Most of the demonstrators came from governorates that were closer to Cairo and were more able to organize, like Giza (with approximately 700 employees), Daqhliya (approximately 1,500 employees), Menufiya (approximately 700 employees), Behira (approximately 400 employees), and Beni Suef (approximately 240 employees) (Said 2011; Moneim 2011; Moheb 2011).[10]

The SCC's strategy was to ask employees to meet in front of the Ministry of Finance building at noon exactly and to not arrive before that time. The goal was to not give any opportunity to security agents to pressure small groups that would trickle in at the beginning and thereby easily demobilize them. As Ramadan (2011) of the Giza organization committee explained,

> Abu Eita told us that whoever arrives early should walk around and not go in front of the building until twelve noon exactly. He even told us straight out that whoever arrives in front of the building before noon, is not one of us, and whoever arrives afterwards is not one of us either.

This underscores the importance of the leaders' prior political experience and its influence on the development of effective mobilization tactics. The employees did as requested, and thousands of demonstrators arrived at the agreed-upon time in front of the building. They demanded the same rights: to return to the Department of Finance ("1, 2, where is the Minister of Finance?"; "We have the same demands, being part of the Ministry of Finance again [Matalibna hiyya nirga' tani lil-maliyya])!"[11]

Central Security forces only surrounded the demonstrators, who numbered less than three thousand, according to Al-Masry Al-Youm, and no repression took place ("Lil-mara al-khamisa" 2007). As with the case of the Mahalla movement, the security agents, who supervised the dynamics of the demonstration from a distance, served as links between the

10. These numbers were gathered during interviews.

11. Mohsen Abd El Razek et al., 2007, "Lil mara al-khamisa, alaf al-muwazafin bil-dara'ib al-a'qariyya yatazaharun lil-mutalaba bi-naqluhum ila al-maliyya" [For the Fifth Time, Thousands of RETA Demonstrate to Demand Their Transfer to the Ministry of Finance], *Al-Masry Al-Youm*, October 22, 2007.

government and the demonstrators. After an hour of demonstrating (i.e., at around 1 p.m.), they invited the movement leaders to form a delegation to meet Momtaz al-Said, a consultant at the Department of Finance, since the minister of finance was traveling. Abu Eita formed a delegation of a dozen people representing the intergovernorate organizing committee for this event. However, al-Said told them that he had no power to act, and that prime minister Ahmed Nazif was the only person who had the authority to resolve their demands (Shaaban 2008, 37–38).

The delegation gave the news to the demonstrators, and Abu Eita suggested that they demonstrate in front of the prime minister's building on Hussein Hegazy Street in downtown Cairo. As Jasper (2014, 69) notes, "Strategic action is full of dilemmas and compromises: each option is promising in some ways, but risky in others." This relatively risky decision was designed to achieve two promising objectives, which Abu Eita succeeded de facto to get: to send a message to the government that they would persist, and to give more media visibility to the protest movement activities. He chanted: "Al-muwazaf al-sharif yigi ma'aya 'and Nazif!" (The brave and honest employee comes along with me to Nazif!; Eweida 2008, 23).

In order to make the movement's protest less visible, the State Security agents tried to pressure the protesters to go to the Council of Ministers by bus instead of on foot, but their efforts were futile, and the demonstrators walked approximately twenty-four kilometers to the Council of Minister's building. Arriving in front of the building at 4:30 p.m., they remained there until 9:00 p.m., waiting for someone to negotiate with them. The Central Security forces surrounded them without using violence. Seeing the fatigue of the demonstrators, and with no negotiation in sight, the coordination committee suggested that they return home and prepare for a longer-term protest that would be capable of putting more pressure on the government (Shaaban 2008, 38).

As a result, this event was terminated with the demobilization of the protest. At the same time, it marked a crucial step in the movement's history: it demonstrated the ability of the SCC to coordinate a national level protest, marking the emergence of a nascent social movement and a player, and it doubled the reach of the SCC and as a result solidified its ability to coordinate action on a national level. In fact, the media coverage of the dynamics of the demonstration, together with the walk to the Council of Ministers, was widely reported by the privately owned media, the foremost of which was *The Ten O'Clock Show* (*Al-'ashira masa'an*), which had an audience of millions and was broadcast on the Dream 2 Channel (Said 2011). Media also increased the movement's visibility at a national level. As Amenta and colleagues (2015a, 302) indicate, media coverage not only constitutes key data in mapping identities among the politically disadvantaged but also provides a possibility of discursive presence and capacity of production of meanings. The media thus helped to form a shared interpretation of the situation among employees and, consequently, to recruit future leaders. Nasser, for example, in the governorate of Qalyubiya, heard about Abu Eita and the demonstrations organized by the movement from the media. He (2011) explained,

> I have read a lot in the newspapers and heard of Abu Eita in the media. I wanted to do everything in my power to get in touch with him. I wanted to know who is this person who defended our rights? After the demonstration in front of the Department of Finance, I tried to meet him and join his team.

It was at this time that Nasser became a member of the SCC and later participated in organizing the sit-in in front of the Federation of Trade Unions (and, later, in front of the Council of Ministers).

In summary, the strategies implemented by the movement's leaders to ensure the successful organization of the first protest on a national scale, as well as their efforts in building the movement, enabled them to bring together RETA employees at the country level for this protest. This collective action organized on a national level led to, or even embodied, a "scale shift" (Tilly and Tarrow 2015, 125). This shift in scale occurred, as contention in the Giza governorate was not only spread across space but also led to the creation of instances for new coordination on the national level: the Strike Coordinating Committee (SCC) which transformed the scattered RETA protests into a hub of social movement, and to a player on the national level that was able to confront regime players in sequences of contentious and strategic interactions. It was thus an *upward scale shift* that took place.[12]

Finally, it remains to be said that the tolerant attitude of the security forces at this time was encouraging in terms of the possibilities of future activism. As discussed earlier, interactions do not begin from scratch but are subject to the definition of the situation that emerges during the course of the strategic interaction itself (Jasper and Volpi 2018, 24). The RETA employees would thus organize a longer-term protest to exert more pressure: a two-day sit-in in front of the Federation of Trade Unions on December 3, 2007—a date that was later changed to November 13, 2007 (Shaaban 2008, 38).

Sit-In in November 13–14: Delegitimization and Activation of Boundaries

The RETA demonstration in front of ETUF's headquarters took place in a context of struggle over legitimation between the regime subplayers (Real Estate Tax Collectors Administration and ETUF) and the movement players, and a contention over the diagnostic framing of the problem of the RETA employees between both sides. ETUF players aimed to delegitimize the movement's protest claims and actions, while the movement leaders sought to legitimize them. The event that actually triggered this war a few days before the demonstration in front of the ETUF on November 13 was the following: on October 24, Momtaz al-Out, director of the office of the Department of Finance, presented a document to the minister of finance in which he requested 78 million EGP. This sum would be received by the employees of the Ministry of Finance in the form of bonuses and premiums, although they were already getting a much higher salary than the employees linked to the different governorates, who were not part of the Ministry of Finance. The Minister of Finance approved this application on November 7, thereby exacerbating the frustration of the RETA employees.

12. Upward scale shift involves coordination of collective action at a higher level (whether regional, national, or even international) than its initiation (Tilly and Tarrow 2015, 125).

The movement's leaders took advantage of this to achieve two objectives. First, they aimed to legitimize their protest actions by constructing a narrative that identified the RETA employees as victims of injustice and placed the blame for that victimization on the government. They thus formulated a diagnostic framing of their grievances as a lack of social justice. Far from stirring up confrontation with the government, this expression of the movement's cause aimed to provoke the political authorities to consider the legitimacy of the claims, given their strictly social and even ethical dimensions.

Second, the leaders used the momentum built to "expand the scope of the movement and the echoes that it could produce in terms of solidarity or sympathy" (Koopmans 2004, 367). In that matter, Emad, a member of the coordination committee, confirmed that they took full advantage of this demonstration, which was widely publicized in the media, and that they even notified the security agents that they met in the street to call attention to their demands and stir up sympathy with them (Said 2011).

Chain reactions took place within the media, and a war of reciprocal delegitimization erupted. Ismail Abdel Rasul, the director of the Real Estate Tax Administration, stated on *The Ten O'Clock Evening Show* that employees opted for escalation. In several privately owned newspapers, the foremost of which was *Al-Masry Al-Youm*, he constructed a diagnostic framing of the RETA employees' problem as being one of impatience, stating that they would just have to wait for the new law on real estate taxation, which was to be submitted to parliament during the next session, on November 7, 2007. In his statement to *Al-Masry Al-Youm*, Farouk Shehata, president of the Bank and Insurance Union, expressed similar sentiments, as he stated that the event that took place in front of the Department of Finance had no legitimacy, and that some of the employees were mobilizing their colleagues to advance their own interests.[13] In the same vein, on October 23, Shehata organized a meeting with all the presidents of the union committees in the different governorates and ordered

13. Rabab Fares, 2007, "Fashal iqna' muwazafi al-dara'ib al-'aqariyya bi-fad al-i'tisam" [Failure to Convince the RETA Employees to End Their Sit-In], *Nahdit Masr*, October 24, 2007.

them to prevent any strike or protest from taking place. In a similar way to the head of the Real Estate Tax Administration in Cairo, his argument was that such strikes have no legitimacy, and that the problem is that the RETA employees were rather impatient—they should just wait, as the real estate taxation law would be enacted very soon (Fares 2007, 1).

Players constantly assess the strengths and weaknesses of their opponents to identify tactics that take advantage of weak spots, or, in Jasper's (2014, 68) terms, "the right key." Movement leaders used Farouk Shehata's negative positions toward demonstrators' demands to delegitimize the official trade union as not representing RETA employees' rights (Said 2011; Magdy 2011). This war of delegitimization, as well as the position of the official trade union, is particularly significant for this analysis because it created/activated a *boundary* between the employees of the RETA and the formal trade union.

This dispute over legitimacy and "activation of boundaries" between the two sides of the contention matches the analysis provided by Tarrow (2013, 15–16) on the dynamics of contentious interactions and their influence on shaping the emergent new actor/player. He pointed out that in a contest between two actors (i.e., a challenger and an opponent), the first actor does not only take advantage of perceived political opportunities to make claims on their opponents, but also attempts to certify themselves as a worthy, powerful, legitimate actor, to which the opponent responds by delegitimizing him, calling him a thug or someone who wants to exploit his followers. Within this hardening identity boundary, the challenger works to frame a consensual appeal to increase their support base, while maintaining a conflictual message across it.

The movement leaders met to organize the sit-in that would be in front of the ETUF on November 13. The reach of the SCC had broadened, particularly with the increase in the number of active new employees from other governorates. Two thousand or so RETA employees gathered in front of the ETUF building on Al-Galaa Street in Cairo (Said 2011). They chanted slogans focusing on the legitimacy and justice of their cause: "The honest employee can't afford to buy bread!" (Al-muwazaf al-sharif mish laqi al-righif); "RETA go to sleep hungry!" (Muwazafin, muwazafin, yama layali namu ga'anin); and "The strike is legitimate in the face of poverty and hunger!" (Al-idrab mashru', mashru' did al-faqr w did al-gu'). They also denounced the minister of finance again: "Botros Ghali, come down from your ivory tower!" (Ya Botros ya Ghali, inzil min burgak al-'ali!).[14] The RETA employees avoided direct confrontation with the government, but they wanted to exert just enough pressure to achieve their demands. They shouted slogans appealing for help from the president of the Republic: "Mr. President, have a look at the property tax officials!" (Ya ra'is al-gumhuriyya bus w tul 'ala al-'akariyya; Azouz 2011). A few hours later, the demonstrators threatened to escalate if the government refused to meet their demands: "Nazif, Nazif, the storm is coming!" (*Ya Nazif, ya* Na'zif, al-tawfan mistanik; Azouz 2011). This was an implicit threat to move the sit-in to the Council of Ministers building.

Toward the end of the first day, members of the organizing committee, under the chairmanship of Kamal Abu Eita, went to meet with the president of the ETUF at the federation headquarters. Mugawer started by persuading them that he would intercede personally on their behalf. When they refused to surrender, however, he resorted to nonviolent coercion to oblige them to give up their claims.

As part of his persuasive efforts, and as a good-will pledge, Mugawer said that he had personally asked finance minister Botros Ghali at the last meeting of the political bureau of the NDP to attach the employees of the RETA to the Department of Finance. It was even said that Botros Ghali replied, in the presence of Gamal Mubarak, the son of the president of the Republic and chairman of the NDP political committee, that he was in favor of such a project (Lachapelle 2011, 66). In return, he asked them to end the sit-in and give him a chance to solve their grievances, his argument being that ending the sit-in would strengthen his position in negotiations with the government: "Give me the chance to help you. It's not logical that you are in my house [referring to the ETUF], and I can't convince you to leave, and at the same time you ask me to represent you and support your demands during the negotiations" (Moneim 2011).

14. Mohamed Azouz, 2011, "I'tisam 7000 muwazafi min al-dara'ib al-'aqariyya" [The Sit-In of 7,000 Employees of the RETA], *Al-Masry Al-Youm*, November 14, 2011.

Since strategic players actively attribute meaning not only to what they are doing but also to what their opponents do and seek to deceive them by destroying the meaning they attribute to their own acts (Jasper 2014, 65–66), Abu Eita formulated an interpretation of the ETUF president's offer as a way to demobilize the RETA movement, as it was annoying the government. In his argument, he focused his colleagues' attention on the absence of any guarantee that these promises would be kept. He wanted to persuade them that it was important to turn down this offer. As Nasser (2011), leader of the Qalyubiya movement and member of the SCC put it:

> As we were going down the stairs after the meeting with Mugawer, Abu Eita asked me my opinion. I told him that I was reluctant and that he wanted to abort (yughid) our movement. Abu Eita congratulated me for this answer, which proved to him that we were on the same wavelength, and that I was going to support his position.

Moneim (2011), leader of the Menufiya movement and member of the SCC, narrated a similar episode:

> The fact that Mugawer affirmed his mediation during the meeting with the NDP has left some people uncertain about whether he would be able to achieve their demands, and as a result, uncertain of the need to continue the sit-in. However, Abu Eita was able to convince them that the president of the ETUF simply wanted to disband them without giving any concrete guarantees in return, and his firm stance reinforced the general opinion that was suspicious of the offer.

The leaders communicated the result of these negotiations to the employees as well as their common interpretation of what had transpired. A vote by show of hands was held to choose to stay. The final decision, after consultation with the members of the movement, was to spend the night in front of the ETUF building until more concrete action was taken by the government.[15] The demonstrators, refusing to disperse, chanted: "We don't

15. Omar Said, 2007, "Al-muwazafin yahtufun did wazir al-dakhiliyya wa al-sitat tandam ilayhum" [Employees Chanting Slogans against the Minister of the Interior and Women Join In], *Al-Badil*, November 15, 2007.

want false promises!"[16] This shows the importance of the leaders' actions in influencing the movement's dynamics and outcomes. Abu Eita's interpretation that Mugawer's suggestion would be harmful to the movement's interests, and his work in convincing members of this, both guaranteed the continued activism of the movement and consolidated its structures.

As night was falling and Mugawer's persuasive acts were not fruitful, he resorted to nonviolent coercive action, ordering that all the rooms in the federation building be closed, especially the restrooms, leaving only the stairways and the sidewalk in front, where the one thousand demonstrators could stay or spend the night (Said 2009). Said (2011), member of the SCC, stated that Mugawer had even called the security agents, asking them to evict the demonstrators, which did not take place. They spent the night on the sidewalk, cordoned off by police. For the movement, this gesture symbolized a betrayal by those who were at least theoretically responsible for representing them. The demonstrators considered the act of closing the restrooms, which was mentioned in almost all the interviews, to be humiliating and even cruel. It solidified the image of an institution that did not represent the employees, and that was even hostile to them. The sentence often repeated during interviews was:

> Can you imagine, Mugawer closed the restrooms and threw us outside? It was so hard because we had to spend the night in Al-Galaa Street [referring to the street where the Federation is located], this institution does not represent us anymore. (Said 2011; Nasser 2011; Moneim 2011)

These emotions and this collective memory of humiliation, shared among movement members, played a pivotal role in shaping a group identity that stood in contrast to the leadership of the ETUF (Bishara 2018), reflecting the beginning of the construction of a *boundary* between the demonstrators and the union. This was a major step in the movement's

16. Mostafa Bassiouni, 2007, "Ba'd thalath sa'at min al-mufawadat bayn Mugawer wa mumathili al-dara'ib al-'aqariyya, al-muwazafin yarfudun inha' al-idrab wa yamdun al-layla amam itihad al-niqabat" [After Three Hours of Talks between Mugawer and Representatives of the RETA, the Employees of the RETA Refuse to Stop the Strike and Spend the Night at ETUF Headquarters], *Al-Dustur*, November 15, 2007.

identity formation process, which was constructed partially in opposition to the official trade union (Lachapelle 2011, 68). As Tilly and Tarrow (2015, 107) explain, "Identities center on boundaries separating us from them. On either side of the boundary, people maintain relations with each other. They also carry-on relations across the boundary; and create collective understandings about the boundary. Together, boundaries, cross-boundary relations, within-boundary relations, and shared understandings make up collective identities."

It is thus that the sit-in, which lasted from November 13 to November 14, was important for the movement's evolution. On the one hand, it affirmed the movement's capacity not only to mobilize at the national level, but also to consolidate its organizational structure for several days (the duration of the sit-in); on the other hand, it created a *boundary* between the movement and the ETUF. As Della Porta and Diani (2006, 112) affirm, the interaction with the authorities represents a significant source of identity; confronting an authority perceived as unfair is a dynamic that creates motivation to act and hostility toward those who hold this authority. Identities become thus *political identities* when authorities become party to them (108). This was exactly the case with the RETA struggle against the ETUF (one of the regime subplayers). Hence, the dynamics of the next sit-in, scheduled for December 3, would continue to promote the process of the movement's political identity formation.

Conclusion

In conclusion, the genesis of structures conducive to the RETA movement's action resulted from a complex and contentious interactional process. The movement's evolution to a national scale was not predestined; rather, it stemmed from the agency of its leaders. Their acumen in identifying the shifting strategy of regime players and interpreting it as an avenue for action, played a pivotal role, and their work in converting their existing social networks into an act of protest proved instrumental in the movement's nationwide expansion. Moreover, the implementation of effective strategies and resonant framings underpinned the protest's success. This encompassed delegitimizing opposing claims and constructing enduring structures over time. Throughout the strategic and contentious interaction, leaders generated new opportunities and prospects for the movement's expansion and the consolidation of its structures. Their agency propelled the gradual formation of the RETA social movement at a national level, overcoming limitations in organizational capacity. The sit-in staged in front of the ETUF set the stage for a more extensive sit-in on December 3, drawing an even larger participant pool and enduring for an extended duration of ten days, as the next chapter will show.

6

The Monster Attacks!

The Success of the RETA Movement and the Creation of an "Independent Union"

Introduction

In this chapter, I explore the successful mobilization of the December 3 sit-in by the RETA movement players, orchestrating a gathering of ten thousand civil servants nationwide in front of the Cabinet's headquarters. The movement strategically opted to establish an independent union, marking a direct challenge to regime players' authority and earning the distinction of being the first union in Egypt to break away from the state corporatist structure since 1957.

In my analysis, I discuss the Strike Coordinating Committee's (SCC) astute choices to avoid repression and the tactical repertoires employed to neutralize the security apparatus during the ten-day sit-in. I argue that their decisions significantly influenced the movement's organizational prowess and survival, and therefore, the outcomes it generated. I also shed light on the way the leaders strategically harnessed media interest to amplify the movement's discursive presence and on the identity-building mechanisms which were triggered during the sit-in, contending that the resultant collective identity facilitated the establishment of a cohesive social movement capable of asserting independence from the Egyptian Trade Union Federation (ETUF).

Moreover, I explore the SCC's decision to establish an independent RETA union outside the ETUF's corporatist framework, delving into the impact of leaders' political careers on their motivation to confront regime players. In my analysis, I illuminate the significance of understanding leaders' biographies and activist trajectories in understanding the movement's development and trajectory.

Finally, I examine the dynamics of the strategic interaction between representatives of the new union and regime players in the arena of trade union affairs. Focusing on the contentious dynamics surrounding legalization and government recognition, I contend that appropriate strategies and the consolidation of the movement's collective identity were pivotal to its success in this contentious process.

Sit-in in Front of the Cabinet Headquarters: The SCC's Preventive Strategies and Tactics

Movement players define their situations and the strategies they adopt based on their previous interactions, and according to the constraints imposed by other players (Jasper and Volpi 2018, 24). The lesson learned by the movement's players through their contentious interactions was that they must exert greater pressure on the regime players if they wanted the latter to meet their demands. In other words, they had to be able to mobilize a greater number of employees and to persist for several consecutive days. A member of the SCC said that they have studied the reasons for their defeat in the previous sit-in and understand that the greater the number of protesters, the greater the chances of success and vice versa. Therefore, they decided to better organize their efforts to be able to increase participation in the next sit-in (Shaaban 2008, 35).

More specifically, the SCC needed to develop strategies and tactics to protect the movement and guarantee its cohesion during the ten-day sit-in period. The SCC met several times in Cairo, notably at the headquarters of the Nasserist Al-Karama Party (of which Abu Eita and Emad were members), to agree on the mobilizing tactics to be implemented. Within each governorate, each of the members of the organizing committee formed during the previous protests was charged with organizing their colleagues. This division of labor was easier in governorates that had organizational structures already in place, such as Giza, Daqhliya, or Menufiya. Gamal Eweida, a member of the Daqhliya governorate's organizing committee and the SCC, explained this division of labor in his booklet on the movement's protests. He stated that for an endeavor to achieve success, a well-defined plan and strategic approach are imperative. On November 24, 2007, the committee of twenty-two members representing RETA employees, corresponding to the twenty-two departments of the property tax administration in Daqhliya governorate, convened. Among these members were the most active participants in prior protests carried out by the RETA movement. The governorate's structure was segmented into five distinct regions, each encompassing several branches or departments of the real estate tax administration within the governorate. In a concerted effort, specific leaders led defined regions, and designated assembly point for RETA members on the day of the sit-in protest. Ensuring seamless logistics, two or three buses were arranged at each gathering point, slated for departure to Cairo at 9:30 a.m. (Eweida 2008).

More RETA employees were expected than at previous protests. In order to avoid a counterattack by security agents, the SCC developed a set of tactics. One tactic was to use several gathering points for the buses heading from each governorate to Cairo. This was to avoid attracting the attention of security agents, who might intervene if they noticed several buses together in the same place, heading in the same direction. During our talks, movement leaders strongly emphasized this point, which in their opinion was crucial to the success of the protest's organization. Moheb (2011), leader in governorate's organizing committee and member of the SCC, explained:

> We were about 240 employees. How could we get everyone out of Beni Suef without anyone knowing it? This was a real problem. We agreed that each of the five scheduled buses would take a different route. Our strategy was successful, because the security agents didn't catch on and let us leave the governorate. The leaders in each bus were told that anyone arriving in Cairo before noon should not go to the place for the sit-in.

Another tactic was to delay the choice of location for the sit-in until the last minute, to surprise state security agents. Just before the buses arrived in Cairo on December 3, Abu Eita told them by phone where the sit-in would take place. Eweida said that the twenty-two buses that came out of Daqhliya governorate with six hundred employees on board arrived in the town of Kafr Shukr, not far from Cairo. Before they arrived there, they did not know where they were supposed to go until Abu Eita gave the order to head to the Cabinet building (Eweida 2008, 30).

According to the newspaper *Al-Badil*, about five thousand demonstrators gathered.[1] They swore that they would not leave the premises until they got their right to parity and began chanting slogans against the prime minister: "Nazif where are you? Are you sleeping, or what?" (Ya Nazif akhbarak 'ih? Inta nayim walla 'ih?)—in reference to his refusal to listen to them (Said 2007, 1), or, "Nazif, wake up, we're suffering!" (Ya Nazif qum w tul, tul 'omrina sharbin al-mur).[2] They also chanted slogans hostile to the minister of finance: "The decision, the decision, we won't leave until there's a decision!" (al-qarar, al-qarar, mish awzin ila al-qarar; Said 2007, 1) and, "We're holding a sit-in against a government that challenges us!" (Mu'tasimin wa al-haq ma'ana did hukuma bithadidna; "10 alaf muwazaf" 2007, 6). They called for the intervention of the president: "President of the Republic, take a look at the Real Estate Tax collectors!" (Ya ra'is al-gumhuriyya bus w tul 'ala al-'akariyya; "10 alaf muwazaf" 2007, 6). In addition to these slogans, they condemned the deterioration of the standard of living among RETA employees. They carried placards that read, "Our salary is equivalent to a pair of shoes or two kilos of meat!" (Muratabna yisawi gazma . . . wa yisawi itnin kilo lahma; Said 2007, 1).

At the end of the first day of the sit-in in front of the Cabinet building, another important choice had to be made: either to sleep on Hegazy Street, in front of the Cabinet headquarters, or go to the ETUF hall and spend the night there to protect themselves from the cold. Abu Eita convinced protesters to spend the night in front of the Cabinet building because of its strategic location.[3] It was the first time that so many protesters had occupied a street in an area where many ministries, the People's Assembly,

1. Omar Said, 2007, "I'tisam al-dara'ib al-'aqariyya amam majlis al-wuzara" [The RETA Sit-In in Front of the Council of Ministers Building], *Al-Badil*, December 4, 2007.

2. "10 alaf muwazaf bi al-dara'ib al-'qariya ya'tasimun amam maglis al-wuzara" [Ten Thousand RETA employees Hold a Sit-In in Front of the Cabinet Building], 2007, *Al-Masry Al-Youm*, December 4, 2007.

3. Al-Sayed El-Turki, 2007, "Hussein Mugawer, azmat rajul muhim" [Hussein Mugawer, the Problem of an Important Man], *Al-Dustur*, December 9, 2007.

and the Advisory Council were all located. This street was also not far from the Ministry of Interior. Choosing this location guaranteed the movement greater media visibility. Kamal Abu Eita asked protesters to decide: those who approved his suggestion had to applaud first, followed by those against. The group that clapped the loudest would win. Given the prior disappointing experience during the sit-in in front of the ETUF, the movement leaders were still able to influence protesters, and their tactical choices had a decisive influence on their ability to exert pressure on the regime players (Morris 2004, 242).[4]

In addition to organizing the sit-in in front of the Cabinet headquarters, the movement used other repertoires of action that were likely to increase pressure on the government. Those who could not go to Cairo organized demonstrations in front of the real estate tax administration buildings in their governorates. On December 4, around 170 employees demonstrated outside the headquarters of the real estate tax administration in Qena ("10 alaf muwazaf" 2007, 6). They chanted slogans against Abdel Rasol, director of the administration in Qena: "We're telling the truth, we want to remove Abdel Rasol!" (Al-haq, al-haq ni'ul 'ayzin nishil Abdel Rasol!).[5] On December 6, in Daqhliya, around 3,000 employees also demonstrated in front of the administration building in Mansoura. Their slogans demanded parity: "Why are the real estate tax collectors forgotten? Why are they neglected?" (Al-darayib al-maliyya lih mitsaba lih mansiyya), and, "Boutros Ghali, come down from your ivory tower!" (Ya Botros ya Ghali, inzil min burgak al-'ali; "I'tisam muwazafi" 2007, 2).

Strategic action is full of dilemmas and compromises, with each option being promising in some ways and risky in others (Jasper 2014, 69). In fact, the strategic choices of the SCC were as important for the survival of the movement as its mobilizing tactics. The refusal to politicize demands and insistence that the sit-in be peaceful allowed the SCC to avoid security

4. Ayman Saleh, 2007, "Tafakuk azmat muwazafi al-dara'ib al-'aqariyya" [The Deteriorating Crisis of The RETA], *Al-Iktisadeya Al-Masreya*, December 9, 2007.

5. "I'tisam muwazafi al-dara'ib al-'aqariyya yadkhul yawmuh al-thalith" [The RETA Sit-In Enters Its Third Day], 2007, *Al-Badil*, December 6, 2007.

intervention. As Goodwin and Jasper (1999, 53) argue, political opportunities are formed by strategic considerations—that is, by the choices that movement leaders make. Their choices thus made it possible for the movement's players to take advantage of the political opportunity presented by the security agents' declining use of violence. The movement's leaders thought that a different choice would have probably changed the regime's tolerant response to the protest. For example, Said (2011), a member of the SCC, said:

> We knew the regime was ready to crush us if it felt that our action was linked to any political organization. We refused that. When members of the "Kifaya movement" came to participate in the sit-in in solidarity with us, we chased them out because they were trying to distribute political leaflets to the employees participating in the sit-in.

Magdy (2011), another movement leader, commented:

> State Security agents mingled with us to monitor us and to understand what it was all about. They only wanted to make sure we did not follow any political party. We knew that emphasizing the fact that we were only demanding a salary increase was appeasing the state's security apparatus.

The presence of these agents at the sit-in was also confirmed by the newspaper *Al-Badil.* They monitored discussions in order to make sure that the movement did not intend to challenge regime players politically.[6] This again shows that the movement leaders' strategic choices, and the tactics they used, affected the movement's success.

Aware of the context they were operating in and its constraints, Kamal Abu Eita and Emad, SCC members and cofounders of the Karama Party, refused any alliance between their movement and political parties/movements that were attempting to ally themselves with the RETA

6. Omar Said, 2007, "Madha ya'mal dubat amn al-dawla fi wasat muwazafi al-dara'ib al-'aqariyya" [What Do Security Officers Do among the Real Estate Tax Collectors?], *Al-Badil*, December 5, 2007.

movement.[7] Abu Eita told *Al-Masry Al-Youm* on December 6 that the employees were facing pressure from political parties and movements that claim to be interceding on their behalf. However, the movement rejected the politicization of its economic demands.[8]

They also refused proposals for intervention by the Muslim Brotherhood. It should be noted here that the Muslim Brotherhood won eighty-eight seats in Parliament following the 2005 parliamentary elections. One of the movement's leaders told *Al-Masry Al-Youm* that the employees refused their intervention because they refused the political exploitation of their cause. The goal of their sit-in was strictly to obtain their rights, which were denied for thirty-four years (Azouz and Razek 2007a, 1).

Far from confronting the regime players, the employees of the RETA repeatedly asked the president of the Republic to intervene to solve their grievances: "Mr. President, have compassion on the RETA!" (Ya ra'is al-gumhuriyya . . . nazrit 'atf lil-'aqariyya); "We are waiting for you, Mubarak, be fair, grant your officials their rights!" (Ya Mubarak mistaniyinak, insh'a haq muwazafinak); "One, two, where is Hosni Mubarak?" (Wahid, ithnayn, Hosni Mubarak fin?); "Our leader, may God keep you, save us from the Minister!" (Ya za'im, Allah yikhalik, irhamna min al-wazir; Azouz and Razek 2007b, 6).

In the same vein, Lotfia, leading member in the independent trade union committee of Cairo (which would be formed later), told me:

> Political parties/movements often infiltrate our ranks to disseminate and shout political slogans, such as "We want the fall of Mubarak (Yasqut, yasqut Hosni Mubarak)! We then chanted even louder, "With our

7. Mohamed Azouz and Mohsen Abd El Razek, 2007a, "Muwazafi al-dara'ib al-'aqariyya yuwasilun al-tahadi: lan nughadir al-shari' dun hal" [The RETA Continue to Challenge: We Will Not Leave the Street without a Solution], *Al-Masry Al-Youm*, December 5, 2007.

8. Mohamed Azouz and Mohsen Abd El Razek, 2007b, "Muwazafu al-dara'ib al-'aqariyya yuhadidun bi-naql al-i'tisam amam al-ri'asa wa yahtefoun ya abou alaa' bos lil'iyal" [The Real Estate Tax Collector Officials Threaten to Transfer Their Sit-In to the Presidency and Chant "Abou Alaa, Tend to the Children"], *Al-Masry Al-Youm*, December 6, 2007.

> spirit and our blood, we will defend the bread of our children!" (Bil-ruh w-al-dam, rizq 'iyalna aham), so that their slogans wouldn't be heard. We wanted to be known as a labor movement, not as a political movement." (Interview with author, October 4, 2011)

In addition, the SCC members feared the possible forced disappearance of Abu Eita by security agencies. They imagined that this could be an option to pressure them to disperse, yet it could also backfire and end up inciting violence. For this reason, they agreed during the preparatory meetings that some of them would take on the responsibility for protecting Abu Eita, to ensure that the sit-in remained peaceful. Moheb (2011), a member of the SCC, explained:

> We were afraid that State Security would kidnap him to pressure us psychologically. If that had been the case, the employees would resort to violence against the security officers who surrounded us. We did not want that. To be very clear, we wanted our sit-in to remain peaceful and non-politicized (Silmi wa ghir musayas). I was the one who took charge of this task. I followed Abu Eita like his shadow to protect him.

Similarly, from the first day, protesters urged "peaceful, peaceful" (silmiya, silmiya; Eweida 2008, 54), so that the security officers encircling the protesters would not have a pretext to intervene and use force. The movement leaders asked their comrades not to use slogans that might provoke security agents. Hussein, a member of the SCC, said, "We asked our colleagues not to use slogans other than those we had agreed upon" (interview with author, October 22, 2011). A member of the SCC told his colleagues that the security agents were also government officials who, like them, were suffering from low wages. The movement used slogans expressing this theme: "We are your children, we are your brothers" (Ihna wiladkum, ihna ikhwatkum; Eweida 2008, 54). Similar slogans were adopted by protesters in the January 25 uprising in 2011. This was not without effect. Some of the security guards sympathized with them. SCC member Magdy (2011) even claimed that some of the agents encouraged them to continue the movement until they were satisfied. This empathy was reciprocal, and participants in the sit-in invented and chanted slogans expressing their gratitude toward security forces: "Minister of the interior, your men are great!" (Ya wazir al-dakhiliyya, rigaltak miyya miyya!); "Employees of the Ministry of Interior, thank you for this help!" (Ya rigal al-dakhiliyya, shukran ʿala al-waqfa diyya).[9]

In light of the above, I can say that two factors facilitated the organization of the movement and protected the protest against possible crackdowns: first, the ability of the leaders to identify the best way to deal with the constraints that the regime players imposed on them (paradoxically, this ability was a necessary precondition for exploiting the opportunities provided by changes in security strategies); and, second, the ability of the leaders to formulate appropriate strategic and tactical choices. This ability was, at least partially, the result of the movement's previous contentious interactions with regime players. These interactive dynamics provided the movement with the know-how to tactically predict, prevent, and adapt to the pressures regime players were likely to exert.

Dynamics of the Sit-In: Media Impact and Identity-Building

The media provided the movement with considerable political opportunities that the SCC did not hesitate to exploit to the maximum. The protest benefited from extensive coverage in the private press, particularly from *The Ten O'Clock Show*, which enjoyed an audience of several million viewers, and which had, in this case, a huge impact. On the evening of the second day of the employees' sit-in on Hegazy Street, the show presented a report about their demands (Said 2011). During his television interview, Abu Eita stressed the depoliticization of the movement and the justness of the cause. He mentioned that the state refused to pay attention to the RETA employees for twenty years when they asked for their rights. He added that they do not belong to any political party; they are protesting simply because they need this wage increase to keep up with the price increases.[10]

9. "Muwazafu al-dara'ib al-ʿaqariyya yarfudun manh Mugawer muhala lil-tafawud" [The RETA Refuse to Give Mugawer an Opportunity to Negotiate], 2007, *Al-Masry Al-Youm*, December 7, 2007.

10. Adel Al-Dergali, 2007, "Al-ʿashira masa'an . . . mumathil itihad al-ʿumal: ʻfi kul qadiyya ʿama la najid man nufawiduh, wa al-dawla la tasmaʻ" [On *The 10 O'Clock Program*, the Representative of the Federation of Trade Unions Declares: "In Every Crisis

The SCC's media strategy was to present the protest action as being driven by social justice and a question of legitimate rights. Its purpose was to engender favorable public opinion and to promote identity-building within the ranks of the RETA employees. Media coverage was crucial in promoting the movement players' goal of creating interests and identities and in providing them with the tools for a strong discursive presence (Amenta et al. 2014, 302). In their statements to the press, movement leaders and members alike emphasized their poor living conditions as the motive for the protest, claiming a legitimate right to equal pay with their peers.[11] For example, SCC member told *Al-Masry Al-Youm* that he had come with his entire family, and that he would not leave the street without obtaining his rights. He stated that after ten years of work, his salary was 350 EGP. He was not afraid for his child who came with him to the sit-in; in any case, he added, they were going to die. He couldn't buy him meat, and when he could, it was just small pieces.[12] His son Islam became popular in the sit-in because of his chants: "We are not afraid, we will not bend, we will not lower our voices!" (Wala binkhaf, wala bintati, ihna kirihna al-sut al-wati; El-Zahi 2007, 6).

Seeing their colleagues on television protesting and campaigning for their common rights, other employees grew bolder and forgot their reluctance to participate (Said 2011). The SCC's media strategy paid off and facilitated the formation of a shared reading and interpretation of events. Media coverage often enables movement players to identify political interests and identities among the politically disadvantaged (Amenta et al. 2014, 302). In addition, the media managed to supersede the lack of

---

We Can't Find Anyone to Negotiate with and the State Is Deaf"], *Al-Masry Al-Youm*, December 5, 2007.

11. Mahmoud El Zahi, Maha El-Behnasawy, and Darine, 2007, "Hikayat min i'tisam 10 alaf muwaṭin amam maqar hikoumat Nazif" [Stories of the Sit-In of 10,000 Citizens in Front of Nazif's Cabinet], *Al-Masry Al-Youm*, December 6, 2007. The article published a dozen interviews with the employees present at the sit-in. All perceived their protest as a claim to a legitimate right, given the deterioration of their social conditions.

12. Mahmoud El-Zahi, 2007, "Al-tifl Islam ja' li-musharakat waliduh al-i'tisam fathar hatif" [The Child Islam Came with His Father to the Sit-In and Led the Slogan-Chanting], *Al-Masry Al-Youm*, December 6, 2007.

organizational structures. They helped mobilize the RETA and encouraged them to participate in the sit-in and join their colleagues. Said (2011) commented on this:

> You cannot imagine how much the Dream2 TV program helped us. It mobilized networks of employees that had not been able to mobilize. Seeing us on TV, our colleagues were very sympathetic to us and decided to join us the next day.

Therefore, according to Said (2011), a few days later, the number of employees participating in the sit-in reached ten thousand employees, then fifteen thousand during the last three days of the sit-in.

The media provided the movement with a chance to expand its social base. This opportunity was also exploited by the SCC to consolidate its existing support and to guarantee its cohesion. The arrival of other employees at the sit-in raised the morale of the strikers and encouraged them to resist. SCC member Nasser (2011) explained:

> On the third day of our sit-in, colleagues from Qalyubiya phoned me. They had seen us on TV. I immediately turned on the speaker on my cell phone so they could hear the slogans we chanted. They told me they wanted to join us. I asked them not to do it and to wait for my arrival in Qalyubiya. I wanted to organize things, organize the gathering so that we'd arrive at the sit-in together. I wanted to send a strong message of solidarity to the strikers who had been sleeping on the street for several days. We were three hundred employees. In order to raise the morale of my sit-in colleagues, we arrived at the scene with a sign on which I wrote, "The RETA of Qalyubiya have arrived, we are all in solidarity with you!"

According to Nasser (2011), Abu Eita followed the same tactics to maintain the movement's coherence. He stood in the middle of the sit-in, with a microphone, and asked his colleagues to calm down to welcome the new protesters coming from the various governorates: "A hearty welcome to the heroes of Qalyubiya, Minya, Baheira, Port Said, Ismailiya, Sharqiya, and Beni Suef!"

A SCC member added:

> As soon as he mentioned the name of a governorate, the RETA whistled and beat the drums to greet them. They all sang: "Welcome, friends! Welcome, friends!" (Ya habayib bil salama . . . Ya habayib bil salama; Eweida 2008, 47)

In addition, the SCC set up two committees to inform the movement of its media coverage: the media committee, whose role was to review the press daily and to update the movement on developments (Lachapelle 2011, 70–71), and the sit-in radio, which was responsible for announcing the latest news about government reactions to the demands and informing the movement every evening of the statements of solidarity that had been sent to the movement's leaders.[13]

To help the movement persist over time, the subsistence committee was also created to support the protesters during this long sit-in. The employees had only brought food for two or three days. As the sit-in lasted longer, this committee collected 10 EGP from each employee to buy food: mainly bread, beans, and cheese. Similarly, residents of Hegazy Street and adjacent streets occasionally brought meals of *molokheya* and *mahshi* (Egyptian comfort food) to the protesters. The movement members used the restrooms of a local mosque and gas station (Eweida 2008, 50).

The government's response was delayed, despite the losses the state was suffering from the sit-in. According to Abu Eita, this amounted to 300 million EGP, because it was tax season in all the villages ("Muwazafi al-dara'ib" 2007, 6). Except for the unsuccessful attempts of the ETUF, the protesters were initially completely ignored by the government. The minister of finance intervened only on the seventh day, December 9. He went to the headquarters of the Council of Ministers and asked the movement leaders to form a representative delegation to negotiate with him. Kamal Abu Eita ensured that the composition of this delegation was representative geographically and religiously (Nasser 2011). At the meeting with the minister, in which a State Security officer participated, the minister

13. Mostafa Bassiouni and Tamer Abu Azab, 2007, "Ma'nawiyat murtafi'a wa wufud tadamun" [High Morale and Solidarity Delegations], *Al-Dustur*, December 9, 2007.

proposed terminating the sit-in in exchange for receiving a financial reward during the Great Bairam holiday and obtaining partial equality with the Real Estate Foundation in Cairo during the parliamentary debate on the draft property tax law for new buildings. He also promised equal status with the Real Estate Foundation administration in Cairo after the enactment of the new law (Eweida 2008, 44).

The delegation made sure to adopt a democratic process. It informed the minister that it had to consult with protesters before making a final decision. Emad and Abu Eita presented the results of the negotiations to the strikers. A vote was organized, and the result was a unanimous rejection of the offer, which was perceived as only partially meeting their demands (Lachapelle 2011, 74). This means that the RETA movement managed, through the occupancy of this symbolic space in front of the Cabinet, to gradually create a public space for deliberation, which became, in the words of Castells (2015, 11), "a political space, a space for sovereign assemblies to meet and to recover their rights of representation, which have been captured in political institutions predominantly tailored for the convenience of the dominant interests and values." In this sense, this sit-in, which gave a space and an opportunity for the emergence of democratic practices, led to the creation of what Alexander calls (2013) "spheres of dissidence" that include social and physical spaces in which ideas that challenge the dominant order can be formulated, and alternative visions of society can be articulated.

Because of the government's delayed response, the sit-in lasted ten days. Multiple daily interactions created a sense of unity among movement members. This led to the development of another identity-building mechanism: the emergence of networks of trust and social bonds between members acting in this complex social environment. These relationships formed the basis for the development of informal social networks and mutual support (Della Porta and Diani, 2006, 94). Participants identified with their leaders and the wider group through mutual solidarity and the family atmosphere they created. For example, one of the RETA employees became a father of twins during the sit-in. He chose to call one of them Kamal and the other Abu Eita in honor of the movement leader (Bassiouni and Abu Azab 2007, 16). Another left the sit-in for a day to celebrate his engagement. The next day he returned to the sit-in to demonstrate with his colleagues, informing his fiancée that he would give her the traditional wedding present (*al-shabka*) after he became an employee of the Ministry of Finance. His colleagues called him "the Sit-In Groom" (*'aris al-i'tisam*; 16).

The longer the sit-in lasted, the more solidarity grew among group members. Many officials returned home to bring back their families, so they could all participate. The children played together, and the parents of different families helped the children with their studies. Women living in the Giza governorate (not far from Cairo) left the sit-in to cook and return with food (Sabah 2011); similar practices were observed in Mahalla. Others brought small ovens and tried to cook at the demonstration. They ate together and shared bread and daily activities (Eweida 2008, 49). The women also showed solidarity with their diabetic colleagues, who were concerned about leaving the sit-in when they needed to use the bathroom several times an hour. Their friends stood next to them, holding signs to cover them while they relieved themselves in inconspicuous street corners ("Qisat 10,000 muwatin" 2007, 6). As time passed, feelings of being part of a group with a common purpose became stronger. A strong collective with a sense of belonging and comradeship was formed, and members became moral role models for each other, developing a sense of being part of something greater (Jasper 2014, 183). They even felt guilty if they left the sit-in to see their families. One of the employees said that he went home to change his clothes and then immediately came back; he added that he and his colleagues will not go home before their demand for parity was met. They all swore they wouldn't do that. He believed that this crisis brought them all closer to each other—Muslims and Christians, men and women. They all became one body (*Kulluh haymid 'iduh fi tabaq wahid*; Eweida 2008, 45).

The leaders ensured a certain public self-representation, through which the movement displayed its "worthiness, unity, numbers, and commitment" to quote Tilly and Tarrow (2015, 153). This public self-representation reaffirmed the collective unity and persistence of the movement. Consistent with the media message it had put forth, which was based on the claim of a legitimate right to social justice, the SCC introduced the movement members as representatives of all Egyptians, victims of the new economic situation, without distinction of sex or religion (Lachapelle 2011). They all represented a social movement that was completely unified in its claim to parity. A member of the SCC said that at the sit-in, they reaffirmed the sense of national unity: no difference between Christians and Muslims, or between men and women, as they were all going through the same ordeal (Eweida 2008, 50).

As Melucci (1996, 340) indicates, movement leaders have a vital communication task in the process of building a collective identity. They present movement members with the image of an identity that could form a basis for solidarity, identification, and emotional gratification. This was indeed the situation during the RETA sit-in, a fact accentuated and strengthened by the coverage provided in privately owned newspapers. For example, the *Al-Masry Al-Youm* newspaper reported on December 6 that "most women spent the night in the street because the tents could not accommodate them. Yet they felt safe alongside their [male] colleagues, whom they considered their brothers" ("Qisat 10,000 muwatin" 2007, 6). In an article published by *Al-Masry Al-Youm*, Samir Ghattas, a writer who lived in a nearby building, also stressed the role of women in this sit-in: "Hundreds of women participated in this sit-in. Some of them spent all ten nights on the ground with their colleagues. Most contributed significantly to the survival of the sit-in in terms of food and daily needs. Similarly, among these women, leaders emerged who participated in the leadership, including the chanting of slogans."[14]

The unity between Christians and Muslims was praised and represented visually on signs showing an interlocking cross and crescent (Bassiouni and Abu Azab 2007, 16). This unity was also affirmed during Friday prayers, in which all employees participated. The preacher said, "Strikers, Muslims and Christians, be patient and persevere!" (Eweida 2008, 45). The motto of the movement that strengthened its cohesion, and of which its members were very proud was "Resistance as a sign of

14. Samir Ghattas, 2007, "Al-durus al-sab'a al-mustafada min i'tisam al-dara'ib al-'aqariyya" [The 7 Lessons of the Sit-In of the Real Estate Tax Collector], *Al-Masry al-Youm*, December 17, 2007.

honesty."[15] The preacher echoed this sentiment as he stated that they all came here to spend nights on the streets and in the cold in order to claim their rights, because they do not want to disobey Allah by stealing or being corrupt. Claiming one's rights was much more honorable than corruption (Eweida 2008, 45).

The government's response came only on the night of the tenth and final day, December 12. State Security generals phoned Kamal Abu Eita and Emad and informed them that the minister had accepted their demand for parity and asked them to meet with him (Said 2011). State Security representatives were the main mediators between the protesters and the ministry. Kamal Abu Eita formed a geographically representative delegation of fifteen employees, who met with the minister at the Institute of Tax Collectors, attached to the Ministry of Finance (Shaaban 2008, 39). As soon as they arrived, the minister told them that he was receiving them here in their home, confirming his agreement to their joining the Ministry of Finance. He added that he would meet all their demands, gradually but quickly: first, they would be upgraded to the level of their peers in the Cairo administration by the beginning of January 2008; second, a bonus of two months' salary would be paid to all employees of the administration on the occasion of the Grand Bayram; third, their financial rights relating to parity were to be transmitted to them gradually, at a premium rate of 316 percent of the initial salary, which was given to them that very day (December 13, 2007), as well as a bonus rate of 651 percent of the initial salary, which would be given to them in 2011.[16] To give an idea of the salary increase that RETA employees managed to acquire in a rather exceptional manner during the Mubarak era, Said, who had been an employee of the RETA for some thirty years, was earning a salary of 600 EGP ($86.50) in 2007. Thanks to the movement's success, his salary more than quadrupled, reaching 3,500 EGP ($505 at that time; Said 2011).

15. Kamal Abu Eita: "Last year, 62 employees committed suicide because of poverty. To survive, the RETA were forced to choose between corruption, bribery, hunger, or suicide. However, we chose another way: activism for our rights." See Eweida 2008, 46.

16. It should be noted that the employees were expecting another wage increase in 2013 (Said 2011).

By analyzing detailed interactions, and the choices various players make during them, we are able to glean a fully dynamic vision of how protests unfold (Jasper 2015a, 23). In this case, the government's choice of "ignoring" the protestors, to quote Bishara (2018, 73) for ten days provided the movement with opportunities to expand and consolidate a collective identity. Collective identity is defined by McGarry and Jasper (2015, 1–2) as "an act of the imagination, a trope that stirs people to action by arousing feelings of solidarity with their fellows and by defining moral boundaries against other categories. It involves both cognition and emotions and can ultimately be traced to the universal human need for attachments to others."

Most of these opportunities were the approximate result of the players/actors' choices and their interactions (Jasper 2011, 17). In other words, the government's choice facilitated the formation of two dynamics favorable to the movement: a broadened media interest, which generated greater solidarity among employees, widening the movement's social base, and the development of a collective identity for the RETA employees, who were previously geographically dispersed. Coming from different governorates, many of them met for the first time in Hegazy Street. As Yuen (2018) asserts, "The place of protest not only provides the spatial foundation for mobilization, but also shapes the groups' collective identity by offering the cultural and symbolic resources for assembling disconnected individuals for an extended period of time and to transform them into new political agencies." Because they were being neglected and left in the street during this period, they managed to share an experience of collective solidarity and to forge strong personal bonds, thus gradually transforming themselves into a united and organized group.

As Tilly and Tarrow (2015, 99) explain, contentious episodes that bring together players who know little or nothing of one another at the outset can lead them, through their interaction and participation in this contentious action, to form a unified actor with an identity, "with boundaries separating them from others, and with a set of unified claims that they put forward against significant targets. In doing so, they become collective political actors." In this sense, the contention between the movement and the regime players led to the formation of a sort of collective consciousness in the form of a commonly shared interpretation of the movement, its interests, and how to achieve them (Taylor and Whittier 1992, 111).

This will be explained in more detail in the next section, which looks at the building of an independent union thanks to the collective identity built during these protests. As McGarry and Jasper (2015, 2) comment: "There is always a great deal of *identity work* within movements that creates, sustains, and transforms identities. Structural positions are never as structural as they seem."

The Construction of an Independent Union: "Political Careers" and the SCC Strategy

In a corporatist state system, the construction of an independent trade union is particularly interesting because of the challenges it presents to the very foundations of this system and its key players. It is generally detrimental to the interests of players who benefit from its perpetuation (in this case, the ETUF), and it opens up possibilities for similar acts to follow. For example, Farouk Shehata, president of the Banking and Insurance Union (affiliated with the ETUF), said in a meeting with the chairpersons of the RETA committees on September 16, 2008, that the main goal in creating this independent trade union was to dispense with the official union. He asked them to be careful and to confront such an initiative forcefully (*bi-hazm*). He also added that the official trade union organization (ETUF) refused trade union pluralism, which, he asserted was not in the interests of the workers/employees.[17] Kamal Abbas, director of Dar al-Khadamat, made statements along similar lines in the *Al-Badil* newspaper on December 22, 2008: that the creation of the RETA trade union is an historic event, the first step toward the deconstruction of trade union authoritarianism. He believed that this initiative would open the door to building other

17. Ibrahim Gaballah, 2008, "Niqabat al-bunuk tuhazir lijan al-dara'ib al-ʿaqariyya min al-taʿamul maʿ al-munazamat al-mustaqilla" [The Banking Union Threatens Trade Union Committees with Contacting Independent Organizations], *Rose-al-Youssef*, September 18, 2008.

independent unions.[18] This is exactly what happened following the 2011 uprising in Egypt, as hundreds of "independent trade unions" emerged out of the framework of the ETUF.

The movement leaders were fully aware of the difficulties they might encounter while deciding to establish this union. They were aware, in particular, that this act constituted a challenge to regime players, and that they would consequently be subject to security pressures. They also believed that it was likely to be badly received by members of the movement, who could fear that it would lead to further repression. Moreover, they knew there would be difficulties in establishing and running it in practice, given the legal and logistical challenges and the geographical dispersion of civil servants. As such, these leaders made a strategic choice during a key period in the movement's history that would change its trajectory. The decision to form a union representing the RETA required an active choice, since other options were also possible, such as the dissolution of the SCC. The discussions actually focused on two options: either to attempt to reform the ETUF (the corporatist structure), or to establish an independent union out of it.[19] The Strike Coordinating Committee issued a statement on May 14, 2008, declaring the establishment of an independent union.[20] As indicated by Jasper (2014, 69), "Creating change is possible when someone suddenly sees the tradeoff as a choice point, when there are two or more different options, generating the possibility to do something different." Accordingly, on December 20, 2008, the RETA leaders organized a conference at the Journalists' Union (Niqabit al-sahafiyyin) to celebrate the formation

18. "Niqabiyun: ta'sis niqaba mustaqilla muwazafi al-qariya khatwa li-tafkik al-istibdad al-siyasi" [Unionists: "The Foundation of The Real Estate Tax Collector Union Is a Step toward the Deconstruction of Political Authoritarianism"], 2008, *Al-Badil*, December 22, 2008.

19. Azza Khalil, 2009, "Halaqat niqash hawl al-niqaba al-mustaqilla lil-dara'ib al-'aqariyya ka-tajruba lil-ta'adudiyya al-niqabiyya" [Roundtable Discussion on the Independent Trade Union as an Example of Trade Union Pluralism], *Tadamon Masr*, June 12, 2009.

20. Laila Nureldine, 2008, "Muwazafi al-dara'ib al-'aqariyya bada'u khatawat al-i'lan 'an niqaba 'ama badila" [The RETA Have Taken the First Steps Leading to the Declaration of an Alternative General Union], *Al-Badil*, May 16, 2008.

of a union with democratically elected leadership. According to *Al-Badil*, 10,000 RETA employees participated in this event. The celebration began with the election of a founding or union executive committee and the fourteen local committees that were formed in the governorates.[21] According to Abu Eita, who was elected president of the union ("Muwazafu al-dara'ib al-'aqariyya" 2008, 5), 27,060 civil servants joined.[22]

The biographies and "political careers" of the movement leaders are key to explaining their choices and decisions during contentious episodes (Jasper 2014, 184–85; Jasper 2015a, 12). As mentioned in the previous chapter, many of them had some history of political activism in oppositional political parties. Kamal Abu Eita was active in the ranks of the Nasserist Karama Party, Said and Nasser in the left-wing Al-Tajammu' Party. For some of the leaders of the Strike Coordinating Committee, this strategic choice regarding the creation of an independent union was part of a political vision that envisaged broader sociopolitical changes (Bishara 2018). Accordingly, creating an independent trade union had to contribute to changing relations between the regime and the working class and to thereby inducing wider political change. The success of the December 2007 sit-in was thus seen as an opportunity to define a more ambitious political agenda. Some leaders criticized historical political organization, considering activists to be disconnected from society and largely elitist. This was expressed by Nasser (2011), a member of the SCC:

> After several years in the Al-Tajammu' Party, I realize today that political activism alone cannot achieve political change. The experience I had during the sit-in and the gains we managed to achieve showed me that organizing society "from the bottom up" was more important—all the more so because we, as political elites, had lost touch with it. I was aware of the consequences that this decision could probably cause: entering into

21. "Muwazafu al-dara'ib al-'aqariyya yu'linun ta'sis awal niqaba mustaqilla munzu 50 'am" [The RETA Declare the Founding of the First Independent Union in 50 Years]," 2008, *Al-Badil*, December 20, 2008.

22. Mahmoud Sabra, 2009, "27.060 'udw min niqabat al-dara'ib al-'aqariyya al-mustaqila" [27,060 Members of the Independent Union of the Real Estate Tax Collectors], *Al-Arabi Al-Nasseri*, April 26, 2009.

> direct and prolonged conflict with the regime. However, succeeding in forming this union not only guarantees the recovery of the rest of our financial rights, it is also the first step to reunite the working class in Egypt.

In the same vein, another movement leader stated:

> I used to be involved in politics, but realized that political activism did not achieve anything. In my experience in the RETA movement, I could see gains every day, tangible gains on the ground. When I saw other independent unions emerge, I became convinced that organizing society from below was more important, and that political elites have lost touch with society. (Interview cited in Bishara 2018, 97)

Along these lines, Abu Eita also stated that the movement managed to win, but it was still not enough. He wanted to continue to advocate for the rest of the employees' financial rights. He also wanted to challenge state policies that went against the interests of employees in general (Shaaban 2008, 40).

The SCC thus put in place a strategy based on the essential elements of developing a narrative premised on the importance of remaining united through the establishment of the new union—with the aim of transforming movements members' potential fears into opportunities—and maintaining the bonds that were forged between members of the movement, and between movements, to prevent demobilization during the process (Bishara 2018).

This narrative entailed three types of framing, linking the financial interests of movement members to the initiative and converting their fears into a willingness to seize rising opportunities and to fight. In the first two framing alignment processes, movement leaders resorted to *frame amplification*, while, in the last one, they resorted to *frame transformation*. Snow and Benford (2000, 264) define "frame amplification" as a process involving the idealization, embellishment, clarification, or invigoration of existing values or beliefs, while "frame transformation" refers to changing old understandings and meanings and/or generating new ones (625).

Leaders thus posited the creation of the union as the only way of sustaining a united entity that was powerful enough to exert pressure on the government to deliver on its promises. Maintaining unity was amplified, and presented, as the only guarantee that the government would respect its commitments and carry out the other stages of the agreement. In fact, this framing proved to find great resonance with members. As Morris and Staggenborg (2004, 184) argue, leaders who have a strong relationship with their base within the movement are likely to formulate more credible and resonant framings. This framing resonated with employees—not just because it echoed their collective experience, but because its credibility was confirmed by their success.

As SCC member Moheb (2011) said:

> As the government fulfilled the demands of the movement . . . the number of employees wanting to join the new union increased.

The same idea was developed by Said (2011), a member of the SCC:

> The employees were crying with joy when they saw the salary increase. This confirmed the conviction of the members who had participated in the sit-in that the unification of the movement is the only guarantee that their future demands would be fulfilled.

The employees who did not participate in the sit-in shared this understanding and felt it was important to be part of this emerging union. They felt guilty for benefiting from all of the gains without having provided any effort. Joining the union was a way to compensate for this. Lotfia (2011), a leading member of the founding committee of the independent trade union and a representative of the trade union committee in Cairo, said:

> Cairo employees did not participate in the sit-in because their financial situation was better than that of employees working in other governorates. I was the only one to do it because activism is part of who I am. As soon as my colleagues in Cairo saw the gains the movement made, and the increase they themselves received without any effort from them, they decided to join the new union. About 2,440 out of 2,700 employees joined all at once. Moreover, the employees in Cairo would play an important role in pressuring the minister of labor to accept the new union's credentials.

The second framing consisted of amplifying the *boundary* already established between the movement and the ETUF. The aim was to strengthen this dividing line between the movement as a separate entity with leaders capable of defending its interests and to stress that the official union was not only unable to do so, but was in fact hostile to these interests. As they carried out their work of persuading others, the movement leaders always emphasized the behavior of the ETUF throughout the contention, especially during their previous sit-in, which was carried out in front of the ETUF headquarters. A SCC member's statements to *Al-Badil* on December 20, 2008, bore witness to this, as he asserted that the official union espoused the regime's position to violate their rights. ETUF's leaders even threatened the employees when they took the initiative to organize a sit-in. They left them on the street and closed the building's restrooms. They did everything to prevent them from receiving their rights, even though they paid a monthly fee to this institution. It was the SCC that gained the employees trust and managed to meet their demands, not this union, which was allied with the state. Therefore, they must continue.[23]

The third framing consisted of transforming and changing the old assertions of regime players that founding new unions was an illegal act into demonstrating that they were legal and totally legitimate (Bishara 2018, 103). The importance of persuading movement members of the legality and legitimacy of establishing a new union was explained by Nasser (2011), leading member of the SCC:

> Having a strong legal and legitimate basis was a very important tool in our work of persuading our colleagues, convincing them to join this union, because most of them refused to take a risk. We know very well that our colleagues want to feel that they are in no way against the law and that the creation of an independent union is as legitimate a demand as that of parity.

Therefore, the SCC sought to found a legal and legitimate alternative to Law 35 of the year 1976, which governed trade union affairs in Egypt, and its amendments in Law 12 of the year 1995.[24] This law banned freedom

23. *Al-Badil*, December 20, 2008.

24. "Waqa'i' mu'tamar al-'amal al-dawli al-sabi' w al-tis'in, al-hala al-masriyya" [The Events of the International Labor Conference Number 97, the Case of Egypt], *Dar El-Khadamat El-Nikabeya Wal Omaleyia*.

of association, stipulating that in order to acquire a legal identity, any new trade union organization must submit an application for membership to the ETUF (in addition to an application for accreditation to the Ministry of Labor). The legal alternatives sought were: Article 56 of the Egyptian Constitution of 1971, which upholds the right to freedom of association and the constitution of trade unions, making Law 35 governing union affairs therefore unconstitutional; international agreements guaranteeing freedom of association, especially Convention 87 of 1948, which guarantees freedom of organization,[25] and the protection of the right to organize; and Convention 98 of 1949, which also guarantees freedom of organization and collective bargaining.[26] These conventions were ratified by Egypt in 1957 and 1954, respectively.[27] Moreover, Article 8.2 of Convention 87 stipulates that national legislation shall not affect the guarantees provided for in this Convention.[28] The SCC would thus insist that these conventions, signed by the Egyptian state, invalidate Law 35 of 1976, and they would therefore consider it sufficient to file an application for accreditation to the Ministry of Labor to acquire a legal identity (Lachapelle 2011, 81). This means that the movement leaders worked on transforming the movement members' beliefs about the act of building a new union, from an illegal and illegitimate act that is unconstitutional into a legal and legitimate action. The movement leaders thus succeeded through their narratives and framing in transforming the threats the movement members feared into challenges to the regime players.

25. For more information, see the articles of Convention 87 of the year 1948: International Labor Organization, http://www.ilo.org/dyn/normlex/en/f?p=NORMLEXPUB:12100:0::NO:12100:P12100_ILO_CODE:C087 (accessed August 21, 2024).

26. For more information, see the articles of Convention 98 of the year 1949: International Labor Organization, http://www.ilo.org/dyn/normlex/en/f?p=NORMLEXPUB:12100:0::NO:12100:P12100_ILO_CODE:C098 (accessed August 21, 2024).

27. For more information, see Egypt's List of Ratifications of ILO Conventions: http://webfusion.ilo.org/public/applis/appl-byCtry.cfm?lang=ENandCTYCHOICE=0690 (accessed August 21, 2024).

28. For more information, see the articles of Convention 87 of the year 1948: http://www.ilo.org/dyn/normlex/en/f?p=NORMLEXPUB:12100:0::NO:12100:P12100_ILO_CODE:C087 (accessed August 21, 2024).

This work of persuasion—affirming the legality as well as the importance of the union—led to the foundation of a committee, which the SCC called "the Awareness Committee" (*lajnit taw'iya*). The role of the committee was to visit the various governorates, such as Alexandria, Beni Suef, Daqhliya, Baheira, and Ismailiya and to explain to the employees what an "independent trade union" meant, because the concept itself was completely new to them (*Al-Badil* 2008, 5); and to organize symposiums in the different governorates to explain to the employees the importance of founding the union and give proves for its legitimacy. In these symposiums, they also responded to the ETUF's counterframing, which sought to delegitimize their purpose (Nasser 2011).

In addition, the SCC accorded a lot of time and importance to maintaining the cohesion of the movement, strengthening the bonds of solidarity that had been formed and working to further consolidate this collective identity. This was all the more important since the geographical dispersion of the movement constituted a risk. Several initiatives aimed specifically at maintaining the vertical and horizontal relationships that had been formed during the sit-in were introduced by the SCC. For example, every two weeks, members of the SCC (and, later, those of the new union executive committee) in a particular governorate organized a small meeting and invited the other governorates to participate in it to exchange the latest news about the creation of the union (Moneim 2011). Movement leader Moneim (2011) said that the movement's members had welcomed the initiative, the proof being that they were paying for travel expenses out of their own pockets. In addition, the SCC launched a nonperiodical review, of which three issues were published before December 20, 2008. This initiative aimed to make members of the movement aware of the new union's achievements, particularly in terms of new memberships, and maintain the link between the SCC and the movement's base (*Al-Badil* 2008, 5).

From what follows, it seems clear that two factors motivated and facilitated the process of forming the independent union: the politicization of some of the movement's leaders, who exploited the opportunity of the movement's victory to achieve their broader sociopolitical agenda; and the leaders' agency during this contentious process and their formulation of narratives that transformed risks the into opportunities that the movement should seize to maintain its power. As stated by Ganz and McKenna (2019, 190–91), "Leadership narrative is a source of individual and collective agency." Through their formulation of a resonant framing for their new initiative of establishing an independent union, the leaders were able to take advantage of this newly formed collective identity and thus convinced the movement's members to join the new union. These narratives and framings empowered the leaders to confront what Jasper (2014, 98) refers to as the "innovation dilemma," a prevalent challenge encountered by movement players during strategic interactions as they strive to push the boundaries of established norms. Simultaneously, they must persuade their followers of the importance and justification for doing so.

The Dilemma of Government Recognition: The Dynamics of Contentious and Strategic Interaction

Having succeeded in collecting 27,060 signatures of support, the SCC then had to attempt to acquire the regime's recognition of the union. This involved acquiring a legal identity by obliging the minister of labor to accept the union's credentials, and getting the Ministry of Finance to recognize the union as a representative of the state employees of the RETA. In other words, they had to convince the minister of finance to grant the union access to the funds designated for the employees' retirement pay and their social security.

The SCC met several times in Cairo to define the best strategy to implement in order to persuade the minister of labor to accept the accreditation papers. Movement players often face the dilemma of pitting safe against risky options (Jasper 2014, 212–13). Abu Eita explained that the movement had two options to choose between: either to deposit the union's foundation papers indirectly through a bailiff's declaration, or to organize a demonstration in front of the office of the minister of labor at the very moment of the presentation of the union's credentials to the authorities (Bishara 2018, 101). The second option was chosen. One of the movement leaders explained the reasons behind the choice:

> We felt that the first option was the riskiest because it increased the minister's chances of finding excuses to reject these papers. That's why we decided to opt for the second. (Interview cited in Bishara, 2018, 101)

Nevertheless, during this process of reflection, an opportunity arose: Abu Eita learned that a mission of the Committee of Experts of the International Labor Organization (ILO) would pay a visit to the Minister of Labor on April 21, 2009. He seized this opportunity to increase pressure on the minister. As SCC member Said (2011) explained:

> Our accreditation papers were ready, but we changed the deadline for submission of the accreditation application when Abu Eita learned through his contacts that the expert committee would be in Egypt on April 21st.

Since some choices are tough, players work hard to back their opponents into a position in which their options are limited (Jasper 2015a, 20). The choice of a politically propitious moment limited de facto the marge of maneuver of the regime players, which was crucial in securing the union's legalization. The submission date for the application for accreditation was not chosen at random. An SCC member explained that the presentation of union papers on the day of the ILO commission's arrival required the political genius of someone like Abu Eita (Lachapelle 2011, 83).

The ILO delegation's visit in April 2009 was planned around the discussion of the Egyptian government's compliance with international standards concerning respect for workers' rights and trade union freedoms, and the possibility of providing technical support with respect to this issue. Moreover, the delegation's visit to Egypt took place in a general context of international pressure on the government over labor issues. In December 2008, the secretary general of the International Trade Union Confederation (ITUC) sent a letter to the Egyptian government supporting the new union and objecting to the difficulties it had faced in becoming established. The letter called for the removal of all obstacles to the union's freedom and the implementation of the ILO Committee of Experts' recommendations, presented in its report of June 2008.[29]

Once the submission date for the accreditation papers was decided, the leaders chose to demonstrate in front of the ministry of labor in order

29. "Al-itihad al-dawli yu'lin tadamunuh ma' niqabat al-dara'ib al-'aqariyya" [The International Federation Declares Itself in Solidarity with the RETA Syndicate], 2008, *Al-Badil*, December 23, 2008.

to increase the pressure on them. About five hundred employees, mostly members of the union's general assembly, participated in this event. Many were employees of the RETA administration in Cairo. They chanted: "Our independent union against an administration that exploits us!" (Niqabitna al-mustaqilla did idara mustaghilla).[30] In response to this pressure, the minister came out to meet the employees and take the papers from them herself ("Muwazafi al-dara'ib" 2009, 5). She accepted the document and was impressed by the work done by the union. I recall that it had managed to recruit about twenty-seven thousand members. Satisfied, the ILO delegation told *Al-Masry Al-Youm* that it considered the ministry of labor's acceptance of the RETA unions' papers as the first step toward democracy and respect for international standards of labor law.[31]

As the movement leaders had succeeded in their battle over legalization of the new union, they moved quickly to the second step of acquiring access to pension and social security funds. On July 6, 2009, representatives of the RETA union met with the deputy minister of finance, the president of the RETA administration, and an assistant minister of finance to negotiate. On July 27, the minister of finance agreed to provide access to the funds. He enacted Decree 425/2009, legalizing the right of the independent trade union to these funds.[32] This meant that the independent trade union was now recognized by the government as representing the employees of the RETA and being responsible for financing the retirement and social security of its members.

30. "Muwazafi al-dara'ib al-'aqariyya yukadimoun awraq awil nikaba mustakila fe masr" [The RETA Employees Present the Papers for the First Independent Trade Union in Egypt], 2009, *Al-Masry Al-Youm*, April 22, 2009.

31. Mohamed Azouz, 2009a, "Ba'that al-'amal al-dawliyya taltaqi munazamat al-mujtama' al-madani ba'idan 'an al-hukuma wa tataraqab al-mowafaqa 'ala niqabet al-dara'ib al-'aqariyya" [The Labor Organization Delegation Meets with Nongovernmental Organizations without the Government and Awaits the Approval of the RETA Union], *Al-Masry Al-Youm*, April 23, 2009.

32. "Wazir al-maliyya yasdur qararan bi-ta'sis sanduq al-ri'aya al-ijtima'iyya lil-'amilin bil dara'ib al-'aqariyya" [The Minister of Finance Publishes a Decision Conferring Social Funds to the Real Estate Tax Collector], 2009, *Al-Akhbar Al-Masriyya*, August 8, 2009.

Nevertheless, since the announcement of the creation of the independent union in December 2008, and its legalization in April 2009 with the filing of its accreditation papers, the ETUF and the Banking and Insurance Union (affiliated with it) fought against it.

Contentious actions against the independent union's representatives followed two repertoires of action: first, with attempts to delegitimize the new union, insisting on the unlawful nature of its creation, in violation of Law 35, and on the international support it received as a sign of foreign intrusion into Egyptian affairs. Mugawer, the head of the ETUF, told *Al-Masry Al-Youm* on December 22, 2008, that the law governing trade union affairs banned the creation of trade unions outside the framework of the ETUF, which had the exclusive recognition of the government and international organizations. He added that the international support for the independent union proved that it was working for foreign interests to the detriment of the country's interests.[33] A few days before the independent union celebrated its first birthday, on December 22, Mugawer said that although Abu Eita was a trade unionist on the political left, he had agreed to throw himself into the arms of the United States, who currently finances his new union.[34]

Second, there were attempts to exert administrative and security pressures on the representatives of the new union. The president of the Banking and Insurance Syndicate took advantage of his contacts with the directors of RETA administrations in the different governorates, and with State Security agents, to exert security pressure on the independent union's representatives (Nasser 2011). The main targets were the employees trying

33. Mohamed Azouz and Amr Abd El Halim, 2008, "Mujawir: niqabat muwazafi al-dara'ib al-'aqariyya kharija 'an al-qanun wa lan na'tarif bi-sha'riyattuha'" [Mugawer: "The Real Estate Tax Collector Union Is Violating the Law and We Will Not Recognize Its Legitimacy"], *Al-Masry Al-Youm*, December 22, 2008.

34. This statement was made on December 17, 2009, during a press conference following the meeting of the Board of Directors of ETUF. "Mujawir yatahim Abu Eita bil-irtima' fi ahdan America wa sariqat al-adwa' min qadat idrab al-dara'ib al-'aqariyya" [Mugawer Accuses Abu Eita of Falling into the Arms of the United States and Stealing the Show from the Leaders of the Property Tax Officials' Movement], 2009, *Al-Wafd*, December 18, 2009.

to form new union committees in governorates that did not have official union representations, such as Qalyubiya, Menufiya, Luxor, and Aswan. Nasser (2011), for example, said that in 2007–8, during the process of construction and legalization of the independent trade union, he was interrogated thirty times by the prosecutor's office (*Al-niqaba al-idariyya*) or by State Security. They attempted to intimidate him, hoping that he would give up and withdraw. In most of the governorates where official union committees already existed, like Beni Suef, there were conflicts between new and old unions. According to Moheb (2011), who had been ousted from the official union committee elections in 2006, members of the official trade union asked the State Security agents to confiscate the petition forms he tried to have his colleagues sign in support of the creation of the independent union.

The conflict worsened as a result of the finance minister's decision to provide the new union with access to pension and social security funds. The ETUF considered this act a direct threat to its monopoly over trade union representation. In addition, the control of funds made the new union attractive to its members. The issue was so vital that the repertoire of tactics against the new union evolved into a direct counterattack to deprive the latter of any governmental recognition.

The president of the ETUF explicitly used his position—as president of the only trade union federation in Egypt—to pressure the minister of finance to go back on his decision. On August 6, 2009, *Al-Masry Al-Youm* reported that Mugawer had sent a letter to the minister of finance listing all the legal and constitutional violations that the ministry had allegedly committed. Mugawer asserted that the minister's recognition of an "illegitimate union" that positioned itself outside the official trade union organization was in complete violation of the law.[35] On August 10, the minister of finance retracted and published an amendment of the decree:

35. "Istiya' bayn a'da' al-niqaba al-mustaqila lil-'amilin bil-dara'ib al-'aqariyya bisabab muhawalat al-maliyya ihlal niqabat al-bunuk wa al-ta'minat mahal niqabathum" [Frustration within the Independent Real Estate Tax Collector Union Because of the Banks and Insurance Union's Attempts to Take Its Place], 2009, *Al-Dustur*, August 7, 2009.

"Correction of an Error in the Decree 425/2009." The term "independent trade union" was replaced by "the general banks and insurance companies union (affiliated with the ETUF)."[36] In other words, the general banks and insurance companies union would be entitled to the pension and social security funds while the negotiations concerning these funds were carried out exclusively by the independent trade union of the RETA.[37] Mugawer and Shehata also lodged a complaint with the attorney general against Abu Eita, accusing him of violating Law 35 governing trade union affairs by founding a union outside the framework of the official trade union organization. They also accused him of presiding over an illegal entity.[38]

Moreover, Mugawer tried to divide the ranks of the RETA movement by seeking to coopt some of them into the ETUF. He proposed the creation of the twenty-fourth union within the ETUF. This new union would exclusively represent the RETA, as well as the customs employees (Niqabit al-'amilin bil-dara'b w al-gamarik).[39] The creation of this new union was, as we can see, an attempt to re-co-opt the RETA under the auspices of the ETUF. From the beginning of 2009, Mugawer had stated many times that there might be a twenty-fourth union. For example, he told *Al-Badil*

36. "Wazir al-maliyya yakhtuf nidal muwazafi al-dara'ib al-'aqariyya" [The Minister of Finance Steals (the Benefits of) the RETA Protests], 2009, *Al-Akhbar Al-Masriyya*, August 11, 2009.

37. The same day, Shehata sent a letter to the governorate RETA administrations that did not have union committees, asking them to help create them. He stated that the receipt of social funds would be reserved exclusively for the employees of the RETA belonging to the banking and insurance syndicate. See "Ra'is niqabat al-ta'minat al-rasimyya yutalib al-dara'ib al-'aqariyya yuqri al-'amilin 'ala 'udwiyyat niqabatahu" [President of the Banking and Insurance Union Obliges Officials to Be Part of His Union], 2009, *Al-Dustur*, April 10, 2009.

38. Dina Gamil, 2009b, "Al-tahqiq ma' naqib al-dara'ib al-'aqariyya wa itihamat bi-'adam shar'iyat al-niqaba" [Inquiry with One of the Members of the Independent Union and Accusations of Illegality], *Al-Shorouk*, September 11, 2009.

39. Technically, this would lead to the division of the Banking and Insurance Syndicate (to which the employees of the RETA were previously affiliated) into two separate entities: the Union of the Public Bank and Insurance employees, and the Union of General Taxes, Land, and Customs.

on March 16, 2009, that he wanted the RETA to adhere to this union.[40] On August 8, 2009, Mugawer told *Al-Masry Al-Youm* that he was setting up a technical committee, whose role would be to prepare the procedures for the creation of the 24th union.[41] These statements carried weight, as the ETUF sought to transfer the pension and social security funds to this union. The strategy of the ETUF was to deprive the independent trade union of its real raison d'être, recognition and access to pension and social security funds, and this would be accomplished by offering a potentially more viable and attractive option.

The president of the ETUF tried to convince two of the SCC members, who were also members of the official trade union committee in Daqhliya and Giza, to disassociate themselves from their colleagues and participate in the construction of the twenty-fourth union. The two leaders who actually embraced this initiative, thus agreeing to work under the umbrella of the ETUF, were Emad, a leading member of the official trade union committee and member of the Karama Nasserite party (with Abu Eita), and Hamdy, a member of the official trade union committee of the Giza governorate and of the NDP. Emad and Hamdy were not convinced by the idea of an independent union. They viewed it as unrealistic, given the possible repression by the security apparatus, and saw its creation as being indicative of the politicization of the movement's demands, which they both refuted, for different reasons. They considered Abu Eita and the SCC's push for the creation of an independent union to be outside the framework of the type of social activism they accepted, which centered strictly on the acquisition of their financial rights (such as the claim of parity). These disagreements converge with the analysis provided by McGarry and Jasper (2015, 10) with regard to the process of negotiating collective identities and the rifts that may occur during such process: "In the process of negotiating collective identity, protesters contest the purpose,

40. Hamada Al-Khashef, 2009, "Mugawer yu'lin 'awdat niqabat al-dara'ib al-'aqariyya al-mustaqilla li-itihad al-'umal" [Mugawer Announces the Return of the RETA Union to the ETUF], *Al-Badil*, March 16, 2009.

41. *Al-Masry Al-Youm*, August 8, 2009.

activities, and substance of the movement, so dilemmas can and will present themselves. The risks of internal conflict are obvious, because they can uncover or create irreconcilable disagreements over goals, tactics. One form of internal disagreement, even within relatively accepted collective identities, revolves around tastes in tactics."

In this respect, both leaders considered this new initiative to be political, coming from a position that was explicitly opposed to the regime players, and using tactics that challenged their power. Emad explained his point of view:

> The Abu Eita union is not an independent union because it will always be dependent on the state in terms of recognition and funding. Otherwise, why does it need the recognition of the minister of labor? Why has he negotiated with the minister of finance to acquire pension and social security funds? (Interview with author, August 25, 2009)

He added:

> The current political situation does not permit us to create this union. We are living in a security state (Dawla bulisiyya) and an authoritarian regime (Nizam sultawi). We won't be allowed to create a union independent of the state. In addition, creating this union implies the ability to compel civil servants to campaign against the state. I am sure that they are not prepared to do so because they are overwhelmed by difficult socioeconomic conditions.

Hamdy's vision reveals a patriarchal logic:

> The state has procured us our rights. We protest because we were deprived of our rights. That is why I called on my colleagues to fight for parity. Now that the state has satisfied our demands, what we should do is thank it and not seek to oppose it. (Interview with author, August 25, 2009)

The opinions of these two leaders, especially Hamdy, fall within the framework of the moral economy: to legitimize the regime and adhere to a patriarchal and clientelist relation with it in return for the economic privileges it provides. This also reveals the significance of the agency of the other movement leaders who initiated the independent trade union, particularly their ability to challenge the structural constraints that limited them.[42]

To counter pressure from the ETUF, the independent union determined to intensify external and internal pressure on regime players. Its strategy was based on a set of components: for example, seeking international recognition to embarrass the government and protect the nascent union (Bishara 2018, 118). "Players assess the strengths and weaknesses of their opponents, trying to identify tactics that will take advantage of those weak spots: the right key" (Jasper 2014, 68). One of the movement's leaders and a member of the SCC argued:

> Outside influence helped. The state was worried about its image abroad. The request to join PSI was accepted on April 23, 2009, and it helped not only in depositing the paperwork but in confronting later attacks on us. (Interview cited in Bishara 2018, 118)

Thus, just after filing the independent union's credentials in April 2009, Abu Eita sent an application for membership to the International Trade Union Confederation (ITUC) and The Public Service International (PSI).[43] On April 25, 2009, the PSI accepted the union's request. The decision was taken at its annual meeting in Switzerland between April 22 and 24,[44] although the banking and insurance union was also a member of the PSI.[45]

42. This also confirms their possession of a sociopolitical agenda for change from below beyond the strictly economic framework to which all the labor protests during that span of time adhered (2004–11).

43. The Public Services International (PSI) is an international trade union federation of about 20 million workers in the public service sector. It comprises 600 unions in more than 150 countries. It has observer status with specialized United Nations agencies, such as the UN Conference on Trade and Development (UNCTAD) and the UN Conference on Education and Culture (UNESCO).

44. Dina Gamil, 2009a, "I'tiraf dawli biniqabat al-dara'ib al-'aqariyya al-mustaqila" [International Recognition of the Independent Union of the Real Estate Tax Collectors], *Al-Shorouk*, April 26, 2009.

45. Mostafa Bassiouni, 2009b, "Al-itihad al-dawli li-'mal al-khadamat yubligh niqabat al-'qariya al-mustaqilla bi-qubul 'udwiyatahum: marhaban bikum" [The International Federation of Service Workers Informs the Independent Union of RETA of the Acceptance of Their Membership: Welcome], *Al-Dustur*, June 12, 2009.

The admission of the RETA union to this international federation made it the first union outside the ETUF to acquire this recognition since 1957.[46] Kamal Abbas, director of the CTUWS, confirmed that this membership increased pressure on regime players because the rejection of an internationally recognized trade union will place them in a difficult situation (Gamil 2009a, 3).

Without a doubt, membership in the IFS, as of April 23, 2009, provided and represented concrete support for the new union in its struggle. The movement leader added:

> The fact that we joined the PSI helped us in many ways. On one occasion, I was transferred for investigation along with some colleagues. The PSI sent a memorandum. On another occasion, Kamal Anu Eita was transferred for questioning. The PSI sent a letter to Mubarak regarding Egypt's international obligations. (Interview cited in Bishara 2018, 118)

In fact, Peter Waldorf, PSI secretary general, sent a letter to the Egyptian prime minister on August 18, during the pension and social security crisis, condemning all the pressure on union leaders. Moreover, the names of the leaders who had been subject to security pressures were explicitly mentioned in the letter. Waldorf also condemned the interference of the ETUF in the affairs of the RETA union, which was founded in accordance with the Egyptian Constitution and the international conventions signed by Egypt. In addition, he explicitly condemned the amendment of Decree 425, issued by the minister of finance on pension and social security funds, and the replacement of the independent union by the union of banks and insurance companies, belonging to ETUF.[47]

46. Mohamed El-Kholi, 2009, "Al-dawli lil khadamat al-'ama yasfa' itihad 'umal Misr: qabilna 'udwiyat al-dara'ib al-'qariya la'inaha tu'ayid mabadi'una w ahdafuna" [The International Federation of Services Slaps ETUF: We Have Accepted the Accession of the RETA Union Because It Adheres to Our Principles and Objectives], *Al-Dustur*, December 17, 2009.

47. Abdel Wehab Khedr, 2009, "Dughut dawliyya 'ala hukumat Nazif li-ihtiram misr lil-itifaqat wa itlaq haq tashkil al-niqabat al-mustaqilla" [Pressure on the Nazif Government to Respect the Conventions and Accept the Creation of Independent Unions], *Al-Ahally*, August 26, 2009.

Another component of the independent union's strategy was its encouragement of RETA employees to resign from the official union in order to demonstrate its incapacity to represent or dictate the actions of its civil servants (Bishara 2018, 119). By January 2009, one month after the founding of the new union, some 3,500 civil servants had already resigned from the banking and insurance union.[48] With the initial successes of the new union, especially after the agreement with the minister of finance, the number of resignations increased again (Said 2011). According to several leading members of the SCC, the governorates that had official committees of the banking and insurance union, such as Giza, Daqhliya, Gharbiya, and Baheira, saw massive resignations and a transfer of the RETA employees to the new union—as all of our interviews show. For example, in the Giza governorate, about 1,000 out of 1,600 employees joined the new union; in the governorate of Daqhliya, about 2,500 out of 2,900 civil servants changed union membership; in Beni Suef, about 2,500 out of 5,000; in Baheira, about 4,000 out of 7,500, and in Gharbiya, about 3,500 out of 8,740. In the other governorates that did not have an official trade union committee, like Cairo or Minya, large numbers of employees also joined the new union: in Cairo, about 2,440 out of 2,700, and in Minya, about 1,500 out of 2,000 (Morsi, interview with author, October 22, 2011; Fathy, interview with author, October 22, 2011; Magdy 2011; Said 2011; Moheb 2011; Hussein 2011; Lotfia 2011).

The contentious interaction that lasted throughout 2008/9 between the independent RETA Union and the ETUF continued to reinforce the "boundaries" that had already been formed between the two sides. During the two years following the RETA's strike, especially during the conflict over social funds, the movement's slogans confirmed their refusal of the official union and their attachment to the new union: "Our union or nothing, we do not need Mugawer!" (Niqabitna ya balash, Mugawer mayilzamnash).[49] This means that, through this interactional process, the

48. Yehia Badawi, 2009, "Abu Eita atlaq al-sharara: istiqalat 3500 muwazaf min niqabat Mugawer" [Abu Eita Ignited the Spark: Resignation of 3,500 Employees from Mugawer's Union], *Al-Karama*, January 26, 2009.

49. Mohamed Azouz, 2009b, "Muwazafu al-dara'ib al-'aqariyya ya'udun li-maqarihim al-i'tisami amam majlis al-wozara' . . . wa yunazimun mohakama sha'biya

sense of a collective identity within the movement intensified. Common experiences of activism helped shape the self-perception and goals of the movement's members. Hence, the emergence of a collective desire and availability for activism from civil servants who did not possess this urge before presents a counterargument to Emad's assumptions that independent union members would not be prepared to step out of line with the regime players because they are overwhelmed by socioeconomic conditions.

Additionally, the independent union organized demonstrations to increase the internal pressure on the regime players. In response to Mugawer's letter to the minister of finance, a protest of about three hundred employees was held on August 6, 2009, in front of the RETA administration in Cairo.[50] Other demonstrations of about one hundred employees each were held in front of RETA administrations in Daqhliya, Gharbiya, and Suez ("Istiya'" 2009, 4). On August 9, the independent trade union issued a statement announcing a sit-in on August 11 in front of the Cabinet headquarters to protest the amendment of the decree.[51] About one thousand employees participated in this event. They put on their face masks and chanted, "These masks are not to protect us from the flu, they're to protect us from Mugawer and Shehata!" The use of masks was a reference to the bird flu crisis in Egypt at the time. They also staged a symbolic trial of Mugawer and Shehata, chanting: "Our union or nothing, we don't need Mugawer! [Niqabitna ya balash, Mugawer mayilzamnash]"; "Farouk, Farouk, we will not leave you the funds!" (Ya Farouk, ya Farouk, mish hansib al-sanduq; Azouz 2009b, 3).

Following this demonstration, the minister of finance promised he would respond positively to their demands. The negotiations resulted in

li-mujawir" [The Real Estate Tax Collectors Return to Their Sit-In in Front of the Cabinet and Organize a Popular Trial for Mugawer], *Al-Masry Al-Youm*, August 12, 2009.

50. Dalia Moussa, 2009, "Al-dara'ib al-'aqariyya yahtajjun 'adam sanduqahum fi niqabat al-bunuk" [The Real Estate Tax Collectors Protest the Separation of Their Funds from the Bank Union], *Al-Shorouk*, August 7, 2009.

51. Laila Nureldine, 2009, "Niqabat al-dara'ib al-'aqariyya tumahhil al-maliyya 3 ayam li-tanfid matalibuha" [The Real Estate Tax Collector Syndicate Gives the Ministry of Finance Three Days to Meet Its Demands], *Al-Wafd*, August 9, 2009.

a compromise: the formation of a board of directors for the social funds, which would include three representatives of the independent union (Azouz 2009b, 3). The tendency of the minister of finance to be more sympathetic toward the employees of the RETA is reflective of opposing interests between various regime players, which was exploited by the independent trade union. The closer security control of the 2006 trade union elections resulted in the ETUF becoming less and less representative of the workers/employees. Since the minister perceived the official union's inability to control the situation, he thought it would be more cost-effective to reach a compromise with the independent union representatives for two reasons: to be able to negotiate with leaders who were representative of the movement, and to guarantee the stability and effectiveness of the employees' performance, especially in dealing with a group that was strategically important for the government in general and the ministry in particular.

Thus, the episode ended with the success of the independent union, which was recognized as a legitimate representative of its members' interests by securing a seat at the negotiations on the administration of funds. The pressure strategy of the movement's leaders brought about positive results. Admittedly, it is difficult to obtain the exact number of members of the twenty-fourth union of the ETUF—it should be recalled that I am analyzing a dynamic that was interrupted a year later with the outbreak of the uprising on January 25, 2011. However, it is clear that the ETUF failed to make the twenty-fourth union more attractive than the independent union, since it did not succeed in depriving it of social funds. It was also unable to effectively co-opt the members of the RETA movement: as previously mentioned, in most of the governorates where trade union committees were established (as well as in those where they did not previously exist), the employees joined the independent union.

Constructing the movement's collective identity in opposition to the ETUF was a key part of its success. As Della Porta and Diani (2006, 94) argue, the construction of an identity implies both a positive definition of those who are part of it and a negative characterization of those who are not only excluded from the group but who actively oppose it. In addition, the delay of the president of the ETUF in formally launching his initiative to create the twenty-fourth union helped to strengthen this identity

(Bishara 2018, 121). The general assembly of the ETUF, which, according to Law 35 has the prerogative to approve the foundation of a new union, would not do so until December 26, 2009.[52] The following day, December 27, more than two thousand employees were already celebrating the first anniversary of their independent union, which even managed to open its headquarters on Faysal Street in the Giza governorate. They chanted, "Long live the independent union against the exploiting union!" (Ashat al-niqaba al-mustaqilla did niqaba mustaghilla).[53] Thus, this slogan explicitly marked their antagonism toward the official union, while demonstrating the attachment of the employees to their new union and their profound sense of belonging to it.

Conclusion

The formation of a social structure compelling regime players to concede to the demand for parity unfolded through an interactive and contentious process. Two pivotal dynamics underpinned the sit-in's success and the movement's triumph in its strategic interactions with regime players in both arenas of labor affairs and street politics: leaders' appropriate tactical adaptations within constraints imposed by regime players developed through an interactional learning process refining organizational and mobilization tactics; and the construction of a public image portraying the movement as a cohesive force, united around social justice, amplified by heightened media coverage.

The confluence of these dynamics prompted a shift in the arena of contention from street politics to trade union affairs, challenging the Egyptian Trade Union Federation (ETUF), a key regime subplayer. Two interconnected dynamics facilitated this shift: first, the creation of a

52. Mohamed Al-Agroudi, 2009, "Ta'sis niqaba lil-'amilin bil-maliyya wa al-dara'ib al-'aqariyya wa al-jamarik lil-himaya al-qanuniyya" [The Founding of the Official Union of the Real Estate Tax Collectors], *Al-Ahram*, December 26, 2009.

53. Hisham Fouad, 2009, "'Alaf al-muwazafin bil-'aqariyya yahtifun: 'ashat al-niqaba al-mustaqilla did niqaba mustaghilla" [Thousands of Property Tax Officials Chanted: "Long Live the Independent Union against an Exploiting Union!"], *Al-Arabi Al-Nasseri*, December 27, 2009.

collective identity during contentious interactions, strengthened by the government's strategic mistake of underestimating the risks of prolonged protests, inadvertently consolidating the movement organizational structures and collective identity. Second, the politicization of some of the movement's leaders, driven by a vision of sociopolitical change, motivated the shift. Without their political impetus, the initiation of the new union idea would be improbable. The critical actions that facilitated success were the persuasive narratives and framing crafted by leaders to garner support for the new union despite risks, and their strategic capacities throughout the contentious process. These strategic efforts proved decisive in establishing Egypt's first independent union since 1957 and securing government recognition.

Conclusion

I outline the internal and external conditions that influenced social movement leaders/players, and their agency in challenging regime players. Taking into consideration the relational and interactional nature of this contention, I shed light on the strategic mistakes that authoritarian regimes might make during these contentious dynamics. Additionally, I present critical empirical and theoretical observations in relation to the impact of the movements' leaders/players on: the emergence of the movement and its success in satisfying its economic demands; and, the movement's opposition to the authoritarian regime players, as well as the success or failure of its attempts.

When Leaders Create Movements

Despite the constraints imposed by the actions of the authoritarian regime players, two labor movements emerged and succeeded in pushing the players of the authoritarian regime to fulfill their socioeconomic demands, despite constraints. In the case of both movements studied in this book, the leaders played an important part in activating the networks they formed during the fraudulent trade union elections of 2006. In both cases, the leaders who were disqualified from these elections played a mobilizing role, by converting their networks and social bases into successful protest campaigns. The support networks that they had formed during these union elections were key to organizing the first protests. The leaders of both movements also worked hard to ensure prolonged protest action and an upward scale shift, transforming scattered protests into a movement of national scale in the case of the RETA movement.

In both movements, the mobilizing role of the leaders was crucial. Nevertheless, an essential difference is worth mentioning in this respect: while the mobilization of social networks and the tactics used by the leaders were necessary for the emergence of these two movements, a third factor was decisive in the case of the RETA movement, which was the movement leaders' interpretation of the strategies of regime players and potential political opportunities that encouraged them to mobilize and act.[1]

This observation is particularly significant in the analysis of social movements in the context of authoritarian rules. Movement leaders' identification of the opportunities available because of regime players' amendments in their strategies when dealing with labor protests is critical for the emergence of movements with weak organizational resources. It is unlikely that the RETA movement could have emerged in a context of authoritarian rule without the movement leaders being persuaded that the regime players' strategy had changed enough to allow greater room for action and protest. In that regard, the leaders of the RETA movement always credited the inspiring influence of the Mahalla labor movement. The mobilization of the latter in 2006 confirmed to RETA movement leaders that the regime players' strategies had changed and gave them signals that there were possibilities to act and to claim their rights. This observation seems all the more important when it comes to the Egyptian bureaucracy, which, unlike the workers in the industrial sector, had neither the infrastructure for organizing protests nor a history of activism. On the other hand, the organizational power of the Mahalla labor movement and its long history of activism allowed it to mobilize and reemerge in 2006 without relying on this change in strategy of the regime players.

Within this framework, which focuses on the agency of worker leaders, I believe that specific actions by the leaders of both movements particularly influenced the contentious process and guaranteed their success: for example, the leaders' ability to implement effective strategies in order to bring about the changes they hoped to achieve. The strategic choice

1. On the contrary, the perception of political opportunities cannot explain the emergence of the Mahalla labor movement.

of the first group of leaders in the Mahalla labor movement, as well as of the leaders of the RETA movement (in all the mobilization preceding the decision to found an independent trade union), in terms of their strict distinction between economic and political demands, helped them to avoid repression and to respond to the needs of the movements they represented.

Thus, beyond the organizational resources of a movement, the choices that its leaders make in their strategic interactions with the players of authoritarian regimes, determines the ability of the movement not only to neutralize the security apparatus but also to preserve the cohesion of the movement. Different choices lead to different results, a fact that was overlooked by structural theories, as movement leaders make choices among several options, which affects the capacity of the movement to mobilize as well as the movement's results (Morris 2004, 242). Leaders' efforts to make certain decisions is not easy. Strategic action is full of dilemmas and compromises, as each option is promising in some ways but risky in others (Jasper 2014, 69). Therefore, the choices that the movement's players/leaders make, in their contentious and strategic interactions with regime players, are crucial for understanding the outcomes that the movement players can bring about.

Moreover, the leaders were able to exploit the political opportunities provided by regime players' actions (or nonaction) during contentious interactions and to utilize tactics that ensured the survival of the movements. The mobilization tactics—including the ways in which the movement leaders managed to publicly represent their interests in a way that guaranteed the perceived worthiness, unity, and commitment of the movement (Tarrow and Tilly 2015, 153), as well as their ability to exploit arising opportunities during the course of the contention—are what enabled the RETA movement both to build its mobilizing structures despite the scarcity of its resources, and to survive despite the constraints put in place by the regime players.

As has been demonstrated, the actions and strategies of the leaders themselves created opportunities that generated new possibilities for expanding the movements. This appeared to be more significant when dealing with a movement with limited organizational resources, as was the case with the RETA movement. Contentious interactions thus create opportunities, which reemerge, depending on the movement leader's strategies, or, in other words, their creative and adaptive ways of turning the movement's relatively scarce resources into the power needed to get what one wants (Ganz and McKenna 2019, 191–92). In the case of a movement with organizational capacities, as was the case with the Mahalla labor movement, resources remain a necessary but insufficient condition to explain the movement's ability to survive and succeed while contentiously interacting with authoritarian regime players. In contrast, the dynamic strategies and tactics deployed by the movement leaders are a necessary prerequisite for success.

These points have several important empirical and theoretical implications for the study of social movements in the context of authoritarian regimes. For instance, analysis of the choices/strategies of leaders interacting with authoritarian regimes (which remains under-studied elsewhere in the literature of social movements) is essential in understanding the success or failure of movement players to achieve their goals. Regime players seek to constrain the choices that movement players have and to block them in specific arenas (Jasper 2021). Not only did Egyptian regime players offer limited opportunities for labor movement players to participate in elections; they also restrained the types of demands that the latter could formulate and constrained their repertoires of actions and tactics. Furthermore, the opportunities that regime players might provide are not just conditioned by the rules they impose, but are also temporal. This implies that each moment of contention is unique, with opportunities that can be actualized or new constraints that may emerge. This is why the strategies that the movement's leaders implemented to circumvent the regime players' pressures, and to exploit emerging possibilities, are decisive in determining the results (positive or negative) that the movement generates. Strategy in this sense is an ongoing process: "It is something you do, not something you have" (Ganz and McKenna 2019, 191–92). Hence, it is not enough to focus on the origins and outcomes of a certain contentious episode, as this overshadows the identification of key turning points in the history of a movement and thereby prevents the detection of counterfactual possibilities that could arise if the leaders of the movement did not take one action over other (Aminzade, Goldestone, and Perry 2001, 128).

Contrary to the case of democratic regimes, the analysis of strategic interactions between the players of a movement and those of an authoritarian regime requires that the researcher analyze how the contentious and strategic interaction may promote the creation of a social movement, or the emergence of a player. In authoritarian contexts, the mobilizing structures of the movement may not be readily available during the initial phase of its formation. This implies that attributing the success of a movement's mobilization solely to its organizational structures may not be accurate, as these structures may only take shape during the mobilization itself or as a result of contentious interactions. Consequently, adopting an interactional and relational perspective becomes a crucial tool for comprehending and analyzing the outcomes generated by social movement actors in their strategic interactions with players within authoritarian regimes in specific arenas.

From an empirical perspective, the analysis of the strategies that the leaders of social movements put forward to confront authoritarian regime players highlights the strategic mistakes that the latter may have committed during some contentious episodes. In this case, it is important to recall the red lines that the Mubarak regime put in place to specify what might or might not pose a "political threat" for its rule. As was shown in the analysis of the April 6, 2008, mobilization of the Mahalla labor movement, the regime players still feared a connection between what it considered "the political," and what it framed as "the social." Regime players thus considered contentious interactions in the arena of politics as threatening to them. However, the analysis of the RETA movement mobilizations demonstrates that the movement's mobilization in the arena of street politics that the players of the regime tolerated represented in itself a threat to the regime players. Yet, by winning over a large portion of the street for a period of time, social ties were formed and a collective and oppositional identity to one of the key regime's subplayers (ETUF) was created. This space (the street) that the government and the security forces (regime subplayers) left to the protesters was exploited, and the time they spent together (at the street sit-ins) was crucial to the development of an oppositional social actor.

When Movement Leaders Contest and Oppose Authoritarian Players and Rules

In the case of the Mahalla labor movement, the internal configuration of the leadership, and their differing positions toward the regime players, influenced, or even built, the movement's oppositional position. Similarly, in the case of the RETA movement, the way it evolved over time, and the influence of its leadership in this process, was also decisive. The simultaneous contentious interactions, in which the movements were involved, led to a process of collective identity construction. Klandermans (2014) recalls that collective identity, rather than being a prerequisite for action, is assembled and fostered through protest and mobilization. It is often through action that certain feelings of belonging are forged and reinforced (Della Porta and Diani 2006, 93). Through the narratives and resonant framing that the leaders developed, they succeeded in transforming this identity into oppositional stances to the regime's players.

In both cases, the decision of the two movements to oppose the players of the authoritarian regime of Mubarak, is explained by the presence of three factors conditioning them: the identification of political opportunities, thanks to the change in strategy of the regime players, thereby allowing the movement to act with a relatively low risk of repression; an assessment of the balance of power between the movement players and the regime players as being in the favor of the former; and the very nature of the leadership, as well as their careers as political activists.[2]

In this regard, the realization of the change in the regime players' strategy, as well as the success of the movement in achieving its economic demands, remained a necessary but insufficient condition to push it to oppose the regime players. However, the relationship of the leaders to politics was indispensable for this oppositional act to occur. The influence of the political careers of the movement leaders is key to explaining their motivations, and, thus, the influence this may have had on the movement's dynamics. Leaders' biographies influence their choices and decisions during

2. This was interpreted as another encouraging sign to raise the level of its demands.

contentious episodes (Jasper 2014, 184–85; Jasper 2015a, 12). In both movements, politicized leaders were present. They advocated for a longer-term vision of social change, involving opposition to the regime players.

Taking the strategic decision to oppose the players of the authoritarian regime wasn't always successful. As I have discussed, the Mahalla workers' movement was repressed and demobilized, while the RETA movement succeeded in creating the first independent trade union in Egypt since 1957. In both cases, the success of the movement's leaders in their oppositional attempts depended not only on the type of leadership and their political positions, but also on their social base within the movement, and their ability to mobilize members. The capacity of social movement players to oppose authoritarian regime players thus depend on the capacity of its politicized leaders to transform their social base into an oppositional force. This was the case with the RETA movement leaders, unlike that of the Mahalla workers. The Mahalla movement leaders, advocating a position that was challenging to the regime players, did not have a sufficient social base within the company to bring about their oppositional vision.

This analysis leads to important theoretical and empirical observations with regard to the conditions under which a mobilization with strictly economic aims might become challenging to the players of an authoritarian regime. The presence of politicized leaders at the top of a social movement, especially if they were able to achieve success in previous contentious episodes, is necessary in order to exploit opportunities. Starting from the second half of the 2000s, when the regime players changed their strategy to be less repressive and more tolerating of action, only social movements that had players/leaders with a history of political activism opted to take advantages of these opportunities and sought to challenge the regime players. This observation is very important in explaining the exceptional oppositional choice that the players of these two movements made in a political context that had witnessed, in general, a depoliticization of the labor movement.

Importantly, the success of this oppositional endeavor in the context of an authoritarian regime doesn't only depend on the presence of politicized leaders at the top of a social movement, but also of them having a strong social base of support within the movement, and, significantly, of them being aware of the importance of acting in times where political opportunities are not closed—or, in other words, in times when the regime players' strategies are more tolerant and less repressive. The insistence of the group of leftist/politicized leaders—who did not have a strong base within the Mahalla labor movement—to push for the challenging demand of the minimum wage at a time when the regime players had adopted a more repressive strategy led to the repression and demobilization of the movement. On the contrary, the group of politicized leaders in the RETA movement, who enjoyed a strong social base within itself, were able to exploit the political opportunities provided by the tolerant strategy of the players of the authoritarian regime of Mubarak. They even managed to create more of them during their contentious and strategic interactions with regime players. This made them able to advance their political project.

In this respect, the formulation of a narrative and a resonant framing is crucial for the success of movement leaders in seizing opportunities. Through the narratives they constructed, the movement leaders managed to turn the threats or risks that the movement was afraid of (i.e., risk of repression) into opportunities to be seized (i.e., remaining united to preserve their power). Narrative thus becomes a source of individual and collective agency (Ganz and McKenna 2019, 190–91). Leaders who have a strong relationship with their bases within the movement are more likely to formulate more resonant narratives and framings (Morris and Staggenborg 2004, 184), which enhances the chances of their adoption by the movement's members. The ways in which the importance of creating an independent union was framed, as being the only way of enabling the movement to remain a united entity, resonated among the rank-and-file employees, and its credibility was confirmed by their previous collective success.

Finally, the political opportunities provided by authoritarian regime players at a certain point of time are sometimes related to the inaccurate estimates that they may conduct, thereby allowing the movement players to better advance their political agendas. While the Mubarak regime players overestimated the risk of a connection between social mobilization and political parties/movements, as well as contention situated in the political arena, I have showed that another risk (besides that of the mobilization in the arena of street politics chosen by the movement) seemed to have been underestimated by the regime players: the presence of politicized leaders in opposition to them (e.g., Kamal Abu Eita) at the head of a social movement with a strong enough foundation to mobilize it for oppositional purposes. Thus, the emergence and constitution of a social actor strong enough to advance its political agenda autonomously of the ETUF was a threat that the players of the regime had not considered carefully enough.

This proved to be true, since the independent union of RETA workers opened the door for the emancipation of the labor movement outside of the ETUF, following the political opportunities and openings provided by the 2011 uprising. Hundreds of independent trade unions thus emerged and were regrouped under the umbrella of several new trade union federations, among which the Egyptian Federation for Independent Trade Unions (EFITU) was established, by Abu Eita, the leader of the RETA movement, at a press conference on January 30, 2011, in Cairo's Tahrir Square.

References

Index

References

Scholarly Books and Articles

Abdalla, Nadine. 2012. "Khasa'is jil al-shabab al-liberali" [Characteristics of liberal youth]. In *Al-anmat ghir al-ṭaqlidiyya li-musharakat al-shabab fi misr* [Nontraditional Forms of Youth Participation in Egypt], edited by Mohamed Al-Ajati, 37–70. Cairo: Rawafid.

Abdalla, Nadine. 2012a. "Social Protests in Egypt before and after the 25 January Revolution: Perspectives on the Evolution of their Forms and Features." *Mediterranean Yearbook Barcelona IEMed*. Accessed August 1. https://www.iemed.org/publication/social-protests-in-egypt-before-and-after-the-25-january-revolution-perspectives-on-the-evolution-of-their-forms-and-features/2024.

Abdalla, Nadine. 2012b. "Egypt's Workers—From Protest Movement to Organized Labor." Berlin: German Institute for International and Security Affairs.

Abdalla, Nadine. 2015. "The Labor and Politics in Egypt." *Middle East Insights* 127. Singapore: Middle East Institute.

Abdalla, Nadine. 2017. "The Egyptian Trade Union Movement in Light of the 2011 Uprising: Co-optation, Containment, and Limits of Resistance." Research report, Essam Fares Institute for Public Policy and International Affairs and Al-Asfari Institute for Civil Society and Citizenship, American Univ. of Beirut.

Abdalla, Nadine. 2020. "From the Dream of Change to the Nightmare of Structural Weakness: The Trajectory of Egypt's Independent Trade Union Movement after 2011." In *Socioeconomic Protests in MENA and Latin America: Egypt and Tunisia in Interregional Comparison*, edited by Irene Weipert-Fenner and Jonas Wolff, 145–68. London: Palgrave Macmillan.

Abdel Latif, Fathy. 2002. *Masirat 'umal al-Mahalla 'abr 100 'am* [The activism of Mahalla Labor through Ten Years]. Cairo: Labor Univ. Press.

Abdulla, Rasha. 2006. "An Overview of Media Developments in Egypt: Does the Internet Make a Difference?" *GMJ: Mediterranean Edition* 1, no. 1:88–100.

Adly, Amr. 2012. *State Reform and Development in the Middle East: The Cases of Turkey and Egypt*. London: Routledge.

Adly, Amr. 2020a. "A Brief History of Nation, State, and Market." In *Routledge Handbook on Contemporary Egypt*, edited by Robert Springborg, Robert Springborg, Amr Adly, Anthony Gorman, Tamir Moustafa, Aisha Saad, Naomi Sakr, and Sarah Smierciak. London: Routledge.

Adly, Amr. 2020b. *Cleft Capitalism: The Social Origins of Failed Market-Making in Egypt*. Stanford, CA: Stanford Univ. Press.

Aidi, Hisham. 2009. *Redeploying the State: Corporatism, Neoliberalism, and Coalition Politics*. London: Palgrave Macmillan.

Al-Banna, Gamal. 1992. *Al-haraka al-niqabiyya al-misriyya, tarikhan wa-ṭanziman, 'abra mi'at 'am 1892–1992* [The History and Organization of the Egyptian Trade Union Movement, 1892–1992]. Cairo: International Islamic Union for Work.

Al-Sayid, Mostafa Kamal. 2006. "Kefaya at a Turning Point." In *Political and Social Protest in Egypt: Cairo Papers in Social Science*, edited by Nicholas Hopkins and Nathalie Bernard-Maugiron, 45–59. Cairo: American Univ. in Cairo Press.

Albrecht, Holger. 2007. "Authoritarian Opposition and the Politics of Challenge in Egypt." In *Debating Arab Authoritarianism: Dynamics and Durability in Nondemocratic Regimes*, edited by Oliver Schlumberger, 59–74. Stanford, CA: Stanford Univ. Press.

Albrecht, Holger. 2013. *Raging against the Machine*. Ithaca, NY: Syracuse Univ. Press.

Alexander, Anne. 2010. "Leadership and Collective Action in the Egyptian Trade Unions." *Work, Employment and Society* 24, no. 2:241–59.

Alexander, Anne. 2013. "Analysing Activist Cultures in the Egyptian Workers' Movement." In *Non-Governmental Public Action and Social Justice*, edited by Jude Howell, 60–85. London: Palgrave Macmillan.

Alexander, Anne, and Mostafa Bassiouny. 2014. *Bread, Freedom, Social Justice, Workers, and the Egyptian Revolution*. London: Zed.

Alissa, Sufyan. 2007. *The Political Economy of Reform in Egypt: Understanding the Role of Institutions*. Washington, DC: Carnegie Middle East Center.

Allam, Rabha. 2012. "Khasa'is jil al-shabab fi al-tayar al-'islami" [Characteristics of Islamist Youth]. In *Al-anmat ghir al-taqlidiyya li-musharakat al-shabab fi misr* [Nontraditional Forms of Youth Participation in Egypt], edited by Mohamed Al-Ajati, 15–42. Cairo: Rawafid.

Almaida, Paul. 2019. *Social Movements: The Structure of Collective Mobilization.* Oakland: Univ. of California Press.

Amenta, Edwin, Neal Caren, and Amber Celina Tierney. 2015b. "Put Me in, Coach? Referee? Owner? Security? Why the News Media Rarely Cover Movements as Political Players." In *Players and Arenas: The Interactive Dynamics of Protest*, edited by James M. Jasper and Jan Willem Duyvendak, 229–50. Amsterdam: Amsterdam Univ. Press.

Amenta, Edwin, Neal Caren, Sheera Joy Olasky, and James E. Stobaugh. 2015a. "Movements in the Media." In *The Social Movements Reader: Cases and Concepts*, edited by Jeff Goodwin and James M. Jasper, 302–17. London: John Wiley & Sons.

Amizade, R. R., J. A. Goldstone, and E. J. Perry. 2001. "Leadership, Dynamics and Dynamics of Contention." In *Silence and Voice in the Study of Contentious Politics*, edited by Ronald R. Aminzade, Jack A. Goldstone, Doug McAdam, Elizabeth J. Perry, William H. Sewell, Sidney Tarrow, and Charles Tilley, 126–54. Cambridge: Cambridge Univ. Press.

Anderson, Lisa. 1995. "Democracy in the Arab World: A Critique of the Political Culture Approach." *Political Liberalization and Democratization in the Arab World*, edited by Rex Brynen, Bahgat Korany, Paul Noble, 77–92. Boulder, CO: Lynne Rienner.

Assaad, Ragui, and Caroline Krafft. 2013. "The Structure and Evolution of Employment in Egypt 1998–2012." Working Paper 805, Economic Research Forum.

Aswani, Alaa. 2011. *On the State of Egypt: What Made the Revolution Inevitable.* Translated by Jonathan Wright. New York: Vintage.

Ayubi, Nazih. 1995. *Over-stating the Arab State.* London: B Tauris.

Barker, Colin, Alan Johnson, and Michael Lavalette, eds. 2001. *Leadership in Social Movements.* Manchester: Manchester Univ. Press.

Bassiouny, Mustafa, and Omar Said. 2008. "A New Worker Movement: The Strike Wave of 2007." *International Socialism*, 118: n.p.

Beinin, Joel. 2008. "Underbelly of Egypt's Neo-Liberal Agenda." Middle East Report Online, April 5, 2008. https://web.archive.org/web/20150905225139/http:/www.merip.org/mero/mero040508.

Beinin, Joel. 2009a. "Neo-liberal Structural Adjustment, Political Demobilization, and Neo-Authoritarianism in Egypt." In *The Arab State and Neo-liberal*

Globalization: The Restructuring of State Power in the Middle East, edited by Laura Guazzone and Daniela Pioppi, 19–46. Berkshire: Ithaca.

Beinin, Joel. 2009b. "Workers' Struggles under Socialism and Neoliberalism." In *Egypt: The Moment of Change*, edited by Rabab El-Mahdi and Philip Marfleet, 68–86. London: Zed.

Beinin, Joel. 2010. *Justice for All! The Struggle for Workers' Rights in Egypt*. Washington, DC: Solidarity Center, AFL-CIO.

Beinin, Joel. 2011. "Workers and Egypt's January 25 Revolution." *International Labor and Working-Class History* 80, no. 1:189–96.

Beinin, Joel. 2012. "The Rise of Egypt's Workers." Carnegie Endowment for International Peace, June 28, 2012. https://carnegieendowment.org/research/2012/06/the-rise-of-egypts-workers?lang=en.

Beinin, Joel. 2015. *Workers and Thieves: Labor Movements and Popular Uprisings in Tunisia and Egypt*. Stanford, CA: Stanford Univ. Press.

Beinin, Joel, and Frédéric Vairel. 2013. "Introduction: The Middle East and North Africa beyond Classical Social Movement Theory." In *Social Movements, Mobilization, and Contestation in the Middle East and North Africa*, edited by Joel Beinin and Frédéric Vairel, 1–30. Stanford, CA: Stanford Univ. Press.

Beinin, Joel, and Frédéric Vairel, eds. 2013. *Social Movements, Mobilization, and Contestation in the Middle East and North Africa*. Stanford, CA: Stanford Univ. Press.

Beinin, Joel, and Hossam El-Hamalawy. 2007a. "Egyptian Textile Workers Confront the New Economic Order." Middle East Report Online, March 25, 2007. https://merip.org/2007/03/egyptian-textile-workers-confront-the-new-economic-order/.

Beinin, Joel, and Hossam El-Hamalawy. 2007b. "Strikes in Egypt Spread from Center of Gravity." Middle East Report Online, May 9, 2007. https://merip.org/2007/05/strikes-in-egypt-spread-from-center-of-gravity/.

Beinin, Joel, and Marie Duboc. 2013. "A Worker's Social Movement on the Margin of the Global Neoliberal Order, Egypt, 2004–2012." In *Social Movements, Mobilization, and Contestation in the Middle East and North Africa*, edited by Joel Beinin and Frédéric Vairel, 205–27. Stanford, CA: Stanford Univ. Press.

Beinin, Joel, and Zachary Lockman. 1988. *Workers on the Nile: Nationalism, Communism, Islam, and the Egyptian Working Class, 1882–1954*. Cairo: American Univ. in Cairo Press.

Bellin, Eva. 2000. "Contingent Democrats: Industrialists, Labor, and Democratization in Late-Developing Countries." *World Politics* 52, no. 2:175–205.

Ben Néfissa, Sarah, and Jean-Yves Moisseron, eds. 2007. "L'Egypte sous pression? Des mobilisations au verrouillage politique." *Politique africaine* 108:5–125.

Ben Néfissa, Sarah. 2007. "'Ça suffit'? Le 'haut' et le 'bas' du politique en Égypte." *Politique africaine* 108:5–24.

Ben Néfissa, Sarah. 2010. "Verrouillage autoritaire et mutation générale des rapports entre l'Etat et la société en Egypte." *Confluences Méditerranée* 75:137–50.

Benford, Robert D. 1993. "Frame Disputes within the Nuclear Disarmament Movement." *Social Forces* 71, no. 3:677–701.

Benford, Robert D. 1997. "An Insider's Critique of the Social Movement Framing Perspective." *Sociological Inquiry* 67:409–30.

Benford, Robert D. 2013. "Frame Disputes." In *The Wiley-Blackwell Encyclopedia of Social and Political Movements*, edited by David Snow, Donatella Della Porta, Doug McAdam, Bert Klandermans, n.p. Hoboken, NJ: Wiley-Blackwell.

Benford, Robert D., and David Snow. 2000. "Framing Processes and Social Movements: An Overview and Assessment." *Annual Review of Sociology* 26:611–39.

Berberoglu, Berch, ed. 2019. *The Palgrave Handbook of Social Movements, Revolution, and Social Transformation*. Cham: Palgrave Macmillan.

Bianchi, Robert. 1989a. *Unruly Corporatism: Associational Life in Twentieth-Century Egypt*. Oxford: Oxford Univ. Press.

Bianchi, Robert. 1989b. "The Corporatization of the Egyptian Labor Movement." *Middle East Journal* 49, no. 3:429–44.

Bishara, Dina. 2012. "The Power of Workers in Egypt's 2011 Uprising." In *Arab Spring in Egypt: Revolution and Beyond*, edited by Bahgat Korany and Rabab El-Mahdi, 83–104. Cairo: American Univ. in Cairo Press.

Bishara, Dina. 2018. *Contesting Authoritarianism: Labor Challenges to the State in Egypt*. Cambridge: Cambridge Univ. Press.

Bosi, Lorenzo, Marco Giugni, and Katrin Uba, eds. 2016. *The Consequences of Social Movements*. Cambridge: Cambridge Univ. Press.

Boudreau, Vince. 2005. "Precarious Regimes and Matchup Problems in the Explanations of Repressive Policy." In *Repression and Mobilization*, edited by Christian Davenport, Hank Johnston, and Carol Mueller, 33–57. Minneapolis: Univ. of Minnesota Press.

Boudreau, Vince. 2015. "Liberal Violence: Strategies of Repression in Transitional Regimes." In *Breaking Down the State: Protestors Engaged*, edited by

James M. Jasper and Jan Willem Duyvendak, 179–205. Amsterdam: Amsterdam Univ. Press.

Brownlee, Jason. 2002. "The Decline of Pluralism in Mubarak's Egypt." *Journal of Democracy* 13, no. 4:6–14.

Brumberg, Daniel. 2002. "The Trap of Liberalized Autocracy." *Journal of Democracy* 3, no. 4:56–68.

Brumberg, Daniel. 2003. *Moyen-Orient: L'Enjeu démocratique.* Paris: Michalon Brumberg.

Bush, Ray. 2012. "Marginality or Abjection? The Political Economy of Poverty Production in Egypt." In *Marginality and Exclusion in Egypt*, edited by Ray Bush and Habib Ayeb, 72–96. London: Zed.

Bush, Ray, and Habib Ayeb, eds. 2008. *Marginality and Exclusion in Egypt.* London: Zed.

Cai, Yongshun. 2008. "Power Structure and Regime Resilience: Contentious Politics in China." *British Journal of Political Science* 8, no. 3:411–32.

Cai, Yongshun. 2010. *Collective Resistance in China: Why Popular Protests Succeed or Fail.* Stanford, CA: Stanford Univ. Press.

Carothers, Thomas. 2002. "The End of the Transition Paradigm." *Journal of Democracy* 13, no. 1:1–17.

Carothers, Thomas, and Marina Ottaway. 2004. "Middle East Democracy." *Foreign Policy* 145:22–28.

Carothers, Thomas, and Marina Ottaway. 2005. *Uncharted Journey: Promoting Democracy in the Middle East.* Washington, DC: Carnegie Endowment for International Peace.

Castells, Manuel. 2015. *Networks of Outrage and Hope: Social Movements in the Internet Age.* Cambridge: Polity.

Chabanet, Didier, and Frédéric Royall. 2014. *From Silence to Protest: International Perspectives on Weakly Resourced Groups.* Farnham: Ashgate.

Champagne, Patrick. 1991. "La construction médiatique des malaises sociaux." *Actes de la Recherche en Sciences Sociales* 90:64–76.

Charles, Tilly. 1986. *La France conteste: De 1600 a nos jours.* Paris: Fayard.

Chraïbi, Mounia B., and Olivier Fillieule. 2003. "Exit, Voice, Loyalty, et bien d'autres choses encore." In *Résistances et protestations dans les sociétés musulmanes*, edited by Mounia B. Chraïbi and Olivier Fillieule, 43–126. Paris: Presses de Sciences Po.

Clément, Françoise. 2007. "Élections ouvrières: Entre fraude et chasse aux "Frères masqués." In *Chroniques égyptiennes, 2006*, edited by Enrique Klause and

Chaymaa Hassabo, 56–86. Cairo: Centre d'Études et de Documentations Économiques, Juridiques et Sociales.

Clément, Françoise. 2009. "Worker Protests under Economic Liberalization in Egypt." In *Political and Social Protest in Egypt: Cairo Papers in Social Science*, edited by Nicholas Hopkins and Nathalie Bernard-Maugiron, 100–116. Cairo: American Univ. in Cairo Press.

Collombier, Virginie. 2012. "Egypt in 2011: A Regime That No Longer Knows How to Adapt? Fluid Conjunctures and Regime Transformations in Perspective." EUI Working Papers.

Craner, Lorne. 2006. "Democracy in the Middle East: Will U.S. Democratization Policy Work." *Middle East Quarterly* (Summer): 3–10.

Croucher, Richard, and Lillian Miles. 2018. "Ethnicity, Popular Democratic Movements and Labour in Malaysia." *Economic and Industrial Democracy* 39, no. 2:294–311.

Davenport, Christian. 2005. "Repression and Mobilization: Insights from Political Sciences and Sociology." In *Repression and Mobilization*, edited by Christian Davenport, Hank Johnston, Carol Mueller, 7–42. Minneapolis: Univ. of Minnesota Press.

Davenport, Christian. 2007. "State Repression and Political Order." *Annual Review of Political Science* 10, no. 1:1–23.

Della Porta, Donatella. 1995. *Social Movements, Political Violence, and the State: A Comparative Analysis of Italy and Germany*. Cambridge: Cambridge Univ. Press.

Della Porta, Donatella, and Herbert Reiter, eds. 1998. *Policing Protest: The Control of Mass Demonstrations in Western Democracies*. Minnesota: Univ. of Minnesota Press.

Della Porta, Donatella, and Kıvanç Atak. 2015. "The Police." In *Breaking Down the State: Protestors Engaged*, edited by James M. Jasper and Jan Willem Duyvendak, 113–33. Amsterdam: Amsterdam Univ. Press.

Della Porta, Donatella, and Mario Diani. 2006. 2nd ed. *Social Movements: An Introduction*. Oxford: Wiley-Blackwell.

Della Porta, Donatella, and Olivier Filleule. 2004. "Policing Social Protests." In *The Blackwell Companion to Social Movements*, edited by David A. Snow, Sarah A. Soule, and Hanspeter Kriesi, 217–41. Malden, MA: Wiley-Blackwell.

De Smet, Brecht. 2015. *A Dialectical Pedagogy of Revolt, Gramsci, Vygotsky, and the Egyptian Revolution*. Leiden: Brill.

Diamond, Larry, Marc F. Plattner, and Daniel Brumberg, eds. 2003. *Islam and Democracy in the Middle East*. Baltimore, MD: John Hopkins Univ. Press.

Diani, Mario. 2003. "Introduction: Social Movements, Contentious Actions, and Social Networks: From Metaphor to Substance." In *Social Movements and Networks: Relational Approaches to Collective Action*, edited by Mario Diani and Doug McAdam, 1–18. Oxford: Oxford Univ. Press.

Diani, Mario, and Ann Mische. 2015. "Network Analysis in Social Movements." In *The Oxford Handbook of Social Movements*, edited by Donatella Della Porta and Mario Diani, n.p. Oxford: Oxford Univ. Press.

Dobry, Michel. 2009. *Sociologie des crises politiques*. Paris: Sciences Po Press.

Duboc, Marie. 2009a. "Journalisme et militantisme: les formes d'engagement dans la couverture médiatique des grèves ouvrières en Égypte." In *En marche vers Tahrir*, edited by Marc Lavergne, n.p. Cairo: Centre d'Études et de Documentation Économiques, Juridiques et Sociales (CEDEJ).

Duboc, Marie. 2009b. "Le 6 avril: un jour de colère sans grèves." In *Chroniques 2008*, edited by Iman Farag, 57–78. Cairo: Centre d'Étude et de Documentation Économiques, Juridiques et Sociales.

Duboc, Marie. 2011. "La contestation sociale en Egypte depuis 2004, Précarisation et mobilisation locale des ouvriers de l'industrie textile." Revue Tiers Monde, accessed June 12, 2024. http://aucegypt.academia.edu/MarieDuboc/Papers/1047635/La_contestation_sociale_en_Egypte_depuis_2004._Precarisation_et_mobilisation_locale_des_ouvriers_de_lindustrie_textile_Revue_Tiers-Monde_Avril_2011.

Duboc, Marie. 2015. "Reluctant Revolutionaries? The Dynamics of Labour Protests in Egypt, 2006–13." In *Revolutionary Egypt: Connecting Domestic and International Struggles*, edited by Reem Abou El-Fadl, 27–42. New York: Routledge.

Dunne, Michelle. 2004. "The United States and Political Reforms in Egypt: A New Era." *Arab Reform Bulletin* 2, no. 5. https://carnegieendowment.org/sada/2008/09/the-united-states-and-political-reform-in-egypt-a-new-era?lang=en&center=middle-east.

Duyvendak, Jan Willem, and James M. Jasper, eds. 2015. *Breaking Down the State: Protestors Engaged*. Amsterdam: Amsterdam Univ. Press.

Duyvendak, Jan Willem, and Olivier Fillieule. 2015. "Conclusion. Patterned Fluidity: An Interactionist Perspective as a Tool for Exploring Contentious Politics." In *Players and Arenas: The Interactive Dynamics of Protest*, edited by James M. Jasper and Jan Willem Duyvendak, 295–318. Amsterdam: Amsterdam Univ. Press.

Earl, Jennifer. 2007. "Leading Tasks in a Leaderless Movement: The Case of Strategic Voting." *American Behavioral Scientist* 50, no. 10:1327–49.

El-Mahdi, Rabab. 2010. "The Workers of Mahalla: The Emergence of a New Labor Movement." In *'Awdat al-siyasa: al-harakat al-ihtijajiyya al-jadida fi misr* [The Return of Politics: The New Protest Movements in Egypt], edited by Dina Shehata, 171–212. Cairo: Al-Ahram Center for Political and Strategic Studies.

El-Mahdi, Rabab. 2011. "Labour Protests in Egypt: Causes and Meanings." *Review of African Political Economy* 38, no. 129:387–402.

El-Mahdi, Rabab. 2012. "Against Marginalization: Workers, Youth, and Class in the 25 January Revolution." In *Marginality and Exclusion in Egypt*, edited by Ray Bush and Habib Ayeb, 133–47. London: Zed.

El-Naggar, Ahmed. 2007. *Al-inhiyar al-iqtisadi fi 'ahd Mubarak* [Economic Collapse in Mubarak's Era]. Cairo: El-Mahroussa.

El-Naggar, Ahmed. 2009. "Economic Policy: From State Control to Decay and Corruption." In *Egypt: The Moment of Change*, edited by Rabab El-Mahdi and Philip Marfleet, 34–50. London: Zed.

El-Shafei, Omar. 1995. "Workers, Trade Unions, and the State in Egypt, 1984–1989." *Cairo Papers in Social Science* 18:2.

El-Shazli, Heba. 2019. *Trade Unions and Arab Revolutions: Challenging the Regime in Egypt*. New York: Routledge.

El-Shobaki, Amr. 2010. "Ihtijajat muwazafi al-dara'ib al-'aqariyya," [Trends among Real Estate Tax Employees]. In *'Awdat al-siyasa: al-harakat al-ihtijajiyya al-jadida fi misr* [The Return of Politics: New Protest Movements in Egypt], edited by Dina Shehata, 213–44. Cairo: Al-Ahram Center for Political and Strategic Studies.

El-Shobaki, Amr, ed. 2011. *Al-harakat al-ihtijajiyya fi al-watan al-'arabi* [Protest Movements in the Arab World]. Beirut: Center of Arab Unity (Markaz al-wihda al-'arabiyya).

Ezz Al-Arab, Mohamed. 2008. "Greasing the Presses: Money and Journalism." Arab Insight, accessed August 22, 2024. http://www.arabinsight.org/pdf/Arab insight27.pdf.

Fahmy, Ninette S. 2002. *The Politics of Egypt: State-Society Relationship*. London: Routledge.

Farah, Nadia R. 2009. *Egypt's Political Economy: Power Relations in Development*. Cairo: American Univ. in Cairo Press.

Farjani, Nadir. 2016. *Arab Revolution in the 21st Century? Lessons from Egypt and Tunisia*. Basingstoke: Palgrave Macmillan.

Favre, Pierre, ed. 1990. *La Manifestation*. Paris: Sciences Po Press.

Ferrié, Jean-Noël. 2005. "Egypte des réformes nécessaires et périlleuses." *Questions internationales* 15:35–49.

Ferrié, Jean-Noël. 2006. "L'Egypte à la jonction de ses agendas intérieurs et extérieurs." Center for International Studies, Paris. Accessed August 22, 2024. http://www.sciencespo.fr/ceri/sites/sciencespo.fr.ceri/files/art_jnf_0.pdf.

Ferrié, Jean-Noël. 2008. *L'Egypte entre démocratie et islamisme. Le système Moubarak à l'heure de la succession*. Paris: Autrement.

Fillieule, Olivier, and Cécile Péchu, eds. 1993. *Lutter ensemble. Les théories de l'action collective*. Paris: L'Harmattan.

Ferrié, Jean-Noël, and Jean-Claude Santucci. 2006. *Dispositifs de démocratisation et dispositifs autoritaires en Afrique du Nord*. Paris: CNRS Editions.

Fillieule, Olivier. 1997. *Stratégies de la rue. Les manifestations en France*. Paris: Sciences-Po Press.

Fillieule, Olivier. 2006. "Requiem pour un concept. Vie et mort de la notion de structures des opportunités politiques." In *La Turquie conteste*, edited by Gilles Dorronsoro, 201–18. Paris: CNRS.

Fillieule, Olivier, and Christophe Broqua. 2020. "Sexual and Reproductive Rights Movements and Countermovements from an Interactionist Perspective." *Social Movement Studies* 19, no. 1:1–20.

Fillieule, Olivier, Lilian Mathieu, and Cécile Péchu, eds. 2009. *Dictionnaires des mouvements sociaux*. Paris: Sciences-Po.

Flacks, Richard. 2004. "Knowledge for What? Thoughts on the State of Social Movement Studies." In *Rethinking Social Movements: Structure, Meaning and Emotion*, edited by Jeff Goodwin and James M. Jasper, 135–53. Lanham, MD: Rowman & Littlefield.

Gamson, William A. 1975. *The Strategy of Social Protest*. Belmont, CA: Wadsworth.

Gamson, William A. 1992. "The Social Psychology of Collective Action." In *Frontiers in Social Movement Theory*, edited by Aldon D. Morris and Carol M. Mueller, 53–76. New Haven, CT: Yale Univ. Press.

Gamson, William A. 2004. "Bystanders, Public Opinion, and the Media." In *The Blackwell Companion to Social Movements*, edited by David A. Snow, Sarah A. Soule, and Hanspeter Kriesi, 242–61. Malden, MA: Wiley-Blackwell.

Gamson, William A. 2015. "Defining Movement 'Success.'" In *The Social Movements Reader: Cases and Concepts*, edited by James M. Jasper and Jeff Goodwin, 382–86. London: John Wiley & Sons.

Gamson, William A., and David S. Meyer. 1996. "Framing Political Opportunity." In *Comparative Perspectives on Social Movements: Political Opportunities, Mobilizing Structures, and Cultural Framings*, edited by Doug McAdam, John D. McCarthy, and Mayer N. Zald, 275–90. Cambridge: Cambridge Univ. Press.

Gamson, William A., and Gadi Wolfsfeld. 1993. "Movements and Media as Interacting Systems." *Annals of the American Academy of Political and Social Science* 528, no. 1:114–25.

Ganz, Marshall, and Elizabeth McKenna. 2019. "Bringing Leadership Back." In *The Wiley-Blackwell Companion to Social Movements*, edited by David Snow, Sarah A. Soule, Hanspeter Kriesi, and Holly J. McCammon, 185–202. London: John Wiley & Sons.

Ganz, Marshall. 2004. "Why David Sometimes Wins: Strategic Capacity in Social Movement." In *Rethinking Social Movements: Structure, Meaning, and Emotion*, edited by Jeff Goodwin and James M. Jasper, 209–38. Lanham, MD: Rowman & Littlefield.

Ganz, Marshall. 2010. "Leading Change: Leadership, Organization, and Social Movements." In *Handbook of Leadership Theory and Practice: An HBS Centennial Colloquium on Advancing Leadership*, edited by Nitin Nohria and Rakesh Khurana, 509–50. Boston: Harvard Business Press.

Giugni, Marco, and Florence Passy. 2001. *Political Altruism? Solidarity Movements in International Perspective*. Lanham, MD: Rowman & Littlefield.

Gobe, Èric. 2006. "Corporatisme, syndicalisme et dèpolitisation." In *La politique dans le Monde Arabe*, edited by Elizabeth Picard, 171–92. Paris: Armand Colin.

Goldberg, Ellis. 1986. *Tinker, Tailor, and Textile Worker: Class and Politics in Egypt, 1930–1952*. Berkeley: Univ. of California Press.

Goldberg, Ellis. 1992. "The Foundations of State-Labor Relations in Contemporary Egypt." *Comparative Politics* 24, no. 2:147–61.

Goldberg, Ellis. 2019. *The Social History of Labor in the Middle East*. 2nd ed. London: Routledge.

Goldstone, Jack A., and Charles Tilly. 2001. *Threat and Opportunity: Popular Action and State*. Cambridge: Cambridge Univ. Press.

Goodwin, Jeff. 2011. *No Other Way Out: States and Revolutionary Movements, 1945–1991.* Cambridge: Cambridge Univ. Press.

Goodwin, Jeff, and James M. Jasper. 1999. "Caught in a Winding, Snarling Vine: The Structural Bias of Political Process Theory." *Sociological Forum* 14, no. 1:30–33.

Gusfield, Joseph R. 1966. "Functional Areas of Leadership in Social Movements." *Sociological Quarterly* 7, no. 2:137–56.

Haas, Richard. 2003. "Toward Greater Democracy in Muslim World." *Washington Quarterly* 26, no. 3:137–48.

Hartshorn, Ian. 2018a. "Marching from All Governorates: Labour Lacunae in Mubarak's Egypt." *Economy and Society* 47, no. 3:343–59.

Hartshorn, Ian. 2018b. *Labor Politics in North Africa: After the Uprisings in Egypt and Tunisia.* Cambridge: Cambridge Univ. Press.

Hashem Rabie, A., ed. 2005. *Al-ta'dil al-dusturi wa intikhabat al-ri'asa 2005* [Constitutional Amendment and the Presidential Elections of 2005]. Cairo: Al-Ahram Center for Political and Strategic Studies.

Hashem Rabie, A., ed. 2006. *Misr wa al-islah ba'd al-intikhabat al-ri'asiyya wa al-barlamaniyya* [Egypt and Reform after Presidential and Parliamentary Elections]. Cairo: Al-Ahram Center for Political and Strategic Studies.

Heydemann, Steven. 2007. "Social Pacts and the Persistence of Authoritarianism in the Middle East." In *Debating Arab Authoritarianism: Dynamics and Durability in Nondemocratic Regimes*, edited by Oliver Schlumberger, 19–38. Stanford, CA: Stanford Univ. Press.

Hunt, Scott, and Robert Benford. 2004. "Collective Identity, Solidarity, and Commitment." In *The Blackwell Companion to Social Movements*, edited by David A. Snow, Sarah A. Soule, and Hanspeter Kriesi, 433–57. Malden, MA: Wiley-Blackwell.

Ikram, Khalid. 2006. *The Egyptian Economy, 1952–2000: Performance, Policies, and Issues.* New York: Routledge.

Jabola-Carolus, Isaac, Luke Elliott-Negri, James M. Jasper, Jessica Mahlbacher, Manès Weisskircher, and Anna Zhelnina. 2018. "Strategic Interaction Sequences: The Institutionalization of Participatory Budgeting in New York City." *Social Movement Studies* 19, nos. 5–6:640–56.

Jasper, James M. 2004. "A Strategic Approach to Collective Action: Looking for Agency in Social Movements' Choices." Accessed June 12, 2024. http://jamesmjasper.org/files/SocialMoves.pdf.

Jasper, James M. 2006. *Getting Your Way: Strategic Dilemmas in the Real World.* Chicago: Univ. of Chicago Press.

Jasper, James M. 2014. *Protest: A Cultural Introduction to Social Movements.* Cambridge: Polity.

Jasper, James M. 2015a. "Introduction: Playing the Game." In *Players and Arenas: The Interactive Dynamics of Protest*, edited by James M. Jasper and Jan Willem Duyvendak, 9–32. Amsterdam: Amsterdam Univ. Press.

Jasper, James M. 2015b. "Introduction: Players and Arenas Formerly Known as the State." In *Breaking Down the State: Protestors Engaged*, edited by Jan Willem Duyvendak and James M. Jasper, 9–24. Amsterdam: Amsterdam Univ. Press.

Jasper, James M. 2021. "Linking Arenas: Structuring Concepts in the Study of Politics and Protest." *Social Movement Studies* 20, no. 2:243–57.

Jasper, James M., and Aidan McGarry. 2015. *The Identity Dilemma: Social Movements and Collective Identity.* Philadelphia: Temple Univ. Press.

Jasper, James M., and Frédéric Volpi. 2018. "Introduction: Rethinking Mobilization after the Arab Uprisings." In *Microfoundations of the Arab Uprisings. Mapping Interactions between Regime and Protestors*, edited by Frédéric Volpi, James M. Jasper, and Jan Willem Duyvendak, 11–40. Amsterdam: Amsterdam Univ. Press.

Jasper, James M. . and Jane Pulsen. 1993. "Fighting Back: Vulnerabilities, Blunders, and Countermobilization by the Targets in Three Animal Rights Campaigns." *Sociological Forum* 8:639–57.

Jasper, James M., and Jan Willem Duyvendak, eds. 2015. *Players and Arenas: The Interactive Dynamics of Protest.* Amsterdam: Amsterdam Univ. Press.

Ketchley, Neil. 2017. *Egypt in a Time of Revolution: Contentious Politics and the Arab Spring.* Cambridge: Cambridge Univ. Press.

Kheir, Ahmed. 2012. "Musharakat al-jumhur fi baramij al-talkshow" [Audience Prticipation in Talk-Show Programs]. In *Al-anmat ghir al-taqlidiyya li-musharakat al-shabab fi misr* [Nontraditional Forms of Youth Participation in Egypt], edited by Mohamed Al-Ajati, 173–206. Cairo: Rawafid.

Kienle, Eberhard. 2001. *A Grand Delusion: Democracy and Economic Reform in Egypt.* London: I. B. Taurus.

Kienle, Eberhard. 2003. "Egypte: le choix réaffirmé de l'autoritarisme." In *Afrique du Nord, Moyen-Orient: Espace et Conflits*, edited by Rémy Leveau, 81–97. Paris: La Documentation Française.

Kienle, Eberhard. 2004. *Transformation without Democratization? Egypt's political future*. Bonn: Internationale Politik und Gesellschaft.

Klandermans, Bert. 1984. "Mobilization and Participation: Social-psychological Expansions of Resource Mobilization Theory." *American Sociological Review* 49:583–600.

Koopmans, Ruud. 2004. "Movements and Media: Selection Processes and Evolutionary Dynamics in the Public Sphere." *Theory and Society* 33, no. 3:367–93.

Koopmans, Ruud. 2005. "Repression and the Public Sphere: Discursive Opportunities for Repression against the Extreme Right in Germany in 1990e." In *Repression and Mobilization*, edited by Christian Davenport, Hank Johnston, and Carol Mueller, 159–88. Minneapolis: Univ. of Minnesota Press.

Krain, Matthew. 2000. *Repression and Accommodation in Post-Revolutionary States*. New York: St. Martin's.

Kriesi, Hanspeter. 2004. "Political Context and Opportunity." In *The Blackwell Companion to Social Movements*, edited by David A. Snow, Sarah A. Soule, and Hanspeter Kriesi, 67–90. Malden, MA: Wiley-Blackwell.

Kurzmann, Charles. 2004. "The Poststructuralist Consensus in Social Movement Theory." *In Rethinking Social Movements: Structure, Meaning, and Emotion*, edited by Jeff Goodwin and James M. Jasper, 108–20. Lanham, MD: Rowman & Littlefield.

Langohr, Vickie. 2004. "Too Much Society, Too Little Politics: Egypt and Liberalizing Arab Regimes." *Comparative Politics* 31, no. 2:181–97.

Lichbach, Mark I. 1987. "Deterrence or Escalation? The Puzzle of Aggregate Studies of Repression and Dissent." *Journal of Conflict Resolution* 31, no. 2:266–97.

Longuenesse, Élisabeth, and Adil Shaban. 1998. "Politique de libéralisation et différenciation de la classe ouvrière: Quelques résultats d'une enquête de terrain." *Egypte/Monde arabe* 33:23–54.

Luce, Stephanie. 2014. *Labor Movements: Global Perspectives*. Cambridge: Polity.

Lynch, Marc. 2011. "After Egypt: The Limits and Promise of Online Challenges to the Authoritarian Arab state." *Perspectives on Politics* 9, no. 2:301–10.

Manski, Ben. 2019. "Methodological Approaches to Movement Waves and the Making of History." In *The Palgrave Handbook of Social Movements, Revolution, and Social Transformation*, edited by Berch Berberoglu. 35–63. London: Palgrave Macmillan.

Mathieu, Lilian. 2002. "Rapport au politique, dimensions cognitives et perspectives pragmatiques dans l'analyse des mouvements sociaux." *Revue française de science politique* 52, no. 1:75–100.

Mathieu, Lilian. 2004. "Des mouvements sociaux à la politique contestataire: Les voies tâtonnantes d'un renouvellement de perspective." *Revue française de sociologie* 45, no. 3:561–80.

McAdam, Doug. 1996. "Conceptual Origins, Current Problems, Future Directions." In *Comparative Perspectives on Social Movements: Political Opportunities, Mobilizing Structures, and Cultural Framings*, edited by Doug McAdam, John D. McCarthy, and Mayer N. Zald, 23–40. Cambridge: Cambridge Univ. Press.

McAdam, Doug. 1995. "Initiator and Spin off Movements: Diffusion Process in Protest Cycles." In *Repertoires and Cycles of Collective Action*, edited by Mark Traugott, 217–39. Durham, NC: Duke Univ. Press.

McAdam, Doug 1984. *Political Process and the Development of Black Insurgency, 1930–1970*. Chicago: Univ. of Chicago Press.

McAdam, Doug, and Gregory Wiltfang. 1991. "The Costs and Risks of Social Activism: A Study of Sanctuary Movement Activism." *Social Forces* 69, no. 4:987–1010.

McAdam, Doug, Sidney Tarrow, and Charles Tilly. 1998. "Pour une cartographie de la politique contestataire." *Politix* 41:7–32.

McAdam, Doug, Sidney Tarrow, and Charles Tilly. 2001. *Dynamics of Contention*. Cambridge: Cambridge Univ. Press.

Mccammon, Holly. 2013. "Discursive Opportunity Structure." In *The Wiley-Blackwell Encyclopedia of Social and Political Movements*, edited by David Snow, Donatella Della Porta, Doug McAdam, and Bert Klandermans, 1–3. Hoboken, NJ: Wiley-Blackwell.

McCarthy, John D., and Meyer Zald. 1977. "Mobilization and Social Theory: A Partial Theory." *American Journal of Sociology* 82, no. 6:1212–41.

Melluci, Alberto. 1994. "The Process of Collective Identity." In *New Social Movements: From Ideology to Identity*, edited by Enrique Laraña, Hank Johnston, and Joseph R. Gusfield, 101–30. Philadelphia: Temple Univ. Press.

Melucci, Alberto. 1996. *Challenging Codes: Collective Action in the Information Age*. Cambridge: Cambridge Univ. Press.

Meyer, David S. 2002. "Opportunities and Identities: Bridge Building in the Study of Social Movements." In *Social Movements: Identity, Culture, and the State*, edited by David S. Meyer, Nancy Whittier, and Belinda Robnett, 3–21. New York: Oxford Univ. Press.

Meyer, David S. 2004. "Protest and Political Opportunities." *Annual Review of Sociology*. http://www.accessmylibrary.com/coms2/summary_0286-4662291_ITM.

Mische, Ann. 2003. "Cross-Talk in Movements: Reconceiving the Culture-Network Link." In *Movements and Networks: Relational Approach to Collective Action*, edited by Mario Diani and Doug McAdam, 258–80. Oxford: Oxford Univ. Press.

Mitchell, Timothy. 1999. "No Factories, No Problems: The Logic of Neo-Liberalism in Egypt." *Review of African Political Economy* 26, no. 82:455–68.

Mohsen, Habiba. 2012. "Hawl al-mosharaqa al siyassiya ghir al-taqlidiyya lel-shabab men tayar al-yassar al-masri." [On the Nontraditional Political Participation of Youth from the Egyptian Left Movement]. In *Al-anmat ghir al-taqlidiyya li-musharakat al-shabab fi misr* [Nontraditional forms of youth participation in Egypt], edited by Mohamed Al-Ajati, 71–95. Cairo: Rawafid.

Morris, Aldon D., and Suzanne Staggenborg. 2004. "Leadership in Social Movements." In *The Blackwell Companion to Social Movements*, edited by David A. Snow, Sarah A. Soule, and Hanspeter Kriesi, 171–97. Malden, MA: Wiley-Blackwell.

Morris, Aldon D. 1992. "Political Consciousness and Collective Action." In *Frontiers of Social Movement Theory*, edited by Aldon D. Morris and Carol Mueller, 351–573. New Haven, CT: Yale Univ. Press.

Morris, Aldon D. 2004. "Reflections on Social Movements Theory: Criticism and Proposal." In *Rethinking Social Movements: Structure, Meaning, and Emotion*, edited by Jeff Goodwin and James M. Jasper, 233–46. Lanham, MD: Rowman & Littlefield.

Nespad, Sharon E., and Bob Clifford. 2006. "When Do Leaders Matter? Hypotheses on Leadership Dynamics in Social Movements." *Mobilization* 11, no. 1:1–22.

Neveu, Érik. 1996. *Sociologie des Mouvements Sociaux*. Paris: La Découverte.

Neveu, Érik. 1999. "Médias et mouvements sociaux." *Réseaux* 98:17–85.

Olson, Mancur J. 1971. *The Logic of Collective Action: Public Goods and the Theory of Groups*. Cambridge, MA: Harvard Univ. Press.

Opp, Karl-Dieter. 2009. *Theories of Political Protest and Social Movements: A Multidisciplinary Introduction, Critique, and Synthesis*. London: Routledge.

Opp, Karl-Dieter, and Roehl Wolfgang. 1990. "Repression, Micro Mobilization, and Political Protest." *Social Forces* 69, no. 2:521–47.

Osa, Maryjane. 2003. *Solidarity and Contention: Networks of Polish Opposition*. Minneapolis: Univ. of Minnesota Press.

Ottaway, Marina. 2003. *Democracy Challenged: The Rise of Semi-Authoritarianism*. Washington, DC: Carnegie Endowment for International Peace.

Ottaway, Marina. 2004. "Democracy and Constituencies in the Arab World." Carnegie Papers, Middle East Series, no. 48, Carnegie Endowment for International Peace.

Ottaway, Marina. 2005. "Evaluating Middle East Reform: How Do We Know When It Is Significant?" Carnegie Papers, Middle East Series, no. 56, Carnegie Endowment for International Peace.

Ottaway, Marina, Jillian Schwedler, Shibley Telhami, Saad Eddin Ibrahim. 2005. "Democracy: Rising Tide or Mirage?" *Middle East Policy* 7, no. 2:1–27.

Owen, R. 1994. "Socio-economic Change and Political Mobilization: The Case of Egypt." In *Democracy without Democrats? The Renewal of Politics in the Muslim World*, edited by Ghassan Salame, 183–99. London: I. B. Tauris.

Paczynska, Agnieszka. 2006. "Globalization, Structural Adjustment, and Pressure to Conform: Contesting Labor Law Reform in Egypt." *New Political Science* 28, no. 1:45–64.

Paczynska, Agnieszka. 2009a. "Economic Liberalization and Union Struggles in Cairo." In *Cairo Contested: Governance, Urban Space, and Global Modernity*, edited by Diane Singerman, 331–49. Cairo: American Univ. in Cairo Press.

Paczynska, Agnieszka. 2009b. *State, Labor, and the Transition to a Market Economy*. Pennsylvania: Penn State Univ. Press.

Passy, Florence. 2003. "Social Networks Matter but How?" In *Social Movements and Networks: Relational Approaches to Collective Action*, edited by Mario Diani and Doug McAdam, 21–48. Oxford: Oxford Univ. Press.

Passy, Florence, and Gian-Andrea Monsch. 2014. "Do Social Networks Really Matter in Contentious Politics?" *Social Movement Studies* 13, no. 1:22–47.

Péchu, Cécile. 2009. "Laissez parler les objets!, De l'objet des mouvements sociaux aux mouvements sociaux comme objets." In *L'Atelier du politiste*, edited by Pierre Favre, Olivier Filleule, and Fabien Jobard, 59–78. Paris: La Découverte.

Peters, Ann Mariel. 2009. "Whither Egypt's Economic Reform?" SADA, Carnegie Endowment, July 7, 2009. http://carnegieendowment.org/2009/07/07/whither-egypt-s-economic-reform/fmxx.

Polletta, Fransesca, and James M. Jasper. 2001. "Collective Identity and Social Movements." *Annual Review of Sociology* 27:283–305.

Posusney, Marsha. 1993. "Irrational Workers: The Moral Economy of Labor Protest in Egypt." *World Politics* 46, no. 1:83–120.

Posusney, Marsha. 1997. *Labor and the State in Egypt: Workers, Unions, and Economic Restructuring*. New York: Columbia Univ. Press.

Posusney, Marsha. 2004. "Enduring Authoritarianism: Middle East Lessons for Comparative Theory." *Comparative Politics* 36, no. 2:126–35.

Pratt, Nicola C. 1998. "The Legacy of the Corporatist State: Explaining Workers' Responses to Economic Liberalisation in Egypt." Durham Middle East Paper, no. 60, Durham Univ.

Pratt, Nicola C. 2001. "Maintaining the Moral Economy: Egyptian State-Labor Relations in an Era of Economic Liberalization." *Arab Studies Journal* 8–9, nos. 2–1:111–29.

Rasler, Karen. 1996. "Concessions, Repression, and Political Protest in the Iranian Revolution." *American Sociological Review* 61, no. 1:132–52.

Reger, Jo. 2007. "Introduction: New Dimensions in the Study of Social Movement Leadership." *American Behavioral Scientist* 50, no. 10:1303–5.

Rey, B. 2005. "Entre nouvelles formes de mobilisations et gestion étatique: L'opposition égyptienne en 2004." In *L'année Chronique 2004*, edited by Florian Kohstall, 25–46. Cairo: Centre d'Études et de Documentation Économiques, Juridiques et Sociales.

Richter, Thomas. 2007. "The Political Economy of Regime Maintenance in Egypt: Linking External Resources and Domestic Legitimation." In *Debating Arab Authoritarianism: Dynamics and Durability in Nondemocratic Regimes*, edited by Oliver Schlumberger, 177–93. Stanford, CA: Stanford Univ. Press.

Robnett, Belinda. 2013. "Leadership." In *The Wiley-Blackwell Encyclopedia of Social and Political Movements*, edited by David Snow, Donatella Della Porta, Doug McAdam, and Bert Klandermans, n.p. Hoboken, NJ: Wiley-Blackwell.

Roll, Stephan. 2013. "Egypt's Business Elite after Mubarak." SWP Research Paper. Accessed August 22, 2024. http://www.swp-berlin.org/fileadmin/contents/products/research_papers/2013_RP08_rll.pdf.

Rucht, Dieter. 2004. "Movement Allies, Adversaries, and Third Parties." In *The Blackwell Companion to Social Movements*, edited by David A. Snow, Sarah A. Soule, and Hanspeter Kriesi, 197–216. Malden, MA: Blackwell.

Rutherford, Bruce K. 2008. *Egypt after Mubarak: Liberalism, Islam, and Democracy in the Arab world*. Princeton, NJ: Princeton Univ. Press.

Savyasaachi, and Ravi Kumar, eds. 2014. *Social Movements: Transformative Shifts and Turning Points*. New Delhi: Routledge India.

Sawyers, Traci M., and David S. Meyer. 1999. "Missed Opportunities: Social Movement Abeyance and Public Policy." *Social Problems* 46, no. 2:187–206.

Schedler, Andreas. 2002. "Elections without Democracy: The Menu of Manipulation." *Journal of Democracy* 13, no. 2:36–50.

Schmitter, Philippe C. 1974. "Still the Century of Corporatism?" *Review of Politics* 36, no. 1:85–131.

Sharara, Magdy A. 2009. *Al-haraka al-niqabiyya al-misriyya: dirasa tahliliyya li-nata'ij intikhabat al-niqabat al-'umaliyya* [The Egyptian Union Movement: An Analytical Study of the Results of the Labor Union Elections]. Cairo: Official Federation of Trade Unions.

Shehata, Dina. 2008. "Youth Activism in Egypt." Arab Reform Initiative, Brief No. 23.

Shehata, Dina. 2010. *Islamists and Secularists in Egypt: Opposition, Conflict, and Cooperation*. London: Routledge.

Shehata, Samer. 2009. *Shop Floor Culture and Politics in Egypt*. Albany: State Univ. of New York.

Smithey, Lee A., and Lester R. Kurtz. 2018. "Smart Repression." In *The Paradox of Repression and Nonviolent Movements*, edited by Lester R. Kurtz and Lee A. Smithey, 185–214. Syracuse, NY: Syracuse Univ. Press.

Snow, David. 2001. "Collective Identity and Expressive Forms." Working papers, Center for the Study of Democracy, Univ. of California, Irvine. Accessed June 12, 2024. http://www.escholarship.org/uc/item/2zn1t7bj#page-2.

Snow, David, and Robert D. Benford. 1988. "Ideology, Frame Resonance, and Participant Mobilization." *International Social Movements Research* 1:197–217.

Snow, David, E. Burke Rochford Jr., Steven K. Worden, and Robert D. Benford. 1986. "Alignment Processes, Micro-mobilization, and Movement Participation." *American Sociological Review* 51, no. 4:467–68.

Snow, David, L. Zurcher Jr., and S. Ekland-Olson. 1980. "Social Networks and Social Movements: A Micro Structural Approach to Different Recruitment." *American Sociological Review*, 45:787–801.

Soliman, Samer. 2011. *The Autumn of Dictatorship: Fiscal Crisis and Political Change in Egypt Under Mubarak*. Stanford, CA: Stanford Univ. Press.

Soule, Sarah A. 2004. "Diffusion Processes within and across Movements." In *The Blackwell Companion to Social Movements*, edited by David A. Snow, Sarah A. Soule, and Hanspeter Kriesi, 294–310. Malden, MA: Blackwell.

Sowers, Jeannie, and Chris Toensing, eds. 2012. *The Journey to Tahrir: Revolution, Protest, and Social Change in Egypt*. London: Verso.

Springborg, Robert. 1989. *The Political Economy of Mubarak's Egypt*. Boulder, CO: Westview.

Staggenborg, Suzanne. 2002. "The 'Meso' in Social Movement Research." In *Social Movements: Identity, Culture, and the State*, edited by David S. Meyer, Nancy Whittier, and Belinda Robnett, 124–39. New York: Oxford Univ. Press.

Tarrow, Sidney. 1995. "Cycles of Collective Action: Between Movements of Madness and the Repertoire of Contention." In *Repertoires and Cycles of Collective Action*, edited by Mark Traugott, 89–116. Durham, NC: Duke Univ. Press.

Tarrow, Sidney. 1996. "States and Opportunities: The Political Structuring of Social Movements." In *Comparative Perspectives on Social Movements: Political Opportunities, Mobilizing Structures, and Cultural Framings*, edited by Doug McAdam, John D. McCarthy, and Mayer N. Zald, 41–61. Cambridge: Cambridge Univ. Press.

Tarrow, Sidney. 1998. *Power in Movement: Social Movements and Contentious Politics*. 2nd ed. New York: Cambridge Univ. Press.

Tarrow, Sidney. 2013. *The Language of Contention: Revolutions in Words, 1688–2012*. Cambridge: Cambridge Univ. Press.

Tarrow, Sidney. 2015. *War, States, and Contention: A Comparative Historical Study*. Ithaca, NY: Cornell Univ. Press.

Taylor, Verta, and Nancy E. Whittier. 1992. "Collective Identity in Social Movement Communities: Lesbian Feminist Mobilization." In *Frontiers in Social Movement Theory*, edited by Aldon Morris and Carol Mueller, 104–29. New Haven, CT: Yale Univ. Press.

Taylor, Verta, and Nella Van Dyke. 2004. "Get Up, Stand Up: Tactical Repertoires of Social Movements." In *The Blackwell Companion to Social Movements*, edited by David A. Snow, Sarah A. Soule, and Hanspeter Kriesi, 262–93. Malden, MA: Blackwell.

Thompson, Lisa, and Chris Tapscott, eds. 2010. *Citizenship and Social Movements: Perspectives from the Global South*. London: Zed.

Tilly, Charles. 1978. *From Mobilization to Revolution*. Boston: Addison-Wesley.

Tilly, Charles. 2008. *Contentious Performances*. Cambridge: Cambridge Univ. Press.

Tilly, Charles, and Sidney Tarrow. 2006. *Contentious Politics*. Oxford: Oxford Univ. Press.

Tilly, Charles, and Sidney Tarrow. 2008. *Politiques du conflit: de la grève à la révolution*. Paris: Presses de La Fondation Nationale des Sciences Politiques.

Tilly, Charles, and Sidney Tarrow. 2015. *Contentious Politics, Second Edition*. Oxford: Oxford Univ. Press.

Uysal, Ayshen. 2006. "Maintien de l'ordre et répression policière en Turquie." In *Police et manifestants*, edited by Olivier Fillieule and Donatella Della Porta, 257–78. Paris: Presses de La Fondation Nationale des Sciences Politiques.

Vairel, Frédéric. 2013. "Protesting in Authoritarian Situations: Egypt and Morocco in Comparative Perspective." In *Social Movements, Mobilization, and*

Contestation in the Middle East and North Africa, edited by Joel Beinin and Frédéric Vairel, 27–42. Stanford, CA: Stanford Univ. Press.

Valenzuela, J. Samuel. 1989. "Labor Movements in Transitions to Democracy: A Framework for Analysis." *Comparative Politics* 21, no. 4:445–72.

Volpi, Frédéric, James M. Jasper, Willem E. Duyvendak, eds. 2018. *Microfoundations of the Arab Uprisings. Mapping Interactions between Regime and Protestors*. Amsterdam: Amsterdam Univ. Press.

Volpi, Frédéric, and Janine A. Clark. 2019. "Activism in the Middle East and North Africa in Times of Upheaval: Social Networks' Actions and Interactions." *Social Movement Studies* 18, no. 1:1–16.

Walgrave, Stefaan, and J. Manssens. 2005. "Mobilizing the White March: Media Frames as Alternatives to Movement Organizations." In *Frames of Protest: Social Movements and the Framing Perspective*, edited by Hank Johnston and John A. Noakes, 113–40. Lanham, MD: Rowman & Littlefield.

Waterbury, John. 1983. *The Egypt of Nasser and Sadat: The Political Economy of Two Regimes*. Princeton, NJ: Princeton Univ. Press.

Waterbury, John. 1985. "The 'Soft State' and the Open Door: Egypt's Experience with Economic Liberalization, 1974–1984." *Comparative Politics* 18, no. 1:65–83.

Whittier, Nanacy. 2002. "Meaning and Structure in Social Movements." In *Social Movements: Identity, Culture, and the State*, edited by David S. Meyer, Nancy Whittier, and Belinda Robnet, 289–307. New York: Oxford Univ. Press.

Wurzel, Ulrich G. 2009. "The Political Economy of Authoritarianism in Egypt: Insufficient Structural Reforms, Limited Outcomes, and a Lack of New Actors." In *The Arab State and Neo-Liberal Globalization: The Restructuring of State Power in the Middle East*, edited by Laura Guazzone and Daniela Pioppi, 97–123. Reading: Ithaca.

Yuen, Samson. 2018. "Contesting Middle-class Civility: Place-based Collective Identity in Hong Kong's Occupy Mongkok." *Social Movement Studies* 17, no. 4:393–407.

Master's Theses

Abdalla, Nadine. 2006. "L'Egypte au cœur de la Doctrine Bush: Elections Présidentielles et Législatives de 2005." Sciences-Po Paris.

Lachapelle, Jean. 2011. "Création d'un syndicat indépendant en Égypte: répertoires, intermédiations et processus de mobilisation." Québec Univ. https://archipel.uqam.ca/3989/.

Unpublished Papers

Abdel Ghafar, Shukr. 2009. "Al-Masry al-Youm wa al-Badil kanamozag tafao'li bayn al sahafa al-mustakila wa al-harakat al- igtima'ia" [Al-Masry al-Youm and Al-Badil as Interactive Model between the Private Press and the Protest Movements]. Presented at the round table organized on July 5–6, 2009 by the Centre des Etudes et de Documentation Ëconomiques, Juridiques et Sociales, the Al-Ahram Center for Political and Strategic Studies, and the Institute of Research for Development in Cairo on Collective Mobilizations, Media and Governance in Egypt.

Reports and Internet Sources

"Al-tanzim al-niqabi bayn 'ilaqat a'mal jadida wa tanzim niqabi qadim" [The Trade Union Structure between New Labor Relation and Old Union Organization]. Center for Trade Union Worker Services. http://www.ctuws.com/content/أوضاع-العمال-فى-مصر-بين-علاقات-عمل-جديدة-وتنظيم-نقابي-قديم-إعداد-كمال-عباس.

"Azmat al-tanzim al-niqabi" [The Crisis of the Syndical Organization]. 2009. Center for Socialist Studies, November 2009. http://www.e-socialists.net/node/5115.

"Business Climate Development Strategy, Phase 1 Policy Assessment—Egypt Dimension 1–2—Privatization Policy and Public Private Partnerships." 2010. MENA-OECD Investment Programme, July 2010. https://www.oecd.org/global-relations/46340470.pdf.

"CTUWS Report." 2009. Center for Trade Union Worker Services, December 7, 2009. http://www.ctuws.com/results.aspx?item=388.

"CTUWS Report." 2010. Center for Trade Union Worker Services, January 18, 2010. http://www.ctuws.com/results.aspx?item=388.

"Egypt: Stop Violating the Rights of the Workers to Organize." 2016. Human Rights Watch, April 30, 2016, https://www.hrw.org/ar/news/2016/04/30/289338.

"Freedom of Association and Protection of the Right to Organise Convention 1948. No. 87." N.d. International Labour Organization. http://www.ilo.org/dyn/normlex/en/f?p=NORMLEXPUB:12100:0::NO:12100:P12100_ILO_CODE:C087.

"President Bush Discusses Freedom in Iraq and the Middle East." 2003. White House remarks by the president at the twentieth anniversary of the National Endowment for Democracy, White House, November 6, 2003. http://www.whitehouse.gov/news/releases/2003/11/20031106-2.html.

"Public Conference at the Center for Trade Union Worker Services Regarding Violations of the Reconciliation Process and Preparations for Labor Elections."

2018. Center for Trade Union Worker Services, May 16, 2018. http://www.ssrcaw.org/ar/show.art.asp?aid=599150.

"Ratifications of ILO Conventions: Ratifications for Egypt." N.d. International Labour Organization. https://www.ilo.org/dyn/normlex/en/f?p=NORMLEXPUB:11200:0::NO::P11200_COUNTRY_ID:102915.

"Report on Workers Protests in 2015." 2016. Economic Center for Economic and Social Rights, January 2016. http://ecesr.org/wp-content/uploads/2016/01/2015-Protests-interactive.pdf.

"Report on Workers' Protests in 2014." 2015. Economic Center for Economic and Social Rights, May 1, 2015. http://ecesr.org/?p=769983.

"Report on Workers' Protests in 2016." 2016. Economic Center for Economic and Social Rights, December 5, 2016. http://ecesr.org/?p=775172.

"Right to Organize and Collective Bargaining Convention 1949. No.98." N.d. International Labour Organization. http://www.ilo.org/dyn/normlex/en/f?p=NORMLEXPUB:12100:0::NO:12100:P12100_ILO_CODE:C098.

"Sawt ʿumal al-Mahalla" [The Voice of the Mahalla Workers]. 2008. Non-periodical magazine issued by Al-Rabta informal organization in Al-Mahalla Company, March 2008.

"Taqrir markaz sawasiya li huquq al-insan w munahadat al tamayuz hawl nata'ig baʿthat taqasi al-haqa'iq alati arsalha ila al-Mahalla fi 6–7 Abril 2008" [The Report Published by the Sawaseya Center for Human Rights and Activism against Discrimination about the Results of Its Truth Commission Sent to the City of Mahalla on April 6 and 7, 2008]. Markaz sawaseya le huquq al-insan we munahadit al-tami'z [Sawaseya Center for Human Rights and Activism Against Discrimination], April 2008, 9.

"Waqa'iʿ ma jara: al-intikhabat al-niqabiyya dawrat 2006–2011" [The Facts: Trade Union Elections of 2006–2011]. N.d. Center for Trade Union Worker Services. http://www.ctuws.com/programs/press/default.aspx?item=186.

Abdel Moati, Ayman. 2015. "Al-haraka al-ʿumaliyya al-misriyya . . . ma al-ʿamal?" [The Egyptian Labor Movement . . . What's Next?]. Democratic Society, October 22, 2015. https://dem-society.com/2015/10/22/الحركة-العمالية-المصرية-ما-العمل؟/.

Adly, Amr. 2014. "Al-azamat al-haykaliyya alati asbahat muliha," [Structural Crises That Have Become Urgent]. Mada Masr, July 6, 2014. https://www.madamasr.com/ar/2014/07/06/opinion/%D8%A7%D9%82%D8%AA%D8%B5%D8%A7%D8%AF/%D8%A7%D9%84%D8%A3%D8%B2%D9%85%D8%A7%D8%AA-%D8%A7%D9%84%D9%87%D9%8A%D9%83%D9%84%D9%8A%D

8%A9-%D8%A7%D9%84%D8%AA%D9%8A-%D8%A3%D8%B5%D8%A8%D8%AD%D8%AA-%D9%85%D9%84%D8%AD%D8%A9/.

Al-Mirghani, Elhamy. 2008. "Ru'ya li-ma hadath fi 6 Abril" [An analysis of What Occurred during the April 6 Strike]. Hisham Mubarak Law Center, September 25, 2008. http://www.hmlc-egy.org/node/850.

Al-Tablawy, Tarek, and Feteha, Ahmed. 2017. "Egypt Inflation Rate Surges to Record after Subsidy Cuts." Bloomberg, August 10, 2017. https://www.bloomberg.com/news/articles/2017-08-10/egypt-urban-inflation-rate-surges-to-record-after-subsidy-cuts.

Eweida, Gamal. 2008. "Malhamat al-dara'ib al-'aqariyya" [The Strike of the Property Tax Workers]. Center for Socialist Studies, 2008. http://www.e-socialists.net/node/1332.

Gabr, Haytham. 2007. "'umal al-Mahalla yuwasilun al-nidal" [The Mahalla Workers Continue Their Fight]. Center for Socialist Studies, February 7, 2007. http://www.e-socialists.net/node/5231.

Gom'a, Mahmoud. 2007. "I'tisam muwazafi al-dara'b al-'aqariyya li-su' ahwalihum" [Property Tax Workers Protest Their Poor Conditions in Egypt]. Al-Jazeera, 2007. http://www.aljazeera.net/News/archive/archive?ArchiveId=1074906.

Ramadan, Fatma. 2012. "Itlala 'ala al-haraka al-'umaliyya 2007–2009" [A Reading of the Labor Movement in Egypt between 2007 and 2009]. Al-Hiwar Al-Mutamaddin, June 6, 2012. http://www.ahewar.org/debat/show.art.asp?aid=313257.

Ramadan, Fatma. 2008. "Nidal al-muwazafin: khibrat wa durus" [The Confrontation of the Civil Servants: Experiences and Lessons]. Center for Socialist Studies, March 27, 2008. http://revsoc.me/workers-farmers/ndl-lmwzfyn-khbrt-wdrws.

Ramadan, Fatma. 2016. "The Corruption of ETUF's leaders . . . Al-Maragehei as an Example." Mada Masr, September 7, 2016. http://www.madamasr.com/ar/opinion/فساد-قيادات-الاتحاد-العام-للعمال-1-جبالي-المراغي.

Rice, Condolezza. 2005. "Remarks at the American University in Cairo." US Department of State, June 20, 2005. https://2001-2009.state.gov/secretary/rm/2005/48328.htm.

Shaaban, Gihan. 2008. "Qisat idrab" [The Story of a Strike]. Center for Socialist Studies, 2008. http://www.e-socialists.net/node/868.

Shaker, Salah. N.d. "13 'aman 'ala idrab ESCO" [13 Years since the ESCO Strike]. Center for Socialist Studies. http://www.e-socialists.net/node/4351.

Blog Articles

Al-Beheiry, Karim. 2007a. "'umal ghazl al-Mahalla yatrudun mas'uli al-hizb al-watani al-muwafidin min al-hukuma lil-tafawud wa tawaghulat amniyya dakhil al-masani'" [The Mahalla Workers Chased out the Representatives of the NDP]. Egy Workers, July 28, 2007. http://egyworkers.blogspot.com/2007/09/blog-post_3533.html.

Al-Beheiry, Karim. 2007b. "Bayanat tadamuniyya ma' 'umal al-Mahalla" [Declaration of Solidarity with the Mahalla Workers]. Egy Workers, September 24, 2007. http://egyworkers.blogspot.de/2007/09/blog-post_330.html.

Al-Beheiry, Karim. 2007c. "Infijar fi wadi al-Mahalla bi-sabab tasrihat al-wazira Aisha Abdel-Hadi" [The Situation Broke out at Mahalla as a Result of the Declaration of Aisha Abdel Hadi]. Egy Workers, September 24, 2007. http://egyworkers.blogspot.com/2007/09/blog-post_4647.html.

Al-Beheiry, Karim. 2007d. "Istmirar i'tisam 27 alf 'amil min 'umal ghazl al-Mahalla lil-yawm al-thani 'ala al-tawali" [The Sit-In of 27,000 workers in Mahalla for the Second Day]. Egy Workers, September 24, 2007. https://egyworkers.blogspot.com/2007_09_01_archive.html.

Al-Beheiry, Karim. 2007e. "Qiyadat ghazl al-Dawar yu'linun al-idrab al-tadamuni al-thulatha' al-qadim" [The Leaders of Kafr al-Dawar Declare a Strike Next Tuesday in Solidarity with the Workers of Mahalla]. Egy Workers, September 24, 2007. http://egyworkers.blogspot.de/2007/09/blog-post_5665.html.

Al-Beheiry, Karim. 2007f. "Khabar 'ajil min al-Mahalla: muzaharat layliyya wa muhawalat min al-amn li-iqṭiham al-sharika" [A Warning from Mahalla: Demonstrations on the Evening and Security Attempts to Attack the Company]. Egy Workers, September 25, 2007. http://egyworkers.blogspot.de/2007/09/blog-post_25.html.

Al-Beheiry, Karim. 2007g. "Al-niqaba al-wataniyya lil-ta'lim wa al-'umal al-mutahidun akbar niqabat janub afriqia wa al-'alam tu'lin tadamunha ma' 'umal ghazl al-Mahalla" [The National Union of Education and United Workers, One of the Largest Unions in South Africa, Declares Its Solidarity with the Workers of Mahalla]. Egy Workers, September 26, 2007. http://egyworkers.blogspot.de/2007/09/blog-post_26.html.

Al-Beheiry, Karim. 2007h. "Istimrar al-idrab lil-yawm al-khamis wa muhawalat fashila min al-hukuma li-hal al-idrab" [Eleven Days and the Failure of Government Attempts to Settle the Strike]. Egy Workers, September 27, 2007. http://egyworkers.blogspot.com/2007/09/blog-post_7069.html.

Al-Beheiry, Karim. 2007i. “Istimrar idrab ghazl al-Mahalla lil-yawm al-khamis” [The Mahalla Workers’ Strike Continues for the Fifth Day]. Egy Workers, September 27, 2007. https://egyworkers.blogspot.com/2007/09/blog-post_7069.html.

Al-Beheiry, Karim. 2008a. “‘umal al-Mahalla yakhtariqun al-hajiz al-amni wa yahtifun yasqut yasqut Hosni Mubarak” [The Mahalla Workers Breach the Security Cordon and chant “Down with Mubarak!”]. Egy Workers, February 17, 2008. http://egyworkers.blogspot.de/2008_02_01_archive.html.

Al-Beheiry, Karim. Egy Workers. 2008b. “Mudawanat ‘Umal Misr takshif al-mukhaṭaṭ al-amniyya li-ijhad idrab ‘umal al-Mahalla” [The Workers of Egypt Blog Reveals Security Plans to Call for the Dissolution of the Mahalla Workers’ Strike]. Egy Workers, April 1, 2008. http://egyworkers.blogspot.de/2008/03/blog-post_1238.html.

Al-Beheiry, Karim. 2008c. “5 bahawat min al-qiyadat al-‘umaliyya ba‘a al-‘umal” [Five Labor Leaders Sold the Labor Cause]. Egy Workers, April 3, 2008. http://egyworkers.blogspot.de/2008/04/blog-post_02.html.

Al-Beheiry, Karim. 2008d. “Mudawanat ‘Umal Misr takshif al-sir al-khafi wara’ ziyarat muhafiz al-Gharbia” [The Workers of Egypt Blog Discovers the Secret behind the Visit of the Governor of Gharbia]. Egy Workers, April 4, 2008. http://egyworkers.blogspot.de/2008/04/blog-post_3394.html.

“Textile Holding Company, Biography of Mohsen al-Gilani.” n.d. http://www.textileholding-gov-eg.com/a-mohsen.htm.

Newspaper Articles

“10 alaf muwazaf bi al-dara’ib al-‘qariya ya‘tasimun amam maglis al-wuzara’” [Ten Thousand RETA Hold a Sit-In in Front of the Cabinet Building]. 2007. *Al-Masry Al-Youm*, December 4, 2007.

“10 alaf muwatin yunazimun muzahara hashida fi al-Mahalla” [Ten Thousand Citizens Organize a Large Demonstration in Mahalla]. 2008. *Al-Masry Al-Youm*, April 7, 2008.

“Abdel Alim ra’isan lil-qabida lil-ghazl khalif Al-Ghilani” [Abdel Alim Succeeds El-Ghilani in the Presidency of El-Sherka El-Kabeda]. 2012. *Al-Youm Al-Sabi‘*, May 28, 2012.

“Al-amn yaqbud ‘ala al-‘asharat fi al-Qahera wa al-muhafazat” [Security Agents Arrest Dozens of People in Cairo and in the Governorates]. 2008. *Al-Masry Al-Youm*, April 7, 2008.

"Al-dakhliyya tahzur min ay muhawala lil-tazahur aw i'aqat 'amal al-yawm . . . wa tatawa'ad bi-ijra'at fawriyya hazima" [The Ministry of the Interior Denounces Any Attempt at Protest or Stoppage of Work]. 2008. *Al-Masry Al-Youm*, April 6, 2008.

"Al-itihad al-dawli yu'lin tadamunuh ma' niqabat al-dara'ib al-'aqariyya" [The International Federation Declares Itself in Solidarity with the Real Estate Tax Collector Syndicate]. 2008. *Al-Badil*, December 23, 2008.

"Al-Mahalla adrabat wa ba'd al-muhafazat tajahalat al-musharaka" [The City of Mahalla is on Strike While the Other Governorates Have Not Participated]. 2008. *Al-Masry Al-Youm*, April 7, 2008.

"Al-niqabat al-mustaqilla tu'lin 'an ta'sis al-jabha al-wataniyya lil-difa' 'an huquq al-'umal," [New Trade Unions Announce the Foundation of the National Front for the Defense of Labor Rights]. 2012. *Al-Youm Al-Sabi'*, October 15, 2012.

"Al-qawmi yawsi bi-raf' al-had al-adna lil-ujur bi-300 junayh shahriyyan" [The National Wage Council Recommends Increase in the Minimum Wage by 300 EGP Per Month]. 2008. *Masrawy*, February 18, 2008.

"Al-sa'at al-akhira qabl idrab al-Mahalla, al-idara wa al-amn wa al-tanzim al-niqabi yuhawilun tahdi'at al-'umal, wa al-'umal 'sawfa nudrib'" [The Final Hours before the Mahalla Company Strike: Management, Security, and Trade Union Organization Attempt to Calm the Workers . . . The Workers Say, "We Are Going to Strike!"]. 2008. *Al-Dustur*, April 5, 2008.

"Al-tashdidat al-amniyya tuhbiṭ idrab muwazafi al-barid" [Security Threats Abort Postal Workers' Strike]. 2009. *Al-Youm Al-Sabi'*, May 7, 2009.

"Al-wizarat wa al-hay'at al-hukumiyya ta'mal bi-kamil taqatuha al-yawm bi-ta'limat mushadada" [Ministries and Governmental Institutions Are Working under Close Monitoring Today]. 2008. *Al-Masry Al-Youm*, April 6, 2008.

"Al-'umal yalja'un lil-qada' li-hal al-lajna al-niqabiyya" [Workers Have Recourse to Justice to Dissolve the Trade Union Committee]. 2007. *Al-Masry Al-Youm*, February 2, 2007.

"Harb al-manshurat tashta'il fi ghazl al-Mahalla" [The War of the Leaflets Breaks out at the Mahalla Company]. 2008. *Al-Badil*, April 4, 2008.

"Idrab. . yurdi jami' al-atraf" [A Strike That Pleases All]. 2008. *Al-Masry Al-Youm*, April 7, 2008.

"Ishtirakiyun: al-quwwa al-'umaliyya 'ajiza 'an insha' itihadat mustaqilla" [Socialists: The Labor Forces Build Trade Union Federations]. 2007. *Al-Masry Al-Youm*, May 3, 2007.

"Istiya' bayn a'da' al-niqaba al-mustaqila lil-'amilin bil-dara'ib al-'aqariyya bi-sabab muhawalat al-maliyya ihlal niqabat al-bunuk wa al-ta'minat mahal niqabathum" [Frustration within the Independent Real Estate Tax Collector Union Because of the Banks and Insurance Union's Attempts to Take Its Place]. 2009. *Al-Dustur*, August 7, 2009.

"Itihamat lil-quwwa al-'amila bi-iqsa' qiyadat al-niqabat al-mustaqilla wa al-wizara tarud" [Before elections, Accusation to the Ministry of Labor of Exclusion of Independent Trade Unions and the Ministry Replies]. 2018. *Masrawy*, May 22, 2018.

"I'tisam muwazafi al-dara'ib al-'aqariyya yadkhul yawmuh al-thalith" [The Real Estate Tax Collector Sit-In Enters Its Third Day]. 2007. *Al-Badil*, December 6, 2007.

"Million junayh khasa'ir alsika al-hadid bisabab idrab al-thalath sa'at" [A Million in Losses Due to the Railway Strike]. 2009. *Al-Masry Al-Youm*, January 24, 2009.

"Mujawir yatahim Abu Eita bil-irtima' fi ahdan America wa sariqat al-adwa' min qadat idrab al-dara'ib al-'aqariyya" [Mugawer Accuses Abu Eita of Falling into the Arms of the United States and Stealing the Show from the Leaders of the Property Tax Officials' Movement]. 2009. *Al-Wafd*, December 18, 2009.

"3600 min muwazafi al-dara'ib al-'aqariyya yujadidun i'tisamuhum lil-muṭalaba bi-maṭalibuhum al-maliyya" [RETA Hold Another Sit-In to Demand Their Financial Rights]. 2007. *Al-Masry Al-Youm*, October 1, 2007.

"Muwazafi al-dara'ib al-'aqariyya yukadimoun awraq awil nikaba mustakila fe masr wa Aisha ta'edohom bra'yaha al-qanouni qariban" [The Real Estate Tax Collectors Present the Papers for the First Independent Trade Union in Egypt and Aisha Promises to Give Her Political Opinion Soon]. 2009. *Al-Masry Al-Youm*, April 22, 2009.

"Muwazafin al-dara'ib al-'aqariyya yanqiluun i'tisamahum lil-Dakahlia" [The RETA Move Their Demonstrations to Dakahlia]. 2007. *Al-Masry Al-Youm*, September 25, 2007.

"Muwazafu al-dara'ib al-'aqariyya yarfudun manh Mugawer muhala lil-tafawud" [The Real Estate Tax Collectors Refuse to Give Mugawer an Opportunity to Negotiate]. 2007. *Al-Masry Al-Youm*, December 7, 2007.

"Muwazafu al-dara'ib al-'aqariyya yu'linun ta'sis awal niqaba mustaqilla munzu 50 'am" [The Real Estate Tax Collectors Declare the Founding of the First Independent Union in 50 Years]. 2008. *Al-Badil*, December 20, 2008.

"Niqabiyun: ta'sis niqaba mustaqilla muwazafi al-qariya khatwa li-tafkik al-istibdad al-siyasi" [Unionists: "The Foundation of the Real Estate Tax Collector Union

Is a Step toward the Deconstruction of Political Authoritarianism"]. 2008. *Al-Badil*, December 22, 2008.

"Hikayatat min i'tisam 10,000 muwatin amam maqar hekoumat Nathif" [The Stories of 10,000 Citizens in Front of Nathif's Cabinet]. 2007. *Al-Masry Al-Youm*, December 6, 2007.

"Qiyadat 'umaliyya: ziyadat wazir al-istithmar la takfi wa hadafuha tafwit maw'id al-idrab" [Labor Leaders: The Minister Of Investment's Increase Is Not Sufficient and Its Sole Purpose Is to Prevent Us Meeting on the Day of the Strike]. 2008. *Al-Dustur*, March 31, 2008.

"Qiyadi fi idrab 6 April yatawaqa' musharakat 150 alf muwatin" [A Leader of the April 6th Strike Expects the Participation of 150,000 Citizens]. 2008. *Al-Masry Al-Youm*, April 6, 2008.

"Raf' badal al-wajbah al-ghiza'iyya fi muhawala li-man' idrab al-ahad" [The Increase in the Meal Allowance for the Mahalla Workers Is an Attempt to Prevent the Strike on Sunday]. 2008. *Al-Badil*, March 31, 2008.

"Sarf al-arbah bi-miqdar shahr wa nisf shahr" [The Payment of Premiums for a Month and a Half before the Beginning of Next February]. 2006. *Al-Ahram*, December 12, 2006.

"Sa'fan: al-intikhabat al-'umaliyya 'ala marhalatayn li-lijan al-niqabiyya ayam 23 wa 24 mayu al-muqbil" [The Trade Union Elections Were Held on the Level of Trade Union Committees on 23 and 24 May 1st Round, and on May 31 Second Round]. 2018. *Al-Ahram*, March 13, 2018

"Tajadud a'mal al-'unf fi al-Mahalla wa mutaradat bayn al-shurta wa al-mutazahirun" [Resumption of the Violence and Confrontation between the Police and the Protesters]. 2008. *Al-Masry Al-Youm*, April 8, 2008.

"Tajawub mahdud ma' da'wat khalik fi-biytak" [A Mediocre Reaction to the Stay at Home Campaign]. 2007. *Al-Masry Al-Youm*, July 24, 2007.

"Waqafat ihtijajiyya lil-tulab al-ishtirakiyyin bi-Helwan wa al-Qahera" [A Demonstration Organized by Socialist Students in Helwan and Cairo]. 2008. *Al-Masry Al-Youm*, April 6, 2008.

"Waqa'i' mu'tamar al-'amal al-dawli al-sabi' w al-tis'in, al-hala al-masriyya" [The Events of the International Labor Conference Number 97, the Case of Egypt]. *Dar El-Khadamat El-Nikabeya Wal Omaleyia*.

"Wazir al-maliyya yakhtuf nidal muwazafi al-dara'ib al-'aqariyya" [The Minister of Finance Steals the Benefits of the Real Estate Tax Collector Protests]. 2009. *Al-Akhbar Al-Masriyya*, August 11, 2009.

"Wazir al-maliyya yasdur qararan bi-ta'sis sanduq al-ri'aya al-ijtima'iyya lil-'amilin bil-dara'ib al-'aqariyya" [The Minister of Finance Publishes a Decision Conferring Social Funds to the Real Estate Tax Collector]. 2009. *Al-Akhbar Al-Masriyya*, August 8, 2009.

"Wazirat al-quwwa al-'amila ta'tarif: al-siyasat al-mutarakima al-khati'a sabab ahdath ghazl al-Mahalla" [The Minister of Labor Admits: Bad Policies Are Behind the Events of the Company of Mahalla]. 2006. *Al-Jumhuriyya*, December 26, 2006.

"Yawmiyat intifadat 'umal al-Mahalla" [The Uprising of the Mahalla Workers from Day to Day]. 2006. *Al-Karama*, December 19, 2006.

"'umal al-Mahalla yarfa'un karnihat al-hizb al-waṭani" [The Mahalla Workers Wave Their National Democratic Party Membership Cards]. 2007. *Al-Masry Al-Youm*, September 28, 2007.

"'umal al-Mahalla yarfudun al-hizb al-watani wa al-ikhwan" [The Mahalla Workers Refuse the NDP and the Muslim Brotherhood]. 2007. *Al-Ahaly*, July 26, 2007.

"'umal al-Mahalla yashabun al-thiqa min al-lajna al-niqabiyya" [The Workers of Mahalla Withdraw Confidence from the Trade Union Committee]. 2007. *Al-Masry Al-Youm*, January 28, 2007.

"'umal al-Mahalla ya'udu lil-i'tisam fi April" [The Mahalla Workers Will Strike in April]. 2008. *Al-Masry Al-Youm*, January 29, 2008.

"'umal al-Mahalla: la taraju' 'an idrab 6 April" [The Mahalla Workers: No Backing Down on the April 6 Strike]. 2008. *Al-Badil*, February 22, 2008.

"10 alaf muwazaf bil-dara'ib al-'aqariyya ya'tasimun amam majlis al-wazara'" [A Thousand Real Estate Tax Collectors Hold a Sit-In in Front of the Council of Ministers Building]. 2007. *Al-Masry Al-Youm*, December 4, 2007.

Abdel Ghani, Sayed. 2012. "Morsi yabhath ma' sanduq al-naqd al-dawli shuruṭ iqtirad 4,8 million dollar" [Morsi Discusses with the IMF the Conditions of the Loan of 4.8 Million Dollars]. *Al-Ahram Al-Masaie'*, n.d.

Abd El Razek, Mohsen, Mamdouh Thabet, Abd El 'Al Tal'at, and Mamdouh Arafa. 2007. "Lil-mara al-khamisa, alaf al-muwazafin bil-dara'ib al-'aqariyya yatazaharun lil-mutalaba bi-naqluhum ila al-maliyya" [For the Fifth Time, Thousands of RETA Demonstrate to Demand Their Transfer to the Ministry of Finance]. *Al-Masry Al-Youm*, October 22, 2007.

Abu Arab, Tamer. 2007. "Muzahara li-alf muwazaf bil-dara'ib al-'aqariyya amam mujjama' al-Jiza lil-mutalaba bi-tahsin ahwalihum wa rabtuhum bil-maliyya" [Demonstration of 1,000 Property RETC in Front of the Mugamma' of Giza to Demand Improvement of Their Work Conditions and Their Annexation to the Department of Finance]. *Al-Dustur*, September 7, 2007.

Abul Dahab, Mohamed. 2008. "Al-jam'iyya al-mumumiyya li-sharikat ghazl al-Mahalla 21 October al-qadim wa masadir: al-arqam al-awaliyya lil-mizaniyya tu'aqid wujud khusarat 144 million junayh" [The General Assembly of the Mahalla Company Convenes Next October 21 and Sources: Preliminary Figures Confirm Losses of 144 Million Egyptian Pounds]. *Al-Dustur*, October 15, 2008.

Abul Dahab, Mohamed. 2007. "idrab al-mahalla yastamir le al-youm al- rabei'" [The Mahalla Workers' Strike Continues for the Fourth Day], *Al-Dustur*, September 27, 2007.

Al-Agroudi, Mohamed. 2009. "Ta'sis niqaba lil-'amilin bil-maliyya wa al-dara'ib al-'aqariyya wa al-jamarik lil-himaya al-qanuniyya" [The Founding of the Official Union of the Real Estate Tax Collectors]. *Al-Ahram*, December 26, 2009.

Al-Dergali, Adel. 2007. "Al-'ashira masa'an . . . mumathil itihad al-'umal: 'fi kul qadiyya 'ama la najid man nufawiduh, wa al-dawla la tasma'" [On *The 10 O'Clock Program*, the Representative of the Federation of Trade Unions Declares: "In Every Crisis We Can't Find Anyone to Negotiate with and the State Is Deaf"]. *Al-Masry Al-Youm*, December 5, 2007.

Al-Desouki, Roshdi. 2008. "Al-da'wa li-idrab 6 April bil-telephone al-ardi wa-email-at wa rasa'il al-chat wa al-kitaba 'ala hitan al-shawari'" [The Call to Strike on April 6 through the Phone, E-mails, and Writing on Street Walls]. *Al-Dustur*, April 5, 2008.

Al-Khashef, Hamada. 2009. "Mugawer yu'lin 'awdat niqabat al-dara'ib al-'aqariyya al-mustaqilla li-itihad al-'umal" [Mugawer Announces the Return of the Real Estate Tax Collector Union to the Official Federation of Trade Unions]. *Al-Badil*, March 16, 2009.

Al-Shazli, Heba F. 2013. "Where Were the Egyptian Workers in the June 2013 Peoples' Coup?" *Jadaliyya*, July 23, 2013.

Al-Turki, Al-Sayed. 2006. "Bil-arqam wa al-watha'iq: khitat al-hukuma li-takhrib sharikat ghazl al-Mahalla li-salih rijal al-a'mal" [With Numbers and Documents: The Plan of the Government to Destroy the Mahalla Company for the Benefit of Businessmen]. *Al-Dustur*, December 20, 2006.

Al-Turki, Al-Sayed. 2007. "Hussein Mugawer, azmat rajul muhim" [Hussein Mugawer, the Problem of an Important Man]. *Al-Dustur*, December 9, 2007.

Al-Zahi, Mahmoud. 2007. "Al-tifl Islam ja' li-musharakat waliduh al-i'tisam fathar hatif" [The Child Islam Came with His Father to the Sit-In and Led the Slogan-Chanting]. *Al-Masry Al-Youm*, December 6, 2007.

Azouz, Mohamed, and Adel Dora. 2006. "27000 ʿamil bi-ghazl al-Mahalla yamtaniʿun ʿan tasalum ujurihum wa yuhadidun bil-iʿtisam" [27,000 Workers at Mahalla Refuse to Take Their Wages and Threaten to Hold a Sit-In]. *Al-Masry Al-Youm*, December 4, 2006.

Azouz, Mohamed, and Amr Abd El Halim. 2008. "Mujawir: niqabat muwazafi al-dara'ib al-ʿaqariyya kharija ʿan al-qanun wa lan naʿtarif bi-shaʿriyattuha'" [Mugawer: "The Real Estate Tax Collector Union Is Violating the Law and We Will Not Recognize Its Legitimacy"]. *Al-Masry Al-Youm*, December 22, 2008.

Azouz, Mohamed, and Mohsen Abd El Razek. 2007a. "Muwazafi al-dara'ib al-ʿaqariyya yuwasilun al-tahadi: lan nughadir al-shariʿ dun hal" [The Real Estate Tax Collectors Continue to Challenge: We Will Not Leave the Street without a Solution]. *Al-Masry Al-Youm*, December 5, 2007.

Azouz, Mohamed, and Mohsen Abd El Razek. 2007b. "Muwazafu al-dara'ib al-ʿaqariyya yuhadidun bi-naql al-iʿtisam amam al-ri'asa wa yahtefoun ya abou alaa' bos lil'iyal" [The Real Estate Tax Collector Officials Threaten to Transfer Their Sit-In to the Presidency and Chant "Abou Alaa, Tend to the Children"]. *Al-Masry Al-Youm*, December 6, 2007.

Azouz, Mohamed. 2008. "Al-amn yaʿtaqil al-ʿasharat wa yuhasir al-shawariʿ wa al-mayadin" [Security Agents Arrest Dozens of People and Block Streets and Traffic Circles]. *Al-Masry Al-Youm*, April 7, 2008.

Azouz, Mohamed. 2011. "Iʿtisam 7000 muwazafi min al-dara'ib al-ʿaqariyya" [The Sit-In of 7,000 RETA]. *Al-Masry Al-Youm*, November 14, 2011.

Azouz, Mohamed. 2007. "Mujawir yatahim "anasir mukhriba' bil-wuquf wara' sahb al-thiqa min al-lajna al-niqabiyya bi-ghazl al-Mahalla" [Mugawer Accuses Outside Forces of Being behind the Labor Attempt to Withdraw Confidence from the Union Committee]. *Al-Masry Al-Youm*, January 31, 2007.

Azouz, Mohamed. 2009a. "Baʿthat al-ʿamal al-dawliyya taltaqi munazamat al-mujtamaʿ al-madani baʿidan ʿan al-hukuma wa tataraqab al-mowafaqa ʿala niqabet al-dara'ib al-ʿaqariiya" [The Labor Organization Delegation Meets with Nongovernmental Organizations without the Government and Awaits the Approval of the RETA Union]. *Al-Masry Al-Youm*, April 23, 2009.

Azouz, Mohamed. 2009b. "Muwazafu al-dara'ib al-ʿaqariyya yaʿudun li-maqarihim al-i'tisami amam majlis al-wozara'... wa yunazimun mohakama sha'biya li-mujawir" [The Real Estate Tax Collectors Return to Their Sit-In in Front of the Cabinet and Organize a Popular Trial for Mugawer]. *Al-Masry Al-Youm*, August 12, 2009.

Azouz, Mohamed. 2007a. "'umal al-Mahalla yashabun al-thiqa min al-lajna al-niqabiyya" [Mahalla Workers Withdraw Confidence from the Trade Union Committee]. *Al-Masry Al-Youm*, January 28, 2007.

Azouz, Mohamed. 2007b. "Muwazafu al-dara'ib al-'aqariyya yusa'idun ihtijajihim wa yuhadidun bi-masira li-majlis al-wuzara"' [The RETC Escalate and Threaten to March against the Cabinet]. *Al-Masry Al-Youm*, November 15, 2007.

Badawi, Yehia. 2009. "Abu Eita atlaq al-sharara: istiqalat 3500 muwazaf min niqabat Mugawer" [Abu Eita Ignited the Spark: Resignation of 3,500 Employees from Mugawer's Union]. *Al-Karama*, January 26, 2009.

Badr, Amr. 2008. "Kamal Abu Eita . . . Al-istiqlal al-tam" [Kamal Abu Eita . . . Total Independence]. *Al-Dustur*, December 23, 2008.

Bassiouni, Mostafa, and Mohamed Abul Dahab. 2008a. "Al-sharika al-qabida tawzi' al-khubz 'ala al-'umal dakhil aswar ghazl al-Mahalla" [The Holding Company Decides to Purchase the Bread within the Company]. *Al-Dustur*, March 20, 2008.

Bassiouni, Mostafa, and Mohamed Abul Dahab. 2008b. "Qiyadat 'umaliyya: ziyadat wazir al-istithmar la takfi wa hadafuha tafwit maw'id al-idrab" [Labor Leaders: The Ministry of Investment's Increase Is Not Sufficient and Their Intention Is to Cancel the Strike]. *Al-Dustur*, March 31, 2008.

Bassiouni, Mostafa, and Mohamed Abul Dahab. 2008c. "'umal al-Mahalla yarfudun nata'ij Mujawir mah qiyadatahum ba'd ijbar khamsa minhum 'ala al-tawqi' 'ala al-ta'ahud bi-'adam al-idrab" [The Mahalla Workers Reject the Results of the Mugawer Meeting with Their Leaders after Pressure Was Exerted on Five of Them to Rescind the April 6 Strike]. *Al-Dustur*, April 4, 2008.

Bassiouni, Mostafa and Mohamed Abul Dahab. 2008d. "Al-sa'at al-akhira qabl idrab al-Mahalla, al-idara wa al-amn wa al-tanzim al-niqabi yuhawilun tahdi'at al-'umal, wa al-'umal sawfa nudrib" [The Final Hours before the Mahalla Company Strike: The Administration, Security, and Union Organization Are Trying to Shout down the Workers . . . the Workers Say: We Are Going to Do the Strike]. *Al-Dustur*, April 5, 2008.

Bassiouni, Mostafa and Mohamed Abul Dahab. 2008e. "30% 'ilawa urs Aspirin li-marad al-saratan" [The 30 Percent Bonus Increase Is an Aspirin for Cancer]. *Al-Dustur*, May 1, 2008.

Bassiouni, Mostafa and Tamer Abu Azab. 2007. "Ma'nawiyat murtafi'a wa wufud tadamun" [High Morale and Solidarity Delegations]. *Al-Dustur*, December 9, 2007.

Bassiouni, Mostafa. 2007. "Ba'd thalath sa'at min al-mufawadat bayn Mugawer wa mumathili al-dara'ib al-'aqariyya, al-muwazafin yarfudun inha' al-idrab wa yamdun al-layla amam itihad al-niqabat" [After Three Hours of Talks between Mugawer and Representatives of the RETC, the Employees of the RETC Refuse to Stop the Strike and Spend the Might at ETUF Headquarters]. *Al-Dustur*, November 15, 2007.

Bassiouni, Mostafa. 2008a. "Al-had al-adna lil-ujur bayn al-matalib al-sha'biyya wa tala'ub al-hukuma" [The Minimum Wage: The People's Demands and Government Tricks]. *Al-Akhbar*, January 31, 2008.

Bassiouni, Mostafa. 2008b. "Qiyadat niqabiyya wa 'umaliyya tutalib bi-iqrar al-had al-adna lil-ujur bi-1200 junayh shahriyyan liyatasawa ma' khat al-faqr al-'alami" [Labor Leaders Demand a Minimum Wage Equal to LE1,200, Compatible with the Poverty Line]. *Al-Dustur*, February 10, 2008.

Bassiouni, Mostafa. 2008c. "24 'amil bi-ghazl al-Mahalla ya'tasimun al-yawm lil-mutalaba bi-ajr 'adil li-muwajahat irtifa' al-as'ar wa takalif al-ma'isha" [Twenty-Four Thousand Workers at the Mahalla Company Stage a Sit-In to Demand a Salary Increase Just to Confront the Increase in Prices]. *Al-Dustur*, February 17, 2008.

Bassiouni, Mostafa. 2009a. "Ra'is niqabat al-ta'minat al-rasmiyya yutalib al-dara'ib al-'aqariyya yuqri al-'amilin 'ala 'udwiyyat niqabatahu" [President of the Banking and Insurance Union Obliges Officials to Be Part of His Union]. *Al-Dustur*, April 10, 2009.

Bassiouni, Mostafa. 2009b. "Al-itihad al-dawli li-'mal al-khadamat yubligh niqabat al-qariya al-mustaqilla bi-qubul 'udwiyatahum: marhaban bikum" [The International Federation of Service Workers Informs the Independent Union of Real Estate Workers of the Acceptance of their Membership: Welcome]. *Al-Dustur*, June 12, 2009.

Bassiouni, Mostafa. 2009c. "Azmat al-tanzim al-niqabi fi Misr" [The Crisis of the Trade Union Organization in Egypt]. The Center for Socialist Studies, November 2009. http://www.e-socialists.net/node/5115.

Bedir, Fathy. 2006. "'umal ghazl al-Mahalla yutalibun bi-muhakamat ra'is al-sharika" [Workers of the Mahalla Company Request the Judgment of the President of the Company]. *Al-Wafd*, December 10, 2006.

El Zahi, Mahmoud, Maha El-Behnasawy, and Darine. 2007. "Hikayat min i'tisam 10 alaf muwaṭin amam maqar hikoumat Nazif" [Stories of the Sit-In of 10,000 Citizens in Front of Nazif's Cabinet]. *Al-Masry Al-Youm*, December 6, 2007.

Fares, Rabab. 2007. "Fashal iqna' muwazafi al-dara'ib al-'aqariyya bi-fad al-i'tisam" [Failure to Convince the RETA to End Their Sit-In]. *Nahdit Masr*, October 24, 2007.

Fouad, Hisham. 2009. "'Alaf al-muwazafin bil-'aqariyya yahtifun: 'ashat al-niqaba al-mustaqilla did niqaba mustaghilla" [Thousands of Property Tax Officials Chanted: "Long Live the Independent Union against an Exploiting Union!"]. *Al-Arabi Al-Nasseri*, December 27, 2009.

Gaballah, Ibrahim. 2008. "Niqabat al-bunuk tuhazir lijan al-dara'ib al-'aqariyya min al-ta'amul ma' al-munazamat al-mustaqilla" [The Banking Union Threatens Trade Union Committees with Contacting Independent Organizations]. *Rose-al-Youssef*, September 18, 2008.

Gamil, Dina. 2009a. "I'tiraf dawli biniqabat al-dara'ib al-'aqariyya al-mustaqila" [International Recognition of the Independent Union of the Real Estate Tax Collectors]. *Al-Shorouk*, April 26, 2009.

Gamil, Dina. 2009b. "Al-tahqiq ma' naqib al-dara'ib al-'aqariyya wa itihamat bi-'adam shar'iyat al-niqaba" [Inquiry with One of the Members of the Independent Union and Accusations of Illegality]. *Al-Shorouk*, September 11, 2009.

Ghattas, Samir. 2007. "Al-durus al-sab'a al-mustafada min i'tisam al-dara'ib al-'aqariyya" [The 7 Lessons of the Sit-In of the Real Estate Tax Collector]. *Al-Masry al-Youm*, December 17, 2007.

Gomaa, Mahmoud. 2007. "I'tisam muwazafi al-dara'ib al-'aqariyya bi misr li-su' awda'ihim" [Egyptian Real Estate Tax Collectors Strike Due to Poor Working Conditions]. *Al-Jazeera*, November 14, 2007.

Hindawy, Tamer, and Khaled El-Adi. 2007. "Wa 'umal al-Mahalla uhadidun bil-i'tisam ba'd khitat al-idara" [The Mahalla Workers Threaten to Strike Again]. *Al-Karama*, January 23, 2007.

Khalil, Azza. 2009. "Halaqat niqash hawl al-niqaba al-mustaqilla lil-dara'ib al-'aqariyya ka-tajruba lil-ta'adudiyya al-niqabiyya" [Roundtable Discussion on the Independent Trade Union as an Example of Trade Union Pluralism]. *Tadamon Masr*, June 12, 2009.

Khedr, Abdel Wehab. 2009. "Dughut dawliyya 'ala hukumat Nazif li-ihtiram misr lil-itifaqat wa itlaq haq tashkil al-niqabat al-mustaqilla" [Pressure on the Nazif Government to Respect the Conventions and Accept the Creation of Independent Unions]. *Al-Ahally*, August 26, 2009.

El-Kholi, Mohamed. 2009. "Al-dawli lil khadamat al-'ama yasfa' itihad 'umal Misr: qabilna 'udwiyat al-dara'ib al-'qariya la'inaha tu'ayid mabadi'una w ahdafuna" [The International Federation of Services Slaps ETUF: We Have

Accepted the Accession of the RETA Union Because It Adheres to Our Principles and Objectives]. *Al-Dustur*, December 17, 2009.

Moussa, Dalia. 2009. "Al-dara'ib al-'aqariyya yahtajjun 'adam sanduqahum fi niqabat al-bunuk" [The Real Estate Tax Collectors Protest the Separation of Their Funds from the Bank Union]. *Al-Shorouk*, August 7, 2009.

Nahdet Masr. 2008. "Idrab 6 April . . . lih?" [The April 6 Strike . . . Why?]. *Nahdet Masr*, April 4, 2008.

Nureldine, Laila. 2008. "Muwazafi al-dara'ib al-'aqariyya bada'u khatawat al-i'lan 'an niqaba 'ama badila" [The Real Estate Tax Collectors Have Taken the First Steps Leading to the Declaration of an Alternative General Union]. *Al-Badil*, May 16, 2008.

Nureldine, Laila. 2009. "Niqabat al-dara'ib al-'aqariyya tumahhil al-maliyya 3 ayam li-tanfid matalibuha" [The Real Estate Tax Collector Syndicate Gives the Ministry of Finance Three Days to Meet Its Demands]. *Al-Wafd*, August 9, 2009.

Rabie, Ahmed. 2007. "Tazahurat tadamun li-Kefaya ma' al-sahafiyin wa 'umal al-Mahalla" [Manifestations of Kefaya in Solidarity with the Journalists and the Workers of Mahalla]. *Al-Itihad*, September 29, 2007.

Reda, Rasha. 2008. "Al-tazahur wa al-idrab laysa al-shakl al-wahid aladhi tahtaj min khilalahu" [Demonstrating and Striking Are Not the Only Ways to Protest]. *Al-Badil*, April 6, 2008.

Sabra, Mahmoud. 2009. "27.060 'udw min niqabat al-dara'ib al-'aqariyya al-mustaqila" [27,060 Members of the Independent Union of the Real Estate Tax Collectors]. *Al-Arabi Al-Nasseri*, April 26, 2009.

Said, Omar. 2007. "Al-muwazafin yahtufun did wazir al-dakhliyya wa al-sitat tandam ilayhum" [Employees Chanting Slogans against the Minister of the Interior and Women Join In]. *Al-Badil*, November 15, 2007.

Said, Omar. 2007. "I'tisam al-dara'ib al-'aqariyya amam majlis al-wuzara" [The Real Estate Tax Collector Sit-In in Front of the Council of Ministers Building]. *Al-Badil*, December 4, 2007.

Said, Omar. 2007. "Madha ya'mal dubat amn al-dawla fi wasat muwazafi al-dara'ib al-'aqariyya?" [What Do Security Officers Do among The Real Estate Tax Collectors?]. *Al-Badil*, December 5, 2007.

Saleh, Ayman. 2007. "Tafakuk azmat muwazafi al-dara'ib al-'aqariyya" [The Deteriorating Crisis of the Real Estate Tax Collector]. *Al-Iktisadeya Al-Masreya*, December 9, 2007.

Salem, Hatem. 2009. "Idariyu al-ta'lim: i'tisamat wa ihtijajat" [Education Employees: Sit-Ins and Protests]. *Al-Youm Al-Sabi'*, August 30, 2009.

Shams, Dalia. 2008. “Echoes of the Factories.” *Al-Ahram*, February 8, 2008. http://hebdo.ahram.org.eg/arab/ahram/2007/5/2/leve2.htm.

Shawada, Seham. 2014. “Ijtima‘ ‘ajil li-‘umal misr al-dimuqraṭi li-sahb al-thiqa min ra’isuh bisabab “tamwilat al-kharij” [An Urgent Meeting for EDLC to Dismiss Its President amid Accusations of Foreign Funding]. *Al-Shorouk*, January 3, 2014.

Taalb, Ebtisam, and Ahmed Zaki Othman. 2007. “Dar al-khadamat al-niqabiyya: 25 ‘aman min al-nidal al-‘umali” [The Center for Trade Unions and Workers’ Services: 25 Years of Labor Activism]. *Al-Badil*, August 17, 2007.

Tantawy, Nagwa. 2006. “Ijma‘ min al-nuwab wa al-hukuma ‘ala tahiyat al-‘umal” [The Agreement of the Parliament and the Government Regarding the Congratulations of the Workers]. *Al-Isbu‘*, December 18, 2006.

Yasin, Mona. 2007. “5000 muwazaf fi al-dara’ib al-‘aqariyya yatazaharun wa yuhadidun bi idrab ‘am” [5,000 RETA Employees Demonstrate and Threaten with a General Strike]. *Al-Masry Al-Youm*, September 11, 2007.

List of Interviews

Afaf, interview with author, February 7, 2010.
Amer, interview with author, August 9, 2009.
Amer, interview with author, January 7, 2009.
Amir, interview with author, January 12, 2016.
Ashraf, interview with author, January 31, 2009.
Ashraf, interview with author, April 15, 2010.
Ashraf, interview with author, April 8, 2010.
Bassem, interview with author, January 24, 2009.
Emad, interview with author, August 25, 2009.
Fathy, interview with author, October 22, 2011.
Fatouh, interview with author, February 7, 2010.
Fatouh, interview with author, January 31, 2009.
Fawzy, interview with author, August 17, 2009.
Hamdy, interview with author, August 25, 2009.
Hassan, interview with author, January 31, 2009.
Hussein, interview with author, October 22, 2011.
Karim, interview with author, July 7, 2009.
Latif, interview with author, April 9, 2010.
Lotfia, interview with author, October 4, 2011.
Lotfy, interview with author, August 15, 2009.

Magdy, interview with author, October 10, 2011.
Maged, interview with author, January, 24, 2009.
Maged, interview with author, August 9, 2009.
Moheb, interview with author, October 22, 2011.
Mohsen, interview with author, April 14, 2010.
Moneim, interview with author, October 19, 2011.
Morad, interview with author, April 14, 2010.
Morsi, interview with author, October 22, 2011.
Nader, interview with author, August 11, 2009.
Nasser, interview with author, October 5, 2011.
Noha, interview with author, June 9, 2012.
Noura, interview with author, June 11, 2017.
Ramadan, interview with author, October 10, 2011.
Ramy, interview with author, June 7, 2012.
Rehim, interview with author, October 5, 2011.
Reyad, interview with author, April 16, 2010.
Reyad, interview with author, August 11, 2009
Reyad, interview with author, January 31, 2009.
Sabah, interview with author, October 10, 2011.
Saher, interview with author, April 16, 2010.
Saher, interview with author, August 4, 2009.
Saher, interview with author, February 7, 2009.
Said, interview with author, August 22, 2009.
Said, interview with author, October 19, 2011.
Samira, interview with author, January 10, 2016.
Seif, interview with author, August 10, 2009.
Seif, interview with author, January 13, 2009.
Shawky, interview with author, April 14, 2010.
Soad, interview with author, February 7, 2010.
Wael, interview with author, August 15, 2009.
Wahid, interview with author, April 11, 2010.
Wahid, interview with author, August 15, 2009.
Wahid, interview with author, September 23, 2010.
Yasser, interview with author, January 31, 2009.
Zaki, interview with author, January 24, 2009.

Index

Nadine Abdalla is an Assistant Professor of Sociology in the Department of Sociology, Egyptology, and Anthropology (SEA) at the American University in Cairo (AUC). In 2015/16, she was a EUME Post-Doctoral Fellow at the Center for Middle Eastern and North African Politics at the Freie Universität of Berlin. In 2006, she received her MA in International Relations from Sciences-Po Paris in France; and in 2014, she received her PhD in Political Science from Sciences–Po Grenoble, with highest honors and committee praise (Très honorable avec félicitation du jury). Her notable achievements have earned her several prestigious awards and fellowships, providing her with opportunities to interact with distinguished academic institutions worldwide. Nadine has actively contributed to esteemed Arab Research Centers, notably the Al-Ahram Center for Political and Strategic Studies (ACPSS) in Cairo, as well as the Arab Forum for Alternative Studies (AFA) in Beirut. Moreover, she has engaged in fellowships at renowned European think tanks, research centers, and universities, including the German Institute for International and Security Affairs (Stiftung Wissenschaft und Politik, SWP) in Berlin, the Peace Research Institute Frankfurt (PRIF) in Frankfurt, the Center for Middle Eastern and North African Politics, Freie Universität in Berlin, the Lausanne Institute of Political and International Studies (IEPI), University of Lausanne (*Unil*) in Lausanne, the Study and Research Center for the Arab and Mediterranean World (Centre pour les Etudes et les Recherches du Monde Arabe et de la Méditerranée, CERMAM) in Geneva, and the Center for Economics, Juridical and Social Studies (Centre d'Etudes et de Documentation Economiques, Juridiques et Sociales, Cedej) in Cairo. Nadine has also actively participated in the research initiatives of the Euro-Mediterranean Study Commission (EuroMeSCo), headquartered in Barcelona, and is an esteemed alumnus of the Arab German Young Academy for Sciences and Humanities (AGYA), situated in Berlin. Her research interests include contentious politics and social movements, specifically labor and youth movements, state-society relations, local politics, and the dynamics of bottom-up approaches to democracy within the MENA region, with a particular emphasis on Egypt. Additionally, her focus extends to Euro-Mediterranean relations, particularly with regard to EU democracy assistance policies. Her research papers and articles have been featured in prestigious academic journals, including *Mediterranean Politics* and the *Journal of North African Studies*, and have been published by well-known publishers such as Palgrave Macmillan and Routledge. Moreover, her insights have reached influential policy platforms, such as the Middle East Institute (MEI) in Washington and Singapore, the German Institute for International and Security Affairs (SWP) in Berlin, the Arab Reform Initiative (ARI) in Paris, the European Institute of the Mediterranean (IEMed), and the Euro-Mediterranean Study Commission (EuroMeSCo), headquartered in Barcelona. Nadine's influence extends beyond academia, as she is an accomplished writer who regularly pens a weekly column for the Egyptian daily *Al-Masry Al-Youm*. Her expertise has also been featured in several articles published in other prominent Egyptian newspapers.

www.ingramcontent.com/pod-product-compliance
Lightning Source LLC
Chambersburg PA
CBHW020903270125
20832CB00001B/2
* 9 7 8 0 8 1 5 6 3 8 5 2 0 *